e a smooth

a·véd \pa-
pavé from
r to pave]

ssible to

dle En-
avimen-

ly cov-
chiefly

ng is

as in

om
ire]

Chiefly British : artfully shrewd : CANNY
pawl \'pȯl\ *noun* [perhaps modification of
Dutch *pal* pawl] (1626)
: a pivoted tongue or sliding bolt on one part
of a machine that is adapted to fall into notches or interdental spaces on another part (as a
ratchet wheel) so as to permit motion in only
one direction — see RATCHET WHEEL illustra-
tion

¹pawn \'pȯn, 'pän\ *noun* [Middle English
pown, from Middle French *poon*, from Medieval Latin *pedon-, pedo* foot soldier, from Late
Latin, one with broad feet, from Latin *ped-,
pes* foot — more at FOOT] (14th century)
1 : one of the chessmen of least value having
the power to move only forward ordinarily
one square at a time, to capture only diagonal-
ly forward, and to be promoted to any piece
except a king upon reaching the eighth rank
2 : one that can be used to further the purposes of another

²pawn *noun* [Middle English *paun*, modification of Middle French *pan*] (15th century)

---

intransitive verb
1 : to discharge a debt
2 : to be worth the
doesn't *pay*)
3 : to suffer the con

— **pay one's d**
position through e
work **2** *also* **pay**
3

☆ SYNONYM
Pay, compe
fy, reimburs
ompense m
alent in retur
discharge of
bills on time
up for serv
attorney w
REMUNER
for servic
paymen
for (pro
handso
son w

PAWNS

Also by Wendell Affield

Muddy Jungle Rivers
A River Assault Boat Cox'n's
Memory Journey of His War in Vietnam and Return Home

Herman
1940s Lonely Hearts Search
Chickenhouse Chronicles: Book I

PAWNS

1950s Nebish, Minnesota, Farm

What one sows, that shall they reap

Chickenhouse Chronicles

Book II

Wendell Affield

Whispering Petals Press, LLC

Published in the United States by Whispering Petals Press, LLC.

Library of Congress Control Number: 2017918971

Pawns, The Farm, Nebish, Minnesota, 1950s
Chickenhouse Chronicles, Book II   Wendell Affield.

Although the author and publisher have made every effort to ensure the accuracy of information contained in this book, we assume no responsibility for errors, inaccuracies, omissions, or inconsistency thereof. Any slights of people, places, or organizations are unintentional. Dialogue is reconstructed.

Paperback ISBN 978-1-945902-03-1

eBook ISBN: 978-1-945902-04-8

Audio book ISBN 978-1-945902-05-5

Printed in the United States of America

info@whisperingpetalspress.com

Photographs are property of the author unless otherwise noted

10 9 8 7 6 5 4 3 2 1   First Edition

ATTENTION CORPORATIONS, UNIVERSITIES, COLLEGES, AND PROFESSIONAL ORGANIZATIONS: Quantity discounts are available on bulk purchases of this book for educational, gift purposes, or premiums for increasing magazine subscriptions or renewals. Special books or book excerpts can also be created to fit specific needs.

For information, contact Whispering Petals Press, an imprint of Hawthorn Petal Press, LLC: PO Box 652, Bemidji, MN 56619-0652

info@whisperingpetalspress.com

For my brother, Randy (1951-1978)

and my son, Jeffrey (1969-2015)

Gone too soon

(1956) Randy, playing in our front yard.

Contents

(Summer 1956) The old garage where we spent so many hours playing.
Farm yard picture taken from atop the house.

(Summer 1953) Wendell Affield, five, in front of the new barn.

From the Author

Memory is a subjective thing—what haunts one may be insignificant and soon forgotten by another. Complicating things further, each time we resurrect a memory, neuroscientists agree, we activate new neurons, creating a new version of the recalled memory.

This *is* a memory story. Thousands of pages from old letters and diaries and hundreds of pictures, many reproduced from cracked and damaged negatives, reawakened dormant memories and added layers to this story. I share many of the memory-triggers as the narrative unfolds so the reader might better understand our life. As with many memories on the farm, seasons blend together into years marked by snow drifts, muddy spring barnyards, summer hay seasons, and autumn hunting, trapping, and butchering. All seasons were anchored to chore time, milking, and staying a step ahead of my parents' unpredictable moods.

In July 1960 Beltrami County Court placed seven of us in foster care—the two oldest had been removed earlier that spring, one to a foster home, the other to Red Wing Reform School. Our mother, Barbara, was committed to Fergus Falls State Hospital. After six months, she was released. Her paperwork said "Recovered," though it did not explain from what.

Over the next three years some of us were reunited. I never again called her mother. It was Barb, or in later years, Barbie. In telling my mother's story, some readers have suggested I refer to her as "Mom" or "Mother" but it doesn't sound right—it sounds dishonest.

Several years ago in a writing workshop, the instructor asked us to write a paragraph about our mother's laugh. I realized that in more than sixty years, I had never heard my mother laugh. The closest expression to mirth was a thin-lipped nod of approval and a subtle "Yes, ummhmm." As a child, I called my stepfather, "Daddy." In telling this story, I refer to him as Herman except when reconstructing childhood dialogue.

Prologue

When you went West [in 1937] I would much rather have had you stay here. I knew I needed you badly because you yourself knew that Barbara [sixteen years old] had already become ill. It was just a few weeks after you left that she tried suicide.

My grandmother, in a 1937 letter she wrote to her mother.

I wrote our mother's obituary. At her funeral dozens of people asked me how a Juilliard-trained pianist came to live on a small farm in Nebish, Minnesota. It's a question my siblings and I grew up with. Barbara sprinkled crumbs of information about her early life across the decades, but didn't leave a lucid path. After she died in 2010 I discovered the answer to the question of how she came to live in Nebish. Locked in the chickenhouse on our old homestead I found answers to many questions we had grown up with, but after eight years of studying her past I've come to realize there's a cavern of contradictions we'll never have answers for.

Barb thrived on adulation. When we were children, she demanded that we call her "Mommy Darling." She often reminded us that she was a sophisticated lady from New York, a blue-blood aristocrat, and a Daughter of the American Revolution (DAR). She self-identified as a concert pianist; that identity was reinforced when her fingers danced across the keyboard of the out-of-tune upright, strains of Bach, Beethoven, or Tchaikovsky rattling dust from tongue-in-groove flooring in the old farmhouse. After playing, she lectured us on notable people she had met when she studied music in Brussels and Paris in the 1930s.

Back to the question, how did Barb come to live on a small farm in northern Minnesota? By 1949, trapped in a small upper flat in New York City, twice divorced with four children, her options had run out and she purchased an advertisement in a singles newspaper. She met Herman Affield through *Cupid's Columns* and promised him the world. In the advertisement she says I'm three years old. Actually I was two, but that's the smallest untruth.

Barb had never lived on a farm or ranch. During her formative years in the 1920s, from the time she was two to about seven years old, she and her family lived in Seattle, Washington. They often ferried across Puget Sound and spent time on Greenbank Dairy Farm, owned by her grandfather, Calvin Philips, along with 10,000 acres of Whidbey Island. More than twenty years later Barb must have carried fond memories of her time at Greenbank and imagined she could recreate that idyllic life for her children.

Herman was a first-generation German immigrant's son. In 1949 he was a forty-three year old bachelor with an eighth grade education living in isolation on his small farm in northern Minnesota. He must have been lonely—perhaps after seeing combat in WWII he became conscious of his mortality. Being frugal, he probably studied Barb's letters in a lantern's glow rather than wasting electricity.

We moved to Minnesota in September 1949 and they were married four months later. For Herman, it must have seemed like a wonderful situation: an instant family and a beautiful wife. For my mother, it must have appeared perfect—her longed-for farm and a safe place to raise her children.

If this one quits me there will never be another. One is enough for me, and if I lose my family I'll sell everything I got as there will be nothing to look forward to, nothing to work for. In plain English I'll just give up, quit.

January 4, 1960,
Herman Affield in a letter
after his wife left with all the children.

Excerpt from my grandmother's 1939 diary:

Friday, August 11, 1939: Dear Bar's birthday and a nice letter from her this a.m., first from Poland. Fascinating description of mountain estate of Eva's where she is visiting. In evening a package of candied fruits came from her from Nice [France].

Tuesday, August 22, 1939: Thank goodness word from Bar from Poland written on the 8th. She talks about German maneuvers across the border in Czechoslovakia in September no more. She is having a wonderful time visiting Aka [Eva Barbacka] in a fashionable resort swimming, mountain climbing, dancing, tennis, and Bridge. The headlines blaze war talk. Germany and Russia have signed a pact.

Wednesday, August 23, 1939: Germany's demand for Poland has reached tremendous headlines and extras. We are awfully nervous for Bar—What a life! to have to be constantly in a state of extreme anxiety. Kay, Pol, and I took a picnic to South Beach Staten Island, all very pleasant.

Saturday, August 26, 1939: !!!X!!! A frightful shock this a.m. in the air mail, mailed by Bar from Poland enclosing a letter from a young Polish Engineer asking us for permission to marry Bar—apparently immediately. We are simply stunned. We don't know what to do—of course our inclination would be to cable to wait until Xmas. Think of her beautiful talent being stored away in Poland, the tension spot of the world and apparently he owns the very oil fields Hitler wants.

2010
Crossing the River

Nineteen days beyond her massive stroke, I knew the end was near. After a night of stroke-racked throes, the doctor didn't replace Barb's feeding tube. By late morning, she'd kicked off the sheet and lay askew, back wedged against the hospital bed rail, legs sprawled. Her diaper had come loose and the catheter dangled, raw urine permeating the room. Her shaved pubes protruded like those of a malnourished corpse in a National Geo magazine. I looked away, but hard as I tried, my eyes crept back to that shaved crotch that had conceived nine children—perhaps ten. I am third oldest.

My mind flashed back more than sixty years to the last time I'd seen that area. She was dancing on the kitchen table, dress pulled to her armpits—naked beneath—screaming at my stepfather, Herman, about his "nigger whore in North Africa."

She groaned and rolled toward me now, curled fetal. Her eyes searched mine, pleading. I'd seen death during my time in Vietnam. Most of the dying did not have the luxury to wind down, to resume the posture they'd taken the first nine months. They had been ambushed, mined, drowned, disintegrated by artillery. I recalled our fatalistic attitude, knowing it was only a matter of time until we got hit. Yet when it did happen, there was always disbelief, incredulous that it was happening to *me*.

I recognized the posture, but denied it. Her knees scrunched against her chest. I saw the jagged scar on her knee and remembered how it had gotten there, more than half a century earlier, and felt guilty. I pulled the sheet and blanket up to her chin and sat down as she dozed off, her fingers cradled in mine.

I was nine that summer. I still recall how the white August sun beat down. It was almost dinnertime and my younger brother Randy and I were tired and thirsty after playing in the woods. We'd take turns climbing trees—mostly young birches and maples—and ride them down while the other chopped at the base. It was always a race to see how high the climber could get before the tree toppled. Over the years we probably cleared ten acres and destroyed a generation of saplings. Decades later, for many years, I set myself a goal of planting at least a hundred trees each spring. Maybe it was subliminal penance.

Eventually, the game lost its thrill. We began betting each other how quickly we could chop the tree down. The climber would reach high on the trunk, pull himself up, pulling his knees up and locking on the trunk; then, while holding with the knees, reach higher—we called it "shinnying up the tree." I think it's a slang derivative of "shimmy," a 1930s dance where the body and butt wiggled—just as we did, climbing.

On that scorching August day, returning home from the woods, hot, hungry, and thirsty, I felt empowered, wielding the whetstone-honed double-edged ax. I chopped thistles, trees, frogs, grass, dead animals I might be lucky enough to find—nothing was off limits. Ax handle cradled loosely in my hand, the blade dragged, slicing a small furrow in the dirt as we walked. Randy and I crawled over the woven wire fence dividing forest and pasture. Two bottle-baby lambs, now weaned in late summer, came up to us. We began pulling cockleburs from their wool, but the lambs ran and hid beneath an abandoned washing machine that Herman had converted to a livestock drinking tank.

The washing machine was beyond repair, so Herman had mounted a cast iron drinking cup at the bottom of the copper tank and placed it in the pasture for watering the sheep. One of Randy's and my chores was to keep the tank filled. It was a hateful project for us to carry pails of water to it each day throughout the hot summer. Eventually, Herman gave up the battle and now thistles and cockleburs enveloped the tank, providing a shaded sanctuary for the lambs.

"I dare you to chop the tub," I said.

"You first," Randy dared.

I swung, and the blade sliced through the verdigris copper side. "Your turn."

Randy chopped a hole and handed the ax back to me. I chopped in a frenzy then, circling the square tub, faster each time, swinging. Finally I stopped, dizzy and exhausted. I walked around it once more to make sure there were holes in all four sides. I slapped the cast iron drinking cup with the flat of the ax and it snapped off with a resounding crack.

I had been so proud to help Herman build the waterer a few summers earlier. He'd discovered the blueprint in a *Successful Farming* magazine and used a pig check to buy the hoses and drinking cup we needed. I helped measure and drill the holes to mount the unit. His arms weren't long enough to hold the wrench on the bottom of the tub, so he asked me to crawl under and hold the wrench on the nuts so they wouldn't turn as he tightened the bolts from above.

Laughing at our destruction, Randy and I continued toward the house.

"Is dinner ready, Mommy? I'm starved," Randy said.

Barb turned around and scowled. "The midday meal is called lunch. Call it lunch. Only peasants refer to it as dinner. In New York City, where I'm from, dinner is the evening meal," Barb said.

"Daddy calls lunch dinner."

"His ancestors were living in barns above cattle in Europe while mine were fighting the Revolutionary War," Barb replied, an oft-repeated refrain to anybody within earshot, including six-year-old Randy.

We sat down to eat, our stomachs rumbling. Throughout the years, mealtime conversations were like weaving through a verbal minefield.

"Pass the Kool-Aid," Tim said.

"Say 'please.' You're not in a barn," Barb told him.

Herman passed the sweating pitcher across the table. "Smells like a damn barn. When you going to clean this place? Need the damn spud to scrape the crap off the floor." The spud was a long-handled sharp chisel we used to scrape the barn floor.

"Take your barn shoes off when you come in and it wouldn't," Barb replied.

"Can I have more noodles and ketchup?" Randy asked.

Herman spooned some onto his plate. "There you go, Sonny." Sonny was Herman's pet name for Randy, his first-born son—a blue eyed, sandy haired, stocky boy.

"Daddy, Windy chopped holes in that old washing machine out in the pasture."

"He what?" Herman's fork lowered as he looked at me.

"He chopped holes with the ax."

"You chopped some, too," I countered.

Randy looked down at his plate and mumbled, "Just one. It was your idea."

Herman's face reddened. "Damn destructive kid—I'll teach you." He jumped from his chair, grabbed a skinny piece of firewood from the nearby wood box, and lunged at me.

"You're not going to beat my son—he's not one of your animals," Barbara shouted, leaping between us. I dodged a blow and bolted out the door. Pushing Barb aside, Herman chased me out, but I had a head start and was across the yard.

"Goddamn kid—I'll get you," he yelled, hurling the stick at me.

I ran down by the hog house, hid in the pig weeds, and watched him stalk out to the pasture. He walked around the washing machine several times and then gave it a vicious kick.

I walked to the windrows—swaths of rocks, stumps and topsoil bulldozed into long rows when the land had been cleared, now thick with wild raspberries—and filled my hat. Herman had a sweet tooth and loved the thickly frosted cakes I made.

When I returned to the house, Barb was in the front room playing the piano, teaching my little sister Laurel some forgotten tune. She looked over her shoulder at me. "Why did you chop that thing?"

"Randy dared me."

"Well, He is furious—you'd better stay clear of Him." Barb refused to call Herman by name. It was He, Him, or That Bald Bastard. She shook her head and went back to the piano.

"I'll make Daddy a raspberry cake. Then he won't be mad at me," I whispered to myself.

Randy came in and reached across the sink full of dirty dinner dishes to turn on the faucet for a drink. "Daddy's really mad—said he's going to give you a taste of the belt."

"Did he belt you?"

"No, but he said he'd get you."

"Well, I'm making him his favorite cake."

"Big deal."

The screen door slammed. I jerked around. "Look, Daddy, I'm making you a cake."

"Don't you ever run from me," he said as he unbuckled his belt.

I stood rigid. A fly squirmed and buzzed on the sticky fly ribbon hanging above the table.

"You're not going to beat my son," Barb screamed, racing from the front room to the kitchen.

"Stay out of my way, bitch. He asked for it."

I dodged the first swing, raced around the table, behind Herman's stuffed chair, and hid under the smoke pipe rising from the back of the cold woodstove. I peeked over the top and watched Barb push against Herman's arm.

"Get the hell out of my way." He swung the belt across her back and her glasses went sailing.

"Stop—if you stop I'll sleep with you tonight." (The past few years she'd been sleeping upstairs with us kids). He switched ends so the buckle would hit me.

The belt lashed forward, missed me and wrapped around the stovepipe. The buckle thudded against the rusty metal. He yanked back and pulled the pipe out of the brick chimney and soot cascaded down on me. I shot out from behind the stove toward the door. Herman took a clean swing at me. Barb blocked it and caught the full force of the brass buckle on her knee. I glanced back at her scream and saw blood flowing down her leg.

"Goddamn bitch," Herman shouted, knocking her to the floor. "I said 'Stay the hell out of my way.'"

I hid in the orchard until I saw him leave on the tractor to mow hay; then I returned to the house and finished the cake. Barb sat in the front room, angry at me, ice packed around her towel-wrapped knee. Laurel was comforting her. I didn't come in for supper—stayed in the garden and ate cucumbers and green crabapples and replayed the conversation Randy and I had earlier in the day when we took a break from chopping trees.

"Why do Mommy and Daddy fight so much?" Randy asked.

"I don't know," I said. "Mommy always starts it."

"He really gets mad when Mommy marches around the table," Randy said. Randy got up and marched stiff-legged back and forth, arm shooting out each time he shouted "Heil Hitler."

"She calls it goose-step."

"I know," I said. "He really gets mad when she says 'Heil Hitler' and calls him a Nazi." All I knew about Nazis was that they were the bad guys. Whenever Chris, Tim, and I played war, I was the Nazi and got killed.

Later that evening while doing chores, I was surprised that Herman didn't grab me. He just ignored me, even though I was extra helpful. I put the De Laval milk separator together, lined the cream cans up, washed the equipment without being told. After milking, the cows were sent to night pasture and everybody returned to the house.

"That was good cake you made—fresh raspberries in the frosting," Herman said to me as I walked alongside him. He didn't seem like a Nazi.

In the nursing home room, my mother rolled toward me, her scarred knee slipping from under the blanket. I cupped her Juilliard-trained fingers, now curled talons, gently in my palm as her dark eyes searched my face. "I don't want to die," she grunted.

She had always been strange about death. She once told me if I had died in Vietnam she would have placed food on my headstone.

I was at a loss. In Vietnam, I had been wounded by a rocket that burned through the armor plating of the riverboat I was driving. As I lay on the deck, stunned and bleeding, I was enveloped in a cocoon of light. All fear and pain disappeared. We Anglos have a term for it—traumatic dissociation—but I believe there's a higher plane that I was privileged to glimpse. I told her that I had seen the other side, that it was profound, timeless peace. That it was okay for her to cross the river. I told her she'd see Randy again.

Her voice wavered. "But I don't want to cross the river."

I sat for a time, sun casting prisms on window moisture buildup, her hand resting in mine. She stirred and her toothless mouth opened and closed soundlessly. From years of watching mouths form words because I can't hear well, I realized what she was asking. I looked into her eyes and whispered, "I forgive you."

Late afternoon her fingers quivered, then relaxed as she drifted into that final private space. I slipped them from my palm and gently brushed my hand down over her face, closing her eyes. Since then I've often wondered if she had slipped back to August 1939, a dark-haired beauty waltzing with an aristocratic Polish soldier on a moon-lit patio, Tchaikovsky's "Swan Lake" drifting through a dacha high in the Carpathian Mountains of southern Poland.

One of Barbara's last letters from her Polish soldier. I had it translated. Enclosed with the packet was Kristaw's marriage proposal.

12 August 1939. Dear and good friend Berti[sic?] (Barbara), I was very sad, that for me it was impossible my dear Bari to stay for your birthday[sic] And I remember fondly the good times[sic] at Chet— [unclear spelling] I'm waiting for any bit of news from you and what you are doing. In accordance with what you said, I'm sending you a proposal of the letter[sic] to your dear parents. But I'm sure that this proposal needs to be corrected. I'm leaving[sic] this to your discretion, my dear Bari. Also many [sic] kisses [unclear words]. Sincerely, Kristaw [sic?]

Inž. Z. KONOPKA
KLECZA GÓRNA Dwór
Poczta, kolej autobus, loco

Klecza 12./8. - 39.

Tres aimable et chère
          Berli: -

          Je etais très triste, que pour
moi etait impossible ma chère Bari
de resté a Ton jour - natal. -
El rapele moi aussi le très belles
jour a Chełmice. Jé entande de Tua
chère Bari une très nouvelles de
Toi, et de sa que Tu fait. _____
Conformént a ce, que nous avont
dissaient, j'envois Tu un project
de la lettre a tes chère parents
          Mais je suis suret que cet
projekt doit etre corrique.
          Je rest cella a Ta disretion ma
chère Beri: - Je ajoint metre sin-
ceres saluts o Toi ma chère Bari.
Aussi beaucoup ambrasses sur Ton
chères maines.   Ton sincive
                              Zurisdeu

Excerpt from my grandmother's 1939 diary:

Sunday, August 27, 1939: All we did was listen to and read war news and worry over Bar and wonder what to do. I have the worse [sic] splitting headache all the time. My news clipping book is up to date. Pol went to Gerta's for the day.

Monday, August 28, 1939: We can't sleep or anything the war news is so bad. The *Normandie* crossed "blacked out" in a zigzag crossing. Polly and I worked until three then went to Kay's for lemonade, marketed then home for a late Bridge with H. I'm so worried about Bar and her war danger and her marriage that I can't see straight or think. I feel suffocated all of the time.

Tuesday, August 29, 1939: The radios are booming hourly war news from all the great European Capitols—War itself could only be some degrees worse. A letter from Poiand from Mme Barbacka, Barb's hostess this morning saying they are not so terrified of war but it was mailed twelve days ago. I sent an air mail to Bar asking her not to think of marrying the Pologuais [sic] until xmas.

Thursday, August 31, 1939: The war tension is very bad. We are nearly crazy worried about Bar. Haven't been sleepy at all in four days—Bar's safety, Polly's school, our place to live. Henry [Barb's father] is holding up well under the strain.

1950
Sanctuary

Burning eyes is my earliest memory. I was standing on a chair. A man with a cigarette tucked in the side of his mouth was fastening my suspenders. My eyes watered and my nose stung. Later in that memory wisp, I was playing on some stairs and the man scolded me. I like to think he was my grandfather because I lived for a time with my grandparents in their New York City apartment. Or it may have been one of my mother's beaus. I am not certain.

(Late February 1949, *left to right*) Chris, Wendell, Barbara holding Laurel, and Tim. My grandmother wrote on the back, "Taken in Central Park which your great, great uncle designed-Fredrick Law Olmsted."

Fast forward a few months. We arrived at the farm in September 1949. Chris recalled our ride out to the farm: "It was dark when the Greyhound reached Bemidji. Tim and I scrunched in the back of the coupe. Barb held Laurel, and you were scrunched between them and Herman in the front. When we got out to the farm, Herman turned the kitchen light on and gave us cold milk and gingersnaps."

Herman was the first stable father-figure my brothers and I had, and we idolized him. We wanted to be like him. We walked with a shuffling gait. We became proficient at holding one nostril closed with a thumb and blowing a snot wad out the other, then switching nostrils. Chris excelled at squirting spit in a fine stream, with the accompanying *Pphhtttuuie*, just like our new father when he spit. We called it, "snuice juice." Chris remembered Tim being especially fond of peeing outside whenever he pleased. In New York we had to use a toilet. Like our new father, Tim modestly turned his back to everybody, peed, and shook it three times. When Herman realized he was being mimicked, he joked at Tim, "If you shake it more than three times, you're playing with it."

"We looked at each other and laughed," Chris told me.

Herman taught us how to fish with a maple sapling pole, braided string, and a bobber baited by the earthworms we captured while weeding the garden. Nebish Lake, a five-minute bike ride from the farm, had a rickety dock made of cedar posts driven into the sand and connected by sawlog slabs. We could often see perch and bullheads swimming beneath the dock. We learned at a young age how to scale and gut perch and skin the dark, red-meat bullheads.

(Summer 1950) Tim, Laurel, Wendell, and Chris.
Going fishing at Nebish Lake in Minnesota.

About a year before Barb died, she and I spent the morning visiting about her first memories of the farm, sixty years earlier. In the beginning, Herman must have shared parts of his early life with her because the first thing she told me was that the first two years the Affield family lived on the homestead, about 1905, they had lived in what we knew as the woodshed. She said that Herman remembered, as a child, that it was his job to take the horse and wagon down to Nebish Lake with water cans to fill the copper boilers and tubs. But that must have been several years later because Herman was born in 1906.

As Barb stared back sixty years, to the autumn we arrived, she saw the front yard the first winter we lived on the farm. "There were long firewood logs lying around the yard. He spent hours each day sawing stove-length pieces by hand with the Swede saw." She mostly remembered the kitchen and the wood-burning cook stove. "We had a sink with running water—only cold," she told me. "The stove was right next to the sink. I had to keep the water reservoir on the cook stove full. We dipped it out with a long-handled ladle that hung from the edge of an open shelf above the stove."

Barb told me it was her responsibility to keep wood in the cook stove. "Herman always kept the wood box near the big stove full. I carried the wood from there to the cook stove. The fire chamber was on the left side."

She talked about other early memories that morning. In the summer, she was responsible for keeping ice in the kitchen ice box. Each morning and evening, Herman rolled the cream separator from the porch into the kitchen to separate the cream from the skim milk. He loved cottage cheese and always kept a pan of skim milk fermenting on top of the stove. He carried the rest of the skim milk to the pigs. She told me that in the winter he stored the cream in the basement so it wouldn't freeze—summer it was placed in the root cellar where the ice was packed in sawdust. "He taught me how to make butter with the hand cranked churn," she told me. "All winter I'd have to push clothes aside to walk through the house because when I washed, I had to hang them inside."

She told me that in the living room there was a leather pull-out couch and a treadle sewing machine. Herman's sister had left a player piano and a crank phonograph. My oldest brother Chris remembered the player piano. "Tim and I wrecked it, and Herman's sister was furious."

I asked Barb about Herman. She must have remembered back to before the anger began. Forty years after his death, she told me that he didn't like to socialize. "He didn't drink, and didn't smoke," she said, as she fidgeted with her coffee cup. "He was clean-shaven, but he chewed snuff so his teeth were brown and his breath was bad."

When Barb told me that, I saw Herman again in my memory, standing in front of the mirror, swirling his damp hog bristle brush in the lather bowl. He set the bowl on the window ledge that Barb would later blow a hole in with the shotgun. I remembered how he sloshed the lathered brush across his face, and if a child came within arm's reach, he'd chuckle and give us a swipe of foam. I don't think Herman ever had a toothbrush—none of us did.

Barb said he had a few friends who came over—one neighbor he cured meat with—they spoke German.

By the time I interviewed Barb in the winter of her years, she had mellowed. As she talked, I wondered if she felt any remorse over the way she had treated Herman. I didn't ask. It was common knowledge that Herman was very frugal. When we were kids, our Uncle Charlie, a master storyteller, once said, "Herman is so tight he'll squeeze a nickel until the buffalo shits."

Barb recalled that upstairs Herman had gunny sacks of seed hanging from the ceiling. "Oats, clover, alfalfa seed," she told me. "He had them hanging so the mice couldn't get at them." She remembered how, all winter, he kept tire chains on the car. "Otherwise we'd never make it through the snowdrifts when we went to town," she said, looking out the window into the past.

I remember the wood burning cook stove—that first winter, sitting on the open door, my bare feet thawing in the oven. By 1954 we had a gas cook stove and an electric refrigerator. A few years later we got a chest freezer. The wood burning cook stove rusted in the blacksmith shop for thirty years. The old icebox was relegated to the porch and used for storage but disappeared a few years later.

Originally, the main part of the house was an old school. In 1908 it was skidded across Nebish Lake and set on a dirt floor basement foundation on the Affield homestead. The following year a two-story addition was constructed on the east end and an upstairs built in the school section. The home became a traditional L-shaped farmhouse with an upstairs that had two bedrooms and a closet in the new section. The upstairs of the school section remained one large open area for many years.

The upstairs rooms had three-foot high walls beneath the sloping uninsulated roof. In the winter, whenever Herman went outside to work, Barb opened the door to the upstairs. When he returned, ten minutes or four hours later, he'd slam the door and mutter, "Wasting heat," and cuss Barb. For all the years I lived at the farm, every winter, pee cans froze and frost formed on sheetrock nail heads.

The main floor was an open design; kitchen and dining area at the west end. A wood-burning stove—the only heat source for the whole house other than the cook stove—was situated in the middle, and the living room and one bedroom finished the east end. In the evening Herman stoked the stove, but with no damper and the door gaskets corroded away, the fire chamber sucked air and by morning the stove was cold and the main floor near freezing. Even with sink cabinet doors open, water pipes often froze, slowly defrosting after Herman rekindled the morning fire.

Each morning, the stove pulled us like a magnet. We clustered around, shivering in our longjohns and flannel pajamas. The warmth spawned an olfactory bouquet composed of leaking smoke, cow manure, and sour milk from the cottage cheese fermenting on the stove top. Those odors fused with the smells of unwashed bodies, baby diapers, dirty laundry and whatever was cooking on the cook stove or baking in the oven. Much of the winter, curing pelts hung behind the stove—muskrats and weasels stretched on V-shaped boards. When we went to school, we must have carried the bouquet with us.

The kitchen sink drain consisted of an elbow connected to a pipe that angled down and out the wall. In the summer, we gave the area a wide berth because the soggy, rancid bare dirt was a breeding ground for flies and mosquitoes. In the winter, wastewater created a corrugated skating rink ten feet from the well. Thanks to gravity, the drain pipe never froze.

I recall one night when I was about eight. I was sick, sleeping on the couch near the stove, when a scratching noise awakened me in the gray dawn. I peeked up and there, on the lip of the sink, perched a white weasel, his black-tipped tail twitching as he grinned at me. He skittered back down the drain hole when I moved.

On sunny days, large south-facing windows warmed the unheated porch, a catch-all for various discards. In winter, trash piled up, until spring sun loosened the odors and eventually the garbage was hauled away and dumped in the woods down around the curve, on state land. Before the indoor plumbing, pee cans and poop cans (for the little kids who might fall through the outhouse holes), were part of the collection. When we first arrived, the porch had a wooden floor with a crawlspace Shep entered from a dog door in the foundation. The spring I was four years old, a skunk wandered in, the dog killed it, and the smell complemented the other odors.

By the mid-1950s the wooden porch floor had rotted to the point that we were stepping through. I remember after Herman ripped out the old floor, we discovered a barnyard of bones and the ossified skunk carcass. Herman wheelbarrowed countless loads of rocks and sand up the steps, dumping and leveling as he filled in the crawl space before he poured concrete.

(Circa 1940s) North side of farmhouse
(Courtesy Elfrieda LaDoux estate)

Like my mother's, *my* early farm memories jumble together, too. During the autumn of 1949 when we arrived in northern Minnesota from New York City, school was already in session, so Chris and Tim were gone all week. I stayed home with my mother, Laurel, and my new father. Laurel was an infant so Barb probably focused on her first daughter in this strange new environment. I tagged along with Herman to the barn morning and evening. Maybe that's why we bonded. He often left the house while I was still wrestling into my boots and parka.

One time as I marched out to the barn, I was passing the chickenhouse and I saw a commotion. A Leghorn rooster sprinted across the snowy yard, red comb flashing in the sun. I stood petrified. He jumped up onto my head, clutched my parka hood in his talons and pecked at my eyes. In my child mind, I remember it happening many times—maybe it did. But that first time, my new father heard my screams, dashed from the barn, and rescued me. Sixty years later, in 2010 when I first opened the chickenhouse door, the faint ammonia-scent of chicken manure triggered that memory and transported me back to a toddler's terror.

 In 1950 the nesting boxes sheltered laying hens—in early spring, an old cluck or two. That's what we called a hen that stopped leaving her nest. She huddled at the back of the box incubating her eggs. Every few seconds, she would "cluck—cluck—cluck," and peck at my hand if I tried to slip it under her to steal an egg. Mostly, the eggs rotted and the cluck ended up in the stew pot. In 2010 the nesting boxes were filled with old books instead of clucks—later I discovered that many of them—the books not the clucks— were published in the1800s, some signed by their authors.

Barb and Herman's wedding took place on January 17, 1950. Chris remembers neighbors arriving in trucks with chain-mounted tires to get through snowbanks. Others arrived in horse-drawn sleds. He said that Tim, Laurel, and I attended the wedding but were sent to bed when the reception started. At the end of the party all the visitors went outside and danced around the house, singing and shouting. Chris called it a shiveree. Barb moved into Herman's bedroom, and we four kids spent that first winter sleeping on the main floor.

Note the name: Barb used "Linda" on the Certificate of Marriage.

There was no honeymoon. We jumped right into farm work. My new father gave me a broken-handled pitchfork so I could "help" load the sled from the concrete silo. After it was piled high with fermented corn silage, he slipped the towrope over his shoulders, leaned forward like a draft horse, and pulled the sled to the barn as I perched on top. The barn was constructed of weathered rough-cut boards. It had a low roof, dirt floor, and wooden stanchions. When we entered with the sled of pungent silage, the cows craned their necks toward us, tongues extended as I helped feed them.

Each day I helped drag forkfuls of hay in. Late in the afternoon I went out with Herman to do the evening chores and milk the cows. I was fascinated by the streams of steaming milk that squirted from the cows' teats. He taught me how to aim and squirt the warm milk directly into my mouth. When I missed, waiting kitties licked the drops from my chin. Herman wasn't quite so loving.

The milk from each cow was poured into an eight gallon can through a funnel-like device with a filter at the bottom. Whenever Herman caught a cat licking the milk strainer, he held the ball of squirming fur between his hands and drop-kicked it across the barn—I suppose a field goal was a splash-down in the gutter. We fed the soggy milk strainer filter to a cat after each milking. Like a boa constrictor, she'd chew and slowly swallow the filter whole. A few days later it would start coming out the other end, often looking like a second tail until it worked through her system.

When Chris and Tim were in school Barb allowed me to ride into town with my new father. We'd bring the cream to the creamery, drive across the street to put a dollar's worth of gas in the car, and go to the Red Owl grocery store. The highlight of the day always happened after we loaded the groceries in the car. Herman dug out a loaf of store-bought white bread, a jar of ketchup, and a package of lunchmeat. With his jack knife—the same one used to castrate piglets—he sliced thick slabs of liverwurst and laid them on a slice of bread, drenched it with ketchup, and covered it with another slice of bread. We'd sit back contentedly eating our sandwiches and wash them down with a shared can of grape soda. After the meal, I'd stuff my gum wad back in my mouth while he read the Bazooka Joe joke I found inside the gum wrapper. One day we shared a can of cold beef stew. When I got home and told Barb about the stew, she hit me because I had shared the spoon with him. It was the first time I remember her knocking me down.

One of my memories from that first spring on the farm is still sweet. It was almost a year before Randy was born. Barb sat at a picnic table shaded by an old growth oak, watching Herman chase Chris, Tim, and me around the house. Herman smelled clean in his faded blue shirt. Bees hummed among the purple clusters of the lilac bushes. Laurel sat in a wooden playpen wearing a ribboned dress that Barb called a pinafore. Mint leaves, picked from the lawn, floated on the ice-cubed lemonade pitcher. Tired of running, I stopped for a drink of icy lemonade and cringed against the instant brain freeze. Barb and Herman were happy.

(Spring 1950) Barb, sitting on the front step of the farmhouse holding Laurel. Barb was quite vain and took her glasses off for pictures.

Old photos are revealing. As a bachelor, Herman apparently didn't do much maintenance around the house. Note the flaking paint and the broken handrail tied to a post. There is also a mass of weeds from the previous year around Barb's legs. Within a few years there was no vegetation within four feet of the steps. I suspect this was due to the way we would stand on the steps and pee, rather than walking twenty-five feet to the outhouse. In the heat of the summer, the front of our house smelled like a urinal at the drive-in theater.

Note the milk cart in the background. Before the new barn was built in 1952, the cart was used to transport the milk cans from the old barn to the house, where the still-warm milk was separated into cream and skim milk. The De Laval separator became the catalyst for countless arguments because Herman was never satisfied with how we scrubbed it after each milking. At first, he taught Barb how to wash all the spouts and discs, but eventually gave up on her and demanded that we children clean it. Over the decades, milk had been splashed on the kitchen wall and spilled on the floor. Again, in the heat of summer, that smell permeated the kitchen corner. The whole area was a mecca for flies.

Herman introduced us to local entertainment and culture the summer of 1950.

(Left to right) Barb holding Laurel, Wendell, Chris behind Tim.
Barb wrote on the back, "At a Rodeo, Bemidji, Minnesota."

Red Lake Nation was only twelve miles north of the farm. In the early 1950s, Ojibwe hunters and fishermen often came to the farm and sold us walleye fillets; in the autumn, venison. Years later, after Chris and Tim bought cars, we drove up to the movie theater in Redby.

I've come to realize that if a person lives long enough, life has a way of coming full circle. As a child, I couldn't know the future impact our Native neighbors would have on my life.

(July 4, 1950) Chris, Laurel, Tim, and Wendell, and an unidentified dancer in regalia at the powwow in Red Lake, MN. We are dressed in New York regalia.

I think back to when I was in Vietnam, how I empathized with the peasants and fishermen who were just trying to live. I didn't realize until many years later that I subconsciously juxtaposed their lives to those of the Natives and our life on the farm. In my memoir, *Muddy Jungle Rivers*, our riverboat squadron is deep in the U Minh Forest on a ten-day operation. My boat is beached near a fisherman's hooch. An ancient Vietnamese man is squatting along the river bank. I wrote, "Back home, on the Indian reservation near our farm in northern Minnesota, there had been an Indian man who sat on the ground, cross-legged on a blanket and listened to the powwow drums—they said he was over one hundred years old."

A few years ago, I spoke at a Veterans Day powwow in Ponemah, Minnesota. I was deeply humbled when two elders made me an honorary member of *O'bahsheeng*, Three Star Warrior Society. Not long ago, another Native veteran friend gifted me an eagle feather. "Every warrior should have one," Bob told me. So, as I say, I feel I've come full circle.

The marriage started with such high hopes. In 1950 Herman made Barb aka Linda co-owner of his farm. I think Herman genuinely tried to make Barb part of his life. I believe he shared details of his military service and early life because later Barb threw that past in his face during arguments. I try to imagine what developed in her mind during those first two years on the farm.

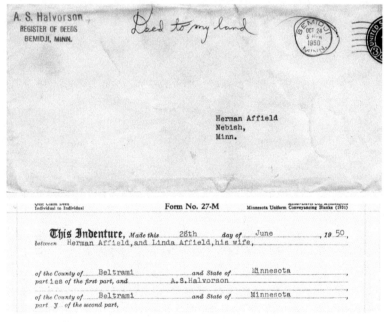

"Deed to my land," Barb wrote at the top of the envelope.

(Summer 1950, *left to right*) Chris, Wendell, Laurel, Tim.
Sitting in the dirt playing with chickens.

Herman and Barbara

I remember Herman's bald head surrounded by a short-cut halo of grayish hair, his scalp often scabbed where he had recently bumped it. His face was ruddy and weathered. Tiny red capillaries spider-webbed his cheeks. He was 5'5" and weighed about 165 pounds. His pale blue work shirt sagged where it was tucked into his baggy dungarees, held up by a leather brass-buckled belt. His shoes, the ones he wore each day working, shined, not from polish but from work. He always insisted on leather laces which he double-knotted each morning. In the winter he wore high-top buckled rubber boots, patched with tire patches from past seasons' wear, and a plaid wool hat with a wilted brim.

During all the years I lived at the farm, Herman's evening routine never varied. After supper and chores, he came into the house and washed up. From beneath a fold-out desk, he'd retrieve a pair of leather slippers. One of the few luxuries he permitted himself was *The Bemidji Pioneer*, a local daily paper which arrived two days late in the mail. Sometimes they'd stack up for a few days. He'd sit in his stuffed chair, adjust his brown-rimmed glasses low on his nose, and arrange the newspapers in chronological order before he read them. Other evenings he'd thumb through a farm magazine or open the desk and work on his farm financial journal. About nine o'clock, he'd stand up, stretch his hands toward the ceiling, and yawn. After a trip to the outhouse, he'd announce, "Lights out," go to his bedroom, and shut the door. That was our cue to finish card games and homework.

He kept his desk locked. The front folded open to a writing platform and revealed a maze of thin vertical storage bins, several horizontal shelves, and a small drawer in the center. The desk housed mysterious papers. Barb was refused entrance. Herman was proud of the fact that, after the war, he had completed an agricultural program the government offered to returning veterans. One aspect of the training was financial planning. Herman recorded all receipts of farm sales and expenses, including money spent on Copenhagen. Sixty years later, I salvaged the desk and had it restored. I rescued many of the papers formerly housed in the desk from a trunk in the attic of the old farmhouse.

On the opposite end of the spectrum, Barb was a talented pianist who could play Brahms, Beethoven, Mozart, and other masters by ear. When she stepped off that Greyhound bus in 1949, her glossy black hair was no doubt well groomed, cheeks rouged, her lips glowing with red makeup. She probably wore a fashionable coat with a beady-eyed mink stole draped around her neck. She carried all her worldly belongings to the farm, including souvenirs of her travels in Europe. She carried post cards of castles and formal gardens, of medieval cathedrals and the mysteries of Spain, the Eiffel Tower and the Swiss Alps. Within a few years the treasures were strewn across the upstairs and mostly destroyed.

She also brought what she thought would be contributions to a farm kitchen, including a sterling silver meat platter that her father had won at the 1927 Orinda Country Club Annual Championship golf tournament.

In the chickenhouse I found supporting evidence of Barb's tales of Poland and Germany and her voyage back to America. (The voyage, in September 1939, had been interrupted when a German U-boat surfaced near them and ordered the captain of the *American Farmer* to pick up survivors from a freighter the U-boat had torpedoed.)

Barb's opera albums, each record tucked in its own protective sleeve, disappeared over the years. We smuggled them out of the house under our shirts and frisbeed Mozart and other classical masters across the yard until they shattered. In the years before we did that, Barb would place one on the Victrola, sit back, demanding complete silence, and drift away as the music filled her farm prison.

In the humid farmhouse with the dirt basement, the silver tea serving set, the silverware, the lazy Susan, and the platter soon succumbed to a mottled charcoal colored film of tarnish. The connection to her past life slowly eroded to memories; the blame, placed on a man who couldn't begin to imagine such an existence. In the end, she bludgeoned Herman with her memories.

Neighbor women had come around visiting in the early days, trying to build friendships with Herman's new wife, but Barb presented a persona of a sophisticated, cultured lady which intimidated the neighbors. They soon stopped visiting and Barb's isolation must have gnawed at her.

From as far back as I can remember, almost every day, Barb complained about severe headaches that could only be soothed by very strong coffee. Her glasses seemed always to be held together with scotch tape or adhesive tape and must have been out of adjustment. I know when mine get out of alignment, I instantly have a headache.

I think now, that by the autumn of 1950 Barb realized she had made a mistake in marrying Herman. She was pregnant with her fifth child and she was hiding from her parents, the only people she could ask for money. I wonder if she was struggling with depression. Chickenhouse documents revealed that two years earlier, when Barb was pregnant with Laurel, I had lived with my grandparents while Barb was under a psychiatric nurse's care in New York City. There were no such mental health resources available to her in northern Minnesota.

A side note: Barb claimed she was ambidextrous and could write with either hand, although she was predominantly right-handed. My sister Laurel and I recently visited about our mother's talent. Laurel thought that because of the complicated music Barb played, her brain strengthened her left hand. I did a bit of research and discovered musicians, especially accomplished pianists, showed superior brain development beyond music. Among other things, the frontal lobe of the brain, the decision maker, operates at a higher rate.

Barb's mother put tremendous pressure on Barb to develop her talent. By the time she was fifteen, Barb gave professional recitals. With her brain so highly developed, how did it impact her behavior over the course of her life? In the isolation of northern Minnesota, did she rebel the only way she knew how?

(May 1936) Barbara, fifteen years old, piano recital in Darien, Connecticut.

Excerpt from my grandmother's 1939 diary:

Friday, September 1, 1939: !!!! Bar has arrived safely in
<u>Brussels!</u> At six a.m. Germany marched on Poland. Bombed
the very spots where B was only a few days before. Never have
we ever had such a thrilling airmail written Tuesday evening
in Brussels the minute she arrived after the most miraculous
escape. With barely enough money she started at 9 a.m. Sat.
having been warned by Eva's papa to flee the moment the
German-Russian Pact was signed. She spent last Sunday in
Warsaw—people were gaily digging trenches and singing. As
she was leaving, the microphone announced "no more trains
across the border." She was let out at 5 a.m. in a Polish frontier
[border] village. A tall Polish American Jew saved her. Talked the
authorities into letting her across and made arrangements for her
in Berlin. She had the same luck in Aachen, Belgian Border—
never were we so thankful. Kay took me out to lunch and then I
went to St. Barts and said prayer.

Saturday, September 2, 1939!!! Another air mail from Bar from
Poland written on August 23, mailed on the 24th. She planned
then to leave on Sept 1—no war fear. Hitler is continuing to
bomb Poland where B was. H, P, and I went to Radio, "Fifth
Avenue Girl" excellent picture—propaganda against all the
troubles in this country.

1951
The Search

For some reason that I have not uncovered, Barb attempted to shield us from our grandparents. Unknown to Herman, Barb was hiding from her parents because she feared that her mother, Elsie, was plotting to have Barb committed to a psychiatric hospital and take custody of us children. Barb's advertisement in *Cupid's Columns* was a last ditch effort to escape from New York and her parents. Randy, Herman's first son, was born January 30, 1951. Herman must have been ecstatic. I wonder how Barb felt with the responsibility of a fifth child.

My grandparents searched frantically for their daughter. I have a computer folder designated for my grandmother's grandiose letter drafts; drafts to King Leopold, Secretary of State Dean Acheson, and others. On April 29, 1950, approximately three months after Barb and Herman were married, Elsie wrote to the governor of New York, asking his assistance in locating Barb. She next appealed to former First Lady Eleanor Roosevelt.

By 1951 the former First Lady was world-renowned for championing humanitarian efforts. She was United States Ambassador to the United Nations Human Rights Council. Elsie despised the First Lady's Democratic Party allegiance but was not above appealing to her for help.

My grandmother knew Eleanor Roosevelt from their shared work thorough Elsie's alma mater, Vassar College, Institute of Euthenics. Near the beginning of the letter, Elsie wrote, "She [Barb] has been missing for over a year." Elsie and Henry first discovered Barb's absence on November 11, 1949. On her appointment calendar, Elsie wrote,

"Armistice Day. Henry and I went out to Far Rock Away [sic]. Barb is not there." That dates Elsie's letter to the former First Lady sometime in the late winter or spring of 1951.

The full text of this undated letter draft, as written by Elsie, follows. I share it so readers can glimpse my grandmother's worldview because, over the years, she became an invisible long-distance influence on our lives and a part of this story.

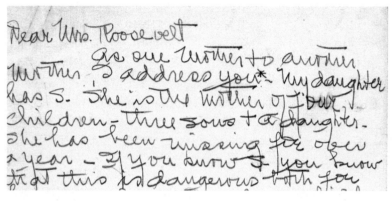

Dear Mrs. Roosevelt

As one mother to another mother, I address you. My daughter has S. [schizophrenia]. She is the mother of four children—three sons and a daughter. She has been missing for over a year. If you know S. you know that this is dangerous both for herself and for her dear children. She was an advanced student studying on scholarships to be a concert pianist when she was blitzed out of Europe by the Second World War. Disconsolate over her music career being ruined by Hitler she went to work in an airplane factory and married the man who worked next to her in the factory. The psychological disorder developed and he deserted her after the first child was born. The second husband got an annulment. She tried suicide (second attempt). We used up what savings we had trying to rehabilitate her. Her father is a veteran of all of our wars. Our forefathers are veterans of all of our wars including the Revolution.

Scz. causes one to withdraw from the World of Responsibilities and people. She started disappearing and going on welfare. The welfare in the county have been wonderful—in Suffolk County they hunted for her, found her, and relieved our anxiety. In Cooperstown, they put her in care of a Psychiatric Nurse, when her fourth baby was coming and had her delivered there to our care for convalescence after.

She disappeared from the Bronx (871 Walton Ave.) over a year ago. The Welfare there was in that communist section. They completely washed their hands of any responsibility. They had just handed her a check for $250. Do you believe that when Congress set up these great Social Agencies it was to disunite the family? In the family unit was America's strength.

Because of the dangerous times in which we live we believe that this poor sick young mother should not be wandering around the country somewhere, where there is no one who has any personal interest in her welfare. If we should be bombed out (Cold War paranoia), she would be entitled to her father's service insurance. To where could it be sent?

It is possible that one of the reasons she is hiding is because she thinks that we think she should be hospitalized. We do not. Only recently Dr. Nolan Lewis, head of New York State Psychiatric Institute of Medical Center 1, 68th St. and Broadway, made this statement that "To date they did not know how to cure scz. Research, of which there should be much more had discovered in that field little more than was known 20 years ago." But we do think that psychiatry could help her and that she owes it to her children and to the good people of our country who give up their savings to support her, that she try to rehabilitate and reestablish herself. She also owes it to herself. She has a high "I Q." If restored to psychological health [she] might become a valuable citizen. Also if she is not, her children as they grow older, nurtured by a neurotic, are very apt to become unhappy and even little criminals.

Would you be willing to write a letter to a Welfare Organization, asking them to contact her with your letter. Would you ask her to see a psychiatrist about her anxieties and those that she is causing her parents, grandparents, and family. And to let her parents know her address. For too long has anti-parents Propaganda gone abroad in our land spread by communist propaganda.

You spoke on the Martha Deane program today of how we could each make our democracy work by doing something about it every day. I do hope you will take five minutes of your valuable time to help these anxious parents. We have exhausted every other channel and can think of nothing else that might so surely set in motion some wheels of progress.

Sincerely Elsie Fratt Philips

Vassar College 1915

*Also as the greatest woman in the world, and also because I believe you are the only woman in the world who can help me—this involves a new humanitarian approach, but as the world's greatest humanitarian I know you are always seeking new approaches.

When Barb and John Curry divorced in 1947, John was ordered to pay child support for my two older brothers. Like Herman, John was enrolled in a higher education program funded by the GI Bill for WWII veterans. A part of that program included an allowance for dependent children. In the chickenhouse I found a carbon copy of a letter dated February 3, 1950, from Calvin Philips, Barb's grandfather, to the Veterans Administration (VA). "I do not have the address of the person [Barbara] referred to in your letter," Calvin wrote. "She wrote me from New York stating that as soon as she was definitely located she will let me know her address." I'm sure Calvin shared that information with Barb's mother.

On March 9, 1950, John, Barb's former husband, wrote to Elsie, "…kindly write to Veterans Administration, Albuquerque, New Mexico, giving my claim #7832977." Elsie was knowledgeable about the VA because her other daughter, Polly, was a WWII veteran and had been diagnosed with paranoid schizophrenia in 1945 while on active duty. Elsie was Polly's guardian and actively worked with the VA to obtain Polly's benefits. My grandmother was like a dog with a bone. I believe that with the bits of information she had accumulated about Barb and knowing Barb's penchant for money, Elsie realized that her daughter would eventually contact the VA. With John's claim number, Elsie began a letter-writing campaign and eventually struck pay dirt through a VA official in Fargo, North Dakota.

On the farm, Barb was completely dependent on Herman for money. During the summer of 1951 he was building a new dairy barn—getting the concrete floor formed and poured for the foundation, gutters, and stanchions. In the dead of winter with the cows dried up, Barb was destitute—destitute to the point of washing and reusing menstrual rags. We grew up dodging them and diapers on the clotheslines strung up in the living room of the old farmhouse. By the summer of 1951 was Barb so desperate for money that she contacted the VA to collect past due child support for Chris and Tim? If so, it was the lead Elsie had been waiting for.

In the autumn of 1951 Elsie and Polly went on a road trip to visit family in Seattle, Washington, and drove back to New York on U.S. Highway 2. In Grand Forks, North Dakota, Elsie deviated from her *AAA TripTik* route and turned south. On October 6 she got in a small accident in Fargo, North Dakota. The man she had turned south to meet, Mr. A. W. Schupieris, was a VA official and an Episcopalian whom Elsie had met through her letter writing campaign. (Elsie and Henry were life-long Episcopalians, very active in their church. One of their closest friends was a bishop.)

Elsie's Diary: October 7, 1951, *Polly and I went to communion service at the Cathedral of Gethsemane, Deacon Birkhead. Who should I sit next to but Mr. A. W. Schupieris, whom I had come to see in Fargo, North*

Dakota? With whom I've had all the correspondence about Barbara. The only one who has had her address in the two years she's been gone. He is a fine man, an usher in the church. He apologized for the way they treated us.

(Written on back of picture) *Sunday, Oct 7, '51. The day I found the means to find Barbara and children. The Episcopal Cathedral, Fargo, North Dakota. Polly and I driving across Continent. A man dented our fender. Mr. A. W. Schupieris, a Vestryman, led the way.*

Elsie's diary continued: October 8, 1951, *One of the most eventful days of my life. Breakfasted at the Powers at 9:15—straight to AAA (American Automobile Association) to find out what company carried our insurance policy. First took car to Buick and they agreed to have the work finished by 2:00 except the paint. I told them I had to drive on schedule. Then to the Vets [Veterans Administration] Attorney General Al Schupieris, who told me as much as he could about Barbara. That she had married Herman Affield Jan. 17, 1950. They live on his farm at Nebish, 22 miles north of Bemidji.*

October 9, 1951, *Duluth—awakened about ten in our beautiful hotel....*

When Elsie left Fargo, she probably drove back up to Grand Forks and continued east on Highway 2. If she did, she passed within twenty miles of the farm where her daughter and grandchildren were living, but she didn't stop. Was Elsie afraid that Barb might physically assault her, as she had done in the past? Or was there a less sinister explanation? Elsie wrote in her diary, *I had to drive on schedule*— I recall when I traveled cross-country with my grandmother in 1967. She was a slave to the *AAA TripTic* schedule, often ruminating on how she would like to revisit points of interest from her past. "We don't have time," she'd lament. Is that what spurred her past Bemidji?

(Autumn 1951) Tim, Barb holding Herman's first son, Randy, and Chris.
(Front) Laurel and Wendell

I always struggled in school. I may have discovered a clue as to why when I studied my older brother's first grade report card, dated May 28, 1951. Over the course of the preceding school year he was absent sixty-four days. His full report card is a litany of "I"—Needs Improvement and "U"—Unsatisfactory. At the end of the school year his teacher wrote, "It is bad for Timothy to miss so much school. I hope that next year his attendance will be more regular." And she passed him to the second grade. Perhaps the most telling part of the report card is the section titled Character Development. I think the marks here are a direct result of our home life.

CHARACTER DEVELOPMENT

	Nine Weeks			
	1	2	3	4
SOCIAL HABITS:				
Plays well with others	u	u	I	S
Is thoughtful of others	I	I	I	I
Is dependable	I	I	I	I
Is learning self-control	I	I	S	S
Respects authority	S	S	S	S
Bus conduct	u	I	I	I
HEALTH HABITS:				
Keeps neat and clean	S	S	S	S
Comes to school rested	S	S	S	S
Is usually happy	S	S	S	S
WORK HABITS:				
Works well with others	I	I	I	I
Works well alone	I	I	I	I
Finishes work on time	I	I	S	S
Listens well	u	I	S	S

SYSTEM OF MARKING
S—Satisfactory   I—Needs Improvement   U—Unsatisfactory
+ Worthy of Special Commendation

PHYSICAL DEVELOPMENT
Height........................... Weight........................ Date.........................
Height....47 1/2 in.... Weight....5 9.......... Date..May 28, 195,

CERTIFICATE OF PROMOTION
This certifies that your child has completed the work of his grade and is hereby promoted to the _second_ grade.
May 31, 19_51_.
Leona E. Nyberg, Teacher

Barb signed all four quarters of the report card Mrs. L. [Linda] Affield.

Some of Barb and Herman's most vicious fights were in the dead of winter. I've always written them off as cabin fever, but was there another dynamic at play?

Today, Minnesota is a recognized leader in SAD (seasonal affective disorder) cases. Is it possible Barb—or Herman—suffered SAD, a form of depression caused by lack of natural sunlight due to short winter days?

If Barb suffered with SAD, did she find solace in her piano and opera albums and just ignore us children? I remember after I started school, digging through heaps of dirty clothes, searching for the least stained, least wrinkled, wadded up shirt and trousers to wear. I found other report cards, from other siblings, with similar grades and attendance records.

Excerpt from my grandmother's 1939 diary:

Sunday, September 3, 1939: !!!! England and France declared war on Germany this morning! It doesn't seem as tho it could really be true! They will immediately go to the aid of Poland. We went to St. Barts to say prayers for Barbara's safe return to Brussels.

Monday, September 4, 1939: A day full of horrible feelings as the Second Great War goes into murderous action. We are relieved to know that Bar has made her miraculous escape from Poland but she is not in complete safety in Brussels.

Saturday, September 9, 1939: Wonder of wonders a cable early this morning from Bar asking for money which means that she is about to leave for home. They are not allowed to cable sailing dates and names of steamers all must be kept in secrecy because of the German U boats sinking so many steamers. *Athenia* with 1500 passengers the first day—almost all lives saved.

Sunday, September 24, 1939: Bar arrives 2 years today (She had left New York on September 24, 1937). We arose and dashed thru breakfast to reach the pier in time. The *Farmer* came in at eleven thirty and there was Bar, the fifth off the steamer. She'd hadn't a cent of money and I hadn't even enough to buy her boat train ticket but got away with it. There was Captain Pederson on the Bridge. They did have the exciting voyage and rescued the crew of a British freighter and saw the British plane sink the German submarine right before them. Barbara isn't well—we brought her mammoth trunk up in the taxi and then took her to Childs in the Plaza for dinner.

1952
First Escape Attempt

Mr. A. W. Schupieris, the vestryman Elsie met in Fargo, connected her
with another Episcopalian, Mr. Rustard, the principal of Bemidji High
School. Mr. Rustard knew of us because Nebish School, where Chris and
Tim attended, was part of the Bemidji school district. Mr. Rustard visited
us at the farm more than once; I don't remember him, but his March,
1952 visit must have terrified Barb—terrified her that her mother was
catching up.

Mon. Mar. 10, 52

Mrs. Henry Olmsted Philips
316 East 58th Street
New York 22, New York

Dear Mr. Rustard,

May I ask your kindness again in giving us any news of our daughter Mrs. Herman Affield? When I telephoned you from Fargo last fall you relieved our worry tremendously by telling me that they were all quite well. We have hoped to hear from our daughter directly this long time, but have just

Mon. Mar. 10, '52

Dear Mr. Rustard, May I ask your kindness again in giving us any news of our daughter Mrs. Herman Affield? When I telephoned to you from Fargo last Fall you relieved our worry tremendously by telling me that they were all quite well. We have hoped to hear from our daughter directly this long time, but have not.

Barb must have felt overwhelmed, tending five children and dealing with a wood-burning cook stove, an outhouse, and no hot water. Being perpetually chilled all winter must have added pressure. That burden was compounded by the companionship of a taciturn man she couldn't possibly understand, a man who shared no cultural values, a man who carried ghosts of his own. And now, her mother was in close pursuit. When did Barb begin forming an escape plan?

I always assumed that the first time she tried to escape the farm was because she found Herman deficient, but as old documents fell into place I came to realize that Herman may have had very little to do with it. Remember that in 1949 Elsie wrote about Barb being under psychiatric nursing care after Laurel was born. With Barb's psychological history, I wonder if she was again dealing with postpartum issues. Was her solution to run from her problems? As she had done in the past, she reached out to her parents—the very people she was hiding from.

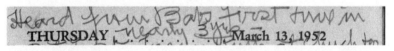

Elsie wrote, *Heard from Babs (Barb), first time in nearly three years.*

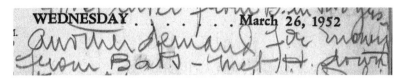

WEDNESDAY . . . . . . March 26, 1952

Two weeks later Elsie wrote, *Another demand for money*. Apparently they sent it and Barb purchased bus tickets.

People are often surprised at how much I remember from my early childhood, but of this I have only vague four-year-old flashes. We were parked at the Bemidji Greyhound Depot, where Barb had first stepped off the bus thirty months earlier. Herman, foot on the clutch, car engine running, shouted at Barb who was sitting next to him holding Randy. Chris remembers that Laurel opened the back door to escape, slipped on the icy curb, and slid under the car. At the same moment, Herman grabbed fourteen-month-old Randy and his foot slipped off the clutch. The car lurched forward and the rear wheel rolled over Laurel's leg. Amazingly, she was only bruised. According to Chris, Herman took Randy over to his sister-in-law's home in Bemidji.

What must have gone through Herman's mind? He probably thought he would never see his son again if he allowed Barb to board the bus. Barb filed a police report about the incident and somehow negotiated Randy's return.

The next day Herman delivered all six of us to the bus station. I was excited about going on a trip. Barb bought us each a Hershey bar. I ate a few squares, folded it shut, tucked it in my pocket, and climbed aboard. Hours later, after I woke from a nap, the Hershey was a melted mass of chocolate on my shirt and Barb slapped me. I think we stopped for a bit in Salt Lake City, Utah, because I have a hazy memory of playing on the steps of the Mormon Tabernacle and visiting a museum where an Egyptian mummy under glass terrified me.

Chickenhouse Chronicles | 49

First we lived in Elko, Nevada. Chris and Tim finished the 1952 spring school year in Elko. Chris remembers that Barb registered them under the last name, Hoganson. Adjacent to the truckstop motel we lived in, there was an auto junkyard, a never-ending source of exploration for Laurel and me while Chris and Tim were in school. When I asked Chris about it, he agreed that we all spent hours in that place, digging through seats in the junk cars, looking for coins. Across the highway from the motel was a range of steep hills with natural holes. Chris, Tim, and I climbed those hills and played hide-and-seek in the holes. I don't recall any snake scares while we lived in Elko even though we spent countless hours playing in their cool dark lairs.

Barb had lived in Nevada before. In studying chickenhouse documents I discovered her old connections. In a letter to her mother in 1941, Barb wrote, … *[we] have been on the go ever since we left Goldfield, Nevada. The telephone line was completed there and this friend asked me to drive his brand new car up to Sacramento.*

"This friend" was John Curry, the man she married a few months later. By 1944, Barb, John, and Chris moved to Henderson, Nevada. The family lived in company housing—Anderson Camp—adjacent to Basic Magnesium, Inc., a critical war industry plant where John worked.

What prompted Barb to return to Nevada the spring of 1952? Elko is three hundred miles from Henderson or Goldfield. Did she attempt to contact her former husband, who was by then, remarried and living in New Mexico? Had she saved a letter from her lonely hearts club correspondence from a prospect in Elko?

In the chickenhouse I discovered this telegram Barb sent to her father on June 22, 1952. Knowing Barb, I'm sure she skipped out on the delinquent rent in Elko. There was no job offer awaiting her in the Cascade Mountains of Washington.

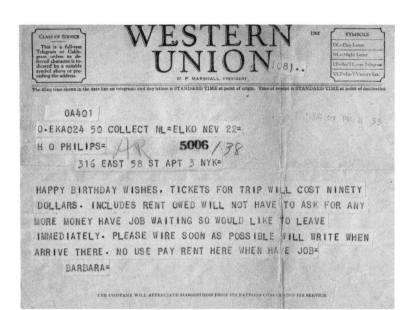

0A401

O·EKA024 50 COLLECT NL=ELKO NEV 22=

H O PHILIPS=   5006 / 38

316 EAST 58 ST APT 3 NYK=

HAPPY BIRTHDAY WISHES, TICKETS FOR TRIP WILL COST NINETY
DOLLARS. INCLUDES RENT OWED WILL NOT HAVE TO ASK FOR ANY
MORE MONEY HAVE JOB WAITING SO WOULD LIKE TO LEAVE
IMMEDIATELY. PLEASE WIRE SOON AS POSSIBLE WILL WRITE WHEN
ARRIVE THERE. NO USE PAY RENT HERE WHEN HAVE JOB=

BARBARA=

Why, after eleven weeks, did we so abruptly leave Elko? Did she reconnect with John? Did he spurn her? Was she afraid that Herman was on her trail? Chris remembered the bus trip to Washington, traveling through snow-covered mountain passes.

Lake Chelan Respite

Tucked in the North Cascade Mountains of Washington is Lake Chelan, a reservoir filled by the Stehekin River and Railroad Creek. Created by the Chelan Dam, it's a string bean shaped lake more than fifty miles long and flows into the Columbia River. Our cabin was a three-hour ferry ride on *Lady of the Lake* from Chelan. Elsie sounded familiar with the house we were squatting in, so I think it's fair to infer that Barb had spent time visiting Lake Chelan as a child in the 1920s.

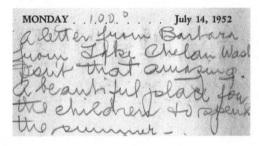

On July 14 Elsie wrote, *A letter from Barbara from Lake Chelan, Wash. Isn't that amazing. A beautiful place for the children to spend the summer.*

Barb's new name was Roseanne Stanley. In late June 1952 we moved into a house on the mountain where pine scent permeated everything. The main entrance was shaded by a screen porch that wrapped around the front of the house. The kitchen was utilitarian. We stored cereal (when we had it) in the icebox, away from mice. There was no ice for the box. Melt water—gravity fed— was piped to the house from higher elevations. Late summer, after it trickled to a stop, we lugged lake water up the sandy trail.

In front of the stone fireplace that covered one wall was a coarse hemp rug that protected our feet from slivers on the living room floor. Panoramic views of Lake Chelan lay beyond the smoke-stained windows. Twice a week *Lady of the Lake* appeared as a speck on the horizon, growing, along with my dream of escape, only to dwindle as she steamed past.

I was four that summer and remember mornings being very bright in the living room. Hiding in a sunbeam behind the old leather armchair, I'd wave at firefly-like dust specks, the drafts nudging them toward the library of books that covered another wall. Now, recalling the dim afternoon coolness, I realize that early morning sun came through those few hours and then was blocked by massive Douglas firs and mountain peaks. Double doors opened to wide steps, bordered by stone banisters. Just beyond, forty feet perhaps, the lake bluff dropped; the water, about thirty feet below.

We were afraid of the rotted outhouse seat so we squatted in the forest and used pine needles to wipe. Randy was eighteen months old and being potty trained. Early each morning, Chris raced down the stairs with Randy in his arms and out into the nearby forest. When Chris talks about those days, he's still in awe of the huge poop pile Randy dropped in the pine needles.

Upstairs had a large screen porch with a big bed that Barb piled in with four of the five children. Sometimes in the evening, from my little cot in the nook above the kitchen near the head of the stairs, I could hear her telling stories.

A trail zigzagged up the mountain; in places through ankle deep sugar sand, at times across rock. It opened to a green meadow with a homestead at the far end. A gnomish woman and her son, Henry, lived there. They had a few milk cows, chickens, and a small orchard. The shriveled lady gave us milk. Sometimes she fed us, and I recall how she never let me put pepper on my fried eggs. "Too expensive," she said.

Chris and Tim often tried to ditch me on the switch-back trail to Henry's homestead. I was a clumsy tag-along. They nicknamed me Ben Tungg (pronounced like the first syllable of tungsten, only dragging the 'g'), and the name stuck for many years. One day on our milk run, they raced ahead on the trail, around a bend, and out of sight. "Hey, Ben Tungg, the grizzlies are gonna get you," Chris shouted over his shoulder.

"More milk for us," Tim yelled, chasing after Chris.

I sat in the trail crying, knowing they'd have to come back. Tired of waiting, scared, I shuffled uphill toward the next curve. As I approached a charred tree trunk—remnant of a lightning strike or a forest fire—deep growls emerged from the base. To my four-year-old mind that looming blackness was a twenty-foot grizzly. I screamed, turned, and ran downhill. Tim and Chris jumped from behind the stump, tore after me with grizzly roars of glee as turds tumbled from my suspendered shorts.

Barb—Mommy Darling we called her in those days—thought it humorous. "Bears wouldn't eat your dirty butt." She sent me down to the lake with a scrub board and a bar of soap.

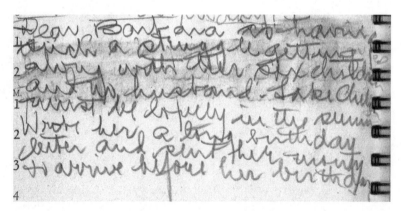

From my grandmother's diary, July 30, 1952: *Dear Barbara is having such a struggle getting along with her six children and no husband. Lake Chelan must be lovely in the summer. Wrote her a long birthday letter and sent her money to arrive before her birthday.*

There's an interesting layer to this entry. As in the past, Elsie again alluded to Barb having one more child than she actually did—there were only five of us that summer. But that's another story—back to Chelan and the milk we carried down the mountain from our neighbor.

We stored the milk in a covered two-gallon can down in the cellar. One day Chris tripped on the stairs and dumped the pail. We soaked it up with rags, rung them into the bucket, and drank the brown milk. Chris received a beating for that.

Barb demanded declarations of love that reached galactic proportions. "Mommy Darling, I love you more than all the water in Lake Chelan. More than the mountains. More than the sky. More than all the stars." We chanted this mantra daily. Yet childhood indiscretions guaranteed the violator a nighttime visit.

Barb purchased orange life vests for us because we spent countless hours playing in Lake Chelan. The lake was primarily melt water from high elevations and very cold. I was terrified of water over my head and Lake Chelan was over 1,400 feet deep. Thank goodness I didn't know that in 1952.

One day Chris, recreating the exploits of Christopher Columbus, captain of the *Santa Maria*, was playing sailboat with a two-handled wash tub when a wind gust curled down from the bluff and whisked his ship into deep water and it sank. That evening he was punched, kicked, and slapped. Later, I listened from my cot as Barb and the four other children cuddled in the big bed on the upstairs screen porch, and she begged her firstborn for forgiveness.

(Summer 1952) Lake Chelan in background. *(Left to right)* Tim, Laurel, Wendell, Randy, Chris

Our bachelor neighbor Henry discovered Chris, Tim, and me playing on his stone quay one afternoon. I don't remember what triggered Henry to throw me off the end of the pier. Without my life jacket, I panicked and screamed as I kicked and swallowed gulps of Lake Chelan. Eventually I clawed my way to the rocky ledge of the quay and pulled myself along the side to shore. From then on, I kept my distance from Henry. I became terrified of water over my head and yet, thirteen years later I qualified as a water survival expert and pilot rescue swimmer for airmen who were shot down in Vietnam and ditched in the Gulf of Tonkin.

Each day we sat on the pine carpeted forest floor while Barb read from *Aesop's Fables* and lectured us on moral pitfalls the stories illuminated. She'd captured a mouse and kept him in a gold bird cage—named him City Mouse. For several weeks she doted on City Mouse, hand-feeding him through the wire bars, dribbling water into his dish. One day Laurel and I were playing with the mouse and I dropped a pencil in. Knowing I'd be punished when Mommy Darling discovered it, I opened the door to retrieve the pencil, and the mouse escaped.

I was upstairs hiding on the screen porch when she found me. "Darling, Laurel told me you've been playing with City Mouse."

"I didn't do it, Mommy Darling," I said, edging around the bed.

"It's okay darling, you're my favorite son."

"I'm sorry, Mommy Darling. I love you more than all the trees on the mountain." I jumped across the bed, ran through the hall, down the stairs, and outside to the woods.

"You little bastard, I'll get you tonight," she shouted after me.

I spent the day hiding at the edge of the yard, beyond the garden. Chris and Tim called me for supper but I refused to answer. I cringed at night noises. Scurrying mice grew into grizzlies. Whistling owl wings were descending goblins. Finally, after the house was quiet and the candles blown out, I crept in. I tucked my pillow beneath the blanket then crawled under the bed. As I dozed off, Barb pounced. Cot springs crushed down on me. She became further enraged by my deception. Holding a candle, she peered under the bed and discovered me hugging the far corner. Grabbing a broom, she jabbed with the handle.

Her rant went something like this. "You lost my pet." Jab. "You little bastard, you lost City Mouse." Jab. "I always wanted my own pet but Mother wouldn't let me." Jab. "Now you let it go." Jab. She continued until she was winded.

Curled fetal, back to her, I wailed, "I love you, Mommy Darling. I'll catch City Mouse again. I'm sorry. I love you. It hurts. Please stop poking me. I love you, Mommy Darling." Eventually, she left. I spent the night in the corner, afraid she would return.

The next morning she asked why I was walking hunched over—I don't recall that she ever mentioned the mouse again. Later in the day she threw the cage in the fireweeds behind the outhouse. I remember lying on the rocky beach, on my stomach, the warm sun soothing on my bruised back.

There were hidden perils beyond our mother's wrath. Over the centuries, wind and weather had eroded the lakeshore bluffs of Lake Chelan. Tree roots supported sod with thin air beneath. One day we three boys were playing near the bluff and I fell through, my outstretched arms stopping me from falling thirty feet to the rocky lakeshore. Chris lay on his stomach, inched his way out to me, and pulled me from my hole.

As summer waned, food grew scarce. A few hundred yards from our house was Moore's Inn, a popular tourist lodge. One day Chris killed a rattlesnake that had frightened a visitor who was hiking past our house. Chris brought the snake home, skinned it, and we ate it.

Our neighbor, Henry Schweke, wrote on back of photo: *1949 with my mother. Lake Chelan and Stehekin Valley in background.*

As I mentioned earlier, in the late 1940s Barb had advertised herself in singles catalogues. Is it possible that Henry sent her this photo? Why else would she have it? Or had she played with Henry when they were children, when the Philips family had visited Lake Chelan in the 1920s? Did Barb have hopes of marrying Henry? I don't recall the two of them spending time together, alone, but that's not part of a four-year-old's worldview.

Gunshots echoed down the mountainside one early autumn night. The next morning we all hiked up the trail to see why Henry had fired his rifle. He'd shot a bear in his apricot tree. We gorged ourselves on the knocked-down fruit. Randy and Laurel sat beneath the tree, sucking apricots, juice running down their chins as ants crawled across their faces. Henry gave us some of the meat and the bear hide. We ate the meat and remnants we scraped from the hide, but our systems were not used to the rich, fatty food. Everybody got diarrhea.

Barb's father sent her the following letter at Chelan. I have only pages three and four.

first consideration in your thinking – for from now on if your theory of life is right, and your living of life is right, then they will mature right – otherwise the reverse is true – Here is a great opportunity to rebuild from past mistakes – which we all make – and build a sound true future – Nothing in life is perfect – No one is perfect – the

... first consideration in your thinking—for from now on if your theory of life is right, and your living of life is right, then they will mature right—otherwise the reverse is true. Here is a great opportunity to rebuild from past mistakes—which we all make—and build a sound true future. Nothing in life is perfect—no one is perfect—the greatest happinesses come from accepting our disillusionments as challenges to make the most of the circumstances we are surrounded by. Go back, take the children back, give Herman a square deal, be a good conscientious sincere wife, be a help-mate—life is difficult for him, too. Use your fine background and intelligence to broaden his mind—not to ever belittle any lack of advantages he has had. Let it be your sole responsibility to make his farm and your home the center of a happy intelligent constructive family center. There is a depth to your being sufficient to override all the trivialities of life, to ignore little frustrations and give to those around you the benefit of a spiritual and moral resurgence that I feel lies very close to the surface, if you will but allow it to come out into the sunlight. Go back and make of your new life a Crusade of Happy Sacrifice to those whose very lives are dependent on you—Mother, Pol, and I send dearest love, and God bless you!

P.S. If you don't think trying to return to Herman is the best idea, write me immediately what you think is a better idea.

I can only imagine what Barb must have written to her father that would generate this response. It must have been something philosophical, questioning life. What did Barb say about us children? What was her father alluding to when he wrote, "...whose very lives are dependent on you." In recent years, we've all read of mothers (and fathers) who have drowned or otherwise destroyed their children in an effort to escape. I wonder how close our mother came to that final solution.

Autumn ebbed. Each day Chris and Tim rode a boat across the lake to school in Lucerne. Barb had registered them with the last name Stanley. As I mentioned earlier, Barb used the alias Roseanne. More than sixty years later Chris remembered how confusing it was to have a new last name.

After school started the autumn of 1952, Chris and Tim couldn't go for the milk, so Henry often delivered it, each time warning Barb about the approaching winter and her lack of food and firewood. There was no money left. Years later, during my interviews with Barb, she reminisced about sitting at the kitchen table after dark, writing letters by candlelight and how deer would nose against the window. I wonder who she was writing to, because in the chickenhouse I found no letters to her parents. Perhaps by autumn she had bled them dry.

We'd eaten the emergency rations the owners had stashed in the cellar. We had eaten the rattlesnake Chris killed. The little garden was gone. Chris and Tim couldn't catch anything with their Gabby Hays fishing equipment, even though Lake Chelan had an abundance of trout, salmon, and bass. Autumn nights turned cold. With no wood to take the chill off the old house, Barb was forced to face reality.

Our last morning, packed, waiting for Henry to ferry us in his old boat, *Tillicome*, to Stehekin where we'd catch *Lady of the Lake* to Chelan, Laurel and I were playing catch in the living room. I hit her in the nose. She screamed for Mommy Darling. I dashed out the double doors and tripped over the hemp rug lying, airing out, on the stairs. I skidded face-down, down to the frost-covered stones at the base of the steps, cheeks scraped raw, nose horribly rope-burned. I rolled over, stunned, and stared through tears and fir limbs into gray sky.

"That will teach you," Barb said, hands on hips at the head of the stairs.

"But I love you, Mommy Darling."

I always assumed that the Lake Chelan house belonged to one of our Seattle relatives because some of them had made their fortunes as turn-of-the-century timber barons and bankers and would have been aware of the pristine wilderness hideaway. In 2010 I discovered this letter in the chickenhouse, written by my great grandfather Calvin Philips to my grandfather Henry.

October 10, 1952, Dear Henry, This must be short as I am out of the sickbed to write it. Mrs. Harry Johnston of Tacoma formerly of Burlington [Delaware] has just been here. Barbara with her five children moved into a furnished house of the Johnston's on Lake Chelan. Because the house had been sold after Barbara moved in, it was necessary to compel her to vacate. Mrs. Johnston sent B a lot of clothing for the children and has more she wants to send if she can learn her address. B told her you had arranged transportation to St. Paul but B said she did not want to go to St. Paul. When B left the house, she took a number of articles belonging to the Johnstons but Mrs. Johnston has no intentions of compelling B to return them. If I learn more I will write you. Love, Father

Calvin Philips was eighty-seven and in failing health when he wrote that letter. In 2010, after Barb died, I purchased an antique steamer trunk at her estate sale. Stenciled on the side is "HH Johnston, WILMINGTON, DEL." Calvin Philips had been raised in Wilmington, son of the Greenbank Mill owners. I'm sure that in late 1800s Wilmington, the Philips and the Johnston families were acquainted—probably friends, and that friendship continued after both families relocated to the West Coast. Because of that, I am quite certain that in the 1920s, Barb and her parents had been guests of the Johnstons at their summer cabin on Lake Chelan. (When Calvin built Greenbank Farm on Whidbey Island, he named it in memory of Greenbank Mill in Delaware.)

Not long after we returned to Herman and the farm, Barb filed with Beltrami County welfare department for Aid For Dependent Children (AFDC) for Chris, Tim, Laurel, and me. I'm sure she had no idea of the far-reaching consequences. Vera Graves, from the Welfare Department, responsible for the supervision of AFDC grants, began visiting us. I discovered her report—an excerpt: "She [Graves] reviewed the condition of the home during her visits which indicated that the house on each occasion was dirty and filthy and that the children were at times dressed in dirty clothes or not adequately clothed."

Vera Graves' appraisement of our living conditions was very accurate. During the 1950s, we children didn't understand anything was unusual—being marginally clothed and fed, living in squalor, was our normal.

I remember when the social worker came out to the house. Barb was rigid and thin-lipped, "Yes, umm-hmmm," she would nod in agreement with the case worker's suggestions. After Graves left, Barb vented, "Who the hell does she think she is, telling a sophisticated lady from New York how to take care of her children?"

With the welfare assistance for the four children she had brought to Minnesota in 1949, Barb now received a steady income that exceeded the farm income six months of the year.

Polly, Elsie, Henry, and Eloise

I have more than one hundred letters my grandfather, Henry, wrote to my grandmother—many while he was away during WWII. He sounded like a deep thinker. His writing was often poetic, passionate, and philosophical. I think he would have been a wonderful minister or professor, but he went into business to please his father. As a businessman, he left a trail of failures. I include this next information so the reader can glimpse the horrific financial pressure my grandfather, a god-fearing Episcopalian layman, was under—and what that pressure drove him to do.

Eloise Thomas Garstin—mentioned earlier—is a name no one in our family had ever heard. In the chickenhouse, about ten feet from my grandfather's urn, I discovered Eloise's existence in a packet of mouse-urine-stained letters. My grandfather and Eloise were first cousins. Over the course of six years, from 1950-1956, Henry defrauded thousands of dollars from Eloise. (Some of the first funds were probably diverted to Barb when we were living in Chelan.)

Eloise first considered putting Henry in charge of her trust in December 1944. Henry's troop ship had been torpedoed and had sunk in the North Sea. After being rescued, while enroute back to the United States, he made a whirlwind visit to his cousin in England—the first time in twenty years they had seen each other. After the visit, Eloise's glowing letters to Henry's wife Elsie and letters to other American relatives, revealed the deep affection and trust Eloise held for Henry.

On May 1, 1946, a month after Henry was discharged from the army, Elsie wrote in her diary, *Henry returns to Wall Street. Henry went back to Lee Higginson from where he left four years ago—how fast time flies—he is glad to be there.* After WWII Henry had returned to his old job as a stock broker at Hares, Ltd. The primary responsibility of a stockbroker is to increase wealth. A second responsibility is to recruit new clients.

Jumping forward almost two years, to June 6, 1948, Eloise, Henry's English cousin, wrote,

17 Walpole Ter.,

Brighton, England

Henry dear, I am writing to ask whether you will take Fred's place in a small business matter which concerns me. As you know Cyrus made money for me and all the securities are with the Bank of California in San Francisco. Around 1928 he drew up a "Voluntary Trust" agreement, – a rather "loose" document which legally would not stand on its own legs in this country. However it has proved extremely useful. During the war [World War II] I believe I told you the Bank of England tried to get this document from the Bank of California with the idea of taking over all my investments and compensating me. The Bank of California steadfastly refused to part with it and after a correspondence lasting the whole of the war, the Bank of England finally dropped the matter. Feeling that my position was a trifle uneasy, although there are many good arguments in my favor, I thought the Trust Agreement might be bolstered up to a certain extent by bringing in an American citizen, so I asked Fred in 1947 if he would agree that his name should be added to a clause stating that I could not remove the capital without his consent. Not that I have any desire to remove the capital – far from it!!

Now that poor Fred has passed away, would you be willing to have your name inserted in his place? You see under this new Act of 1947, called "The Exchange Control Act" I ought to have declared that I hold my securities in the Bank of California but I have not done so, and do not intend to do so, or to cross any bridges until I come to them.

On the assumption that you will be willing to do this, I am enclosing a note to the Bank of California which perhaps you will mail on to them. I am not too keen on writing them direct, as all business letters from here to the United States are opened or x-rayed.

Henry, in the role of stockbroker, convinced Eloise to turn her investment portfolio over to him. On February 16, 1949, Eloise wrote,

My dear Henry,

I have continued to think the matter over very carefully and have been discussing it with Barclays Bank Income Tax Manager who is a very good friend to me and who is the only person on this side conversant with my affairs as he prepares my Income Tax Statement each year for the Inland Revenue, and has done so for the past 16 years.

Well, Henry dear, I am almost ready to take the plunge and write to the Bank of California to redeem the bonds and send the proceeds to you. I certainly know you would have my affairs more at heart than the Bank of California ever would and that you would always be very quick to act. It is most generous of you to be willing to do all this for me, but when the thing gets going, I must insist that you take for yourself a very proper remuneration out of the funds.

The last sentence in that letter will come back to haunt Eloise. Before Eloise transferred the funds to Henry, she arranged for a monthly stipend of one hundred dollars be paid to her two spinster cousins, Estelle and Julia Thomas, who lived in Philadelphia, Pennsylvania. Making this monthly payment to the sisters became one of Henry's responsibilities.

My grandparents were struggling with another issue beyond Barb and her troubles: Polly, Barb's younger sister, was schizophrenic. She was living at home and acting out. The following brief entries from Elsie's diary led up to Polly's disappearance.

Nov 25, 1952—Pol away—skipped seeing W.C. [Wesley Culver, her psychologist]. *Called Culver, turned in missing person's report.*

Dec 8—Herald (Polly's beaux) *called about Polly, said she called him with a strange conversation.*

Dec 10—Our 35th wedding anniversary. Polly not here

Dec 11—All afternoon at V.A. Dr. Jim Howard nice—no answers. W.C. no answer. See me in two weeks. [Polly is at this time, under the supervision of Veterans Administration health care.]

Dec 20—We bought a lovely big Christmas tree. Surely miss Polly but are carrying on anyway.

Dec 23—W.C. talked about Polly's strange disappearance. We have no clues.

And so Polly's absence continued on into 1953 and must have put tremendous stress on her parents. Polly served as an army nurse during WWII. As I mentioned earlier, Polly was diagnosed schizophrenic and discharged in 1945. For the next decade, she was in and out of institutions. In the chickenhouse I discovered an envelope with receipts showing that Henry and Elsie made payments to private institutions for Polly's care. Eventually the Veterans Administration began paying Polly a disability pension. But during that decade, Polly's medical bills drove Henry to defrauding Eloise.

My grandmother Elsie was a spendthrift. As a child, she was surrounded by maids and gardeners. (Today, her family home, the Charles

D. Fratt Mansion in Everett, Washington, is a historic landmark.) Elsie never learned to cook—a deficiency she passed on to Barb. Hundreds of documents, from the 1920s forward, reveal Elsie's extravagant lifestyle and Henry's desperate struggle to finance it. He loved her and couldn't say no. In one 1940s letter, Elsie mentioned leaving him, so perhaps fear motivated his quest to keep her happy. In Elsie's defense, she returned that love. By the end of 1952 there's no doubt that Henry was diverting Eloise Garstin's funds for his personal use. Here is an excerpt from a letter Eloise wrote:

28 December 1952

My Dear Henry, A Happy New Year to You, Elsie and Polly!! Now we must leave pleasure for a moment and turn to business.

Upon pondering over things, especially with regard to the small sums of money you are perhaps earmarking for me for France next year, it occurs to me to wonder exactly where this amount of interest comes from? You remember of course that a few years ago I sold shares to the value of about 1000 pounds and sent the proceeds to you to keep for me for sending abroad from year-to-year, to avoid complications with the British Authorities. Then came the question of transferring a sum to Estelle and Julia. Well, now, what I want to know is—did I make it plain to you that the sum transferred to Estelle and Julia was a free gift to them? That is what I meant it to be but it has occurred to me to wonder whether you understood, or whether you thought the Capital still remained mine and only the interest theirs? The reason I ask is because I am wondering whether you just merged the second transfer into the first, and that is why from time to time you lay aside and odd 30 pounds or so for me? The two are really quite separate. I do not want to take any interest whatever from the sum which is given to Estelle and Julia. If the two sums are merged into one—well, then, it must all be in Estelle and Julia's name and they must have the full interest, not me. It is entirely my fault if I did not make it clear in the first place. After all, I can always have the Bank of California send me part of my quarterly income abroad. It was merely my fear of committing a crime which caused me to transfer some to you in the first place. So, Henry dear, if all you hold is now inextricably mixed into one lot, please put it with the names of Estelle and Julia Thomas. By the way, in whose name is it now? Do forgive all these bothersome questions but I'm having a good clear-out in my mind.

I think without doubt the Capital should be legally made over to Estelle and Julia if not already done so, and that they should hold some document to prove they are the owners, don't you? This life being the uncertain thing it is, if the money is not already in their name, if either I or you meet with a fatal accident, they might never be able to prove the Capital is theirs.

Another thing on my mind off and on for a long time and to which you never reply when I ask you (bad boy) is: do you pay yourself a proper commission on all the transactions you transact? Do please answer this for you know it is my wish and I feel sure it would be theirs [the cousins] *for you to do so—we do not want to exploit your kind heart, so please let me know.*

Well, I think that is all that is on my mind at the moment except to say that if "the girls" do not already hold a document of some sort, would it not be as well, when sending them one, to state in which bank the money is lodged and also the amount of the present Capital? I must confess I myself don't know these two answers! You will think me a strange being indeed to suddenly pour all these ponderings on you. I hope it is not my Swan Song as I'm feeling particularly bright and fit! It's just that I suppose at times we all of us reflect on our affairs.

And now back to pleasure! ....

Below is the draft of a letter Henry wrote in reply to Eloise's letter. Note the ambiguity and the unanswered questions.

Dear Eloise,

To answer your questions regarding the monies caring for Estelle and Julia, no, that has not been merged with the previous amount. As a matter of fact your wish to transfer to Estelle and Julia now the amount caring for them is different than your original instructions for me to so invest this amount to care for them and repay me for doing so. A long-term program was accordingly set up, and at present, without a marked rise in our markets until the Republicans have been in office for some years, it could only be done with loss to you, to them, and to me. I have had no commissions out of it, as under the rules of New York Stock Exchange I, who work for a firm member of the Exchange, am precluded from taking commission from their account. We do indeed live in a dangerous age. I have taken every precaution to see that this income goes on uninterrupted to them, and I suggest though you have done so, that your will cite the facts of this income to Estelle and Julia. Sincerely, Henry

Republican Dwight D. Eisenhower was elected president in 1952. From my grandfather's letter, it sounds as if he was counting on Eisenhower's new economic policies to bail him out. I can only speculate on what Henry did with Eloise's funds that were now legally in his name. In the chickenhouse I discovered an envelope containing stock certificates and many buy/sell orders, all in Henry Philips' name. I took the stock certificates to a local broker. Of course, they were valueless. The stocks, Transstates Petroleum Inc., Transgulf Corporation, Potlatch Oil and Refining, and New Era Mines, represented the wild speculation during that era of natural resource exploration.

For every fortune made, thousands of small investors lost money. I believe that my grandfather, the eternal optimist, squandered a portion of Eloise's money in this way.

Garden and Other Winter Supplies

On the farm, our garden provided thousands of meals, just as it had for the early settlers. When the first Affields arrived in Nebish, they must have been thrilled to discover a young orchard, planted by the original homesteaders, on the east side of the one-acre garden. More than four decades later, when we arrived in 1949, the orchard had become an overgrown jungle of wild plums, pectin apple trees, grass, cockle burrs, and two mature crab apple trees. There were a few domestic plum trees that produced large purple plums, but they never survived our hungry mouths to make it to the pressure cooker. There were also two stunted apple trees, maybe an early variety of today's Honeycrisp apples, which produced a few dozen every other year.

The garden was located about twenty yards east of the woodshed and the root cellar. The woodshed was a rough-hewn log building with the outhouse leaning against the east side. It was, in fact, the first homesteader dwelling on the property, built about the same time as Old Nebish was developed half a mile away on the east shore of Nebish Lake in the 1890s. As a woodshed, the building was inefficient; one small door to carry the wood from shed to house, and one small opening at the other end to throw the cut logs into the building.

The hillside root cellar, probably one of the first improvements when the land was homesteaded, was dug into the clay on the north slope, behind the woodshed and outhouse. It was a natural location, sheltered from summer sun and winter winds. Chris remembers the root cellar. Listening to him, memory fragments flickered in my mind—memories of hiding in the dim coolness of summer, of ice melting in my mouth, splinters chipped from blocks buried beneath damp sawdust.

Chris remembered Herman harvesting ice from Maple Lake and dragging it across the snowy fields on a sled the first winter we were at the farm. "He wouldn't let me go to the lake with him," Chris told me. "I might fall through a hole."

Spring garden planting followed a routine. Rhubarb beds at the top of the clay hill began to break ground while snowbanks were still melting on the shaded side of the house. The pale green knobs pushed up from the still-brown earth, small green leaves reaching for sunlight. Within a month the hills of rhubarb were surrounded by a plush carpet of poison ivy. To harvest the rhubarb was a guaranteed case of the itchy rash—I seemed especially sensitive. The risk was worth it. Tart rhubarb sauce spooned over white bread was the first food from the garden each season.

I imagine that Herman followed his father's garden management. Each spring he spread weed-seed-infested cow manure on the garden and then plowed, disked, and harrowed it. After harrowing, we dragged a homemade two-row marker back and forth, laying out the grid for vegetable rows. A lifetime later I remember the layout that paralleled the orchard. Two rows of onions; two rows of assorted veggies—cucumbers, kohlrabies, tomatoes and lettuce; two rows of carrots and cabbages; one row of string beans and two rows of rutabagas. The last dozen rows were planted in potatoes.

Shriveled russets trailing anemic yellow-green vines—potatoes left from last season's harvest—were brought up from the basement, cut into pieces, two eyes on each section. Herman walked the pre-marked garden rows, full seed potato bucket hanging from his belt. With the hand planter his father had used, he dropped a seed potato into the top of the funnel as he stepped on the foot peg and pressed the point into the ground. With a push forward of the wrist, the jaw of the planter opened and the seed potato was released four inches below ground. He took a sliding step forward and dirt was pushed over the hole and sealed, the process already in motion for the next potato set. As the family grew, we planted several rows of potatoes on the edge of the corn field to supplement the garden.

Our "sweet corn" came from the field corn. We harvested bushels, husked it, stood the naked cobs on end and sliced the kernels off for canning. We threw the husks and stripped cobs to the hogs. Beside the potatoes in the cornfield, the other staple was beans. In autumn, the bushes were pulled from the earth and shelled through the threshing machine, then cleaned of weed seeds and stones in the fanning mill. Bean-size stones filtered through the machines and into the beans, often resulting in chipped teeth when we ate bean soup.

Herman took satisfaction in canning a few things—no doubt a carry-over from his bachelor years. Pickles and pickled crabapples were packed away for winter. The bushels of potatoes, carrots, and rutabagas that we weeded all summer were harvested late in the autumn, carried down to the dirt-floor basement, and stored in large bins.

Beyond the thousands of hours we children spent working the garden, I recall the humorous side of canning. In the early days, Herman had taught Barb how to use the pressure cooker—an essential tool for canning. One summer day the steam valve on the locked-down lid whistled wildly. Suddenly an explosion ripped through the house. The lid blew—blew up and tore the cupboard doors off.

Pickled crabapples were a treat. Randy and I once smuggled a quart jar up out of the basement and went out on the porch to eat it. Randy's face hovered above the jar as I unscrewed the band and started to pry the lid off with my little jackknife. Bacteria had built up in the jar and the lid blasted off. Apple shrapnel dripped from Randy's face as we both laughed and he licked his lips. I'm guessing we ate the contents—wouldn't let a little thing like the fear of food poisoning stop us.

Wild fruit was a treat. A few Sunday afternoons each summer, the whole family piled into the car and drove about ten miles east to a pine forest thick with blueberries. By evening everybody was chewed up by mosquitoes. The berries were dumped in the sink and rinsed in cold water. We skimmed off the green berries, stems, and bugs that rose to the surface. No blueberries were preserved for future use. We devoured them fresh, one of the few times Herman allowed us the treat of a dribble of cold cream and a sprinkle of sugar.

As I mentioned, Barb's canning skills left something to be desired. For Herman it was part of the season, no different than storing forage for the animals. Late summer we each strapped a calf feeding pail to our belt and went in search of chokecherries. By mid-August the little trees drooped like weeping willows, heavy with purple clumps of small berries. One hand pulled the limb down until the clump hung over the pail. The other hand stripped the berries off and we moved on to the next tree.

A few gallons of chokecherries were boiled until they became mush. We poured the contents into a colander lined with cheese cloth and filtered the juice from the pitted berries. The cheese cloth was tightened and squeezed until only damp seed and skin pulp remained. The juice was then reheated, sugar and pectin added, and poured into jars.

Once cooled, blocks of paraffin were melted and a thin layer of wax was poured over each jar to seal it. The jars were then carried down to the cool basement and shelved beside other winter supplies.

Late into the 1950s, each autumn, we made gallons of sauerkraut, brine-cured in earthenware crocks. Fried kraut was a winter staple.

Schwinns and Broken Toys

The earliest correspondence I found between Herman and my grandparents was a Christmas card Herman sent them on December 19, 1952—just a few months after our return from Chelan. I imagine that after Barb left the farm, Herman searched the belongings she left behind and discovered Henry and Elsie's New York address. From the tone of the letter my grandfather sent Barb in Chelan, it sounded as if he had communicated with Herman. In later years Herman's correspondence with Barb's mother triggered many arguments.

I think it was Christmas 1952 when Tim and Chris each received a cherry red Schwinn bicycle—probably purchased with one of Barb's early AFDC checks. Tim's was a stripped version; favored son, Chris, was given a deluxe model. His Schwinn had a chrome passenger seat mounted over the rear fender and red, white, and blue streamers flowing from the handlebars. It had a headlight and a filler with white racing stripes that concealed the top tube. I'd cried and begged for one, too. Barb promised me one for my birthday the following October. I vowed to be the perfect son. I started calling her Mommy Darling several times a day. I felt like a fraud because my allegiance was to Herman.

Since returning from Chelan, Barb refused to sleep with him. She sent me down and she moved upstairs with the kids. Today when I look back, I wonder how much Barb cared about my well-being. The worst Herman ever did was kick me for farting too much after a bean soup supper. He snored, so after a few weeks, I moved back upstairs and burrowed in with Randy.

Over the next year I maneuvered to gain Barb's approval. I made double batches of bread, kneading the dough an extra hundred times to make sure all the flour lumps were out. I made cakes and chocolate pudding pies. I peeled potatoes without being told. By early October, I knew I was on the fast-track to getting my Schwinn. Barb knew the model I wanted—a Red Rover. The Sears catalogue page hung in my room where I studied it each morning and evening.

One morning, Laurel, standing on a chair to reach, was helping me pass shirts through the wringer on the Maytag washing machine. Her fingers got pulled in, she screamed, and I hit the spring-loaded release. The top of the wringer sprang up, hit her in the chin, and bloodied her mouth. The chair flew out from under her and she lay on the floor screaming. From behind, Barb grabbed me and threw me to the floor and kicked me. "No bike for you," she said, and shoved me to the side with her foot as she scooped Laurel up.

Christmas was fast approaching and I doubled my efforts. I kept the stove filled with wood. I ironed clothes other than my own. I mopped tracked-in melted snow puddles. By Thanksgiving, she was promising me the Red Rover again. By the mid-December afternoon when we brought the tree in, I was confident I'd get my bike.

I remember how Chris and Tim took turns breaking trail in our search for the Christmas tree. I followed, dreaming about my Schwinn. We found the perfect tree north of Maple Lake. Once home, in the woodshed, I held it straight while they lay beneath the bottom branches and drove wedges—chips left from splitting firewood—between the tree trunk and the sides of the hole it stood in, in the homemade tree stand. We carried it into the house, to the front room, eager to decorate it.

That evening, Chris made the popcorn. Making good popcorn was an art. Melt a glob of lard in the warped frying pan, watch it spit as it puddled in the center—let it heat on high until it bubbled, then sprinkle kernels in, covering the bottom. When the first kernel popped, Chris slammed the lid on and shook the pan until it went silent. He poured the fluffy white popcorn into the cut-glass punch bowl Barb had carried with her from New York. We gathered around, threaded needles in hand, and made popcorn chains. With the last popped kernel secure, we nibbled old maids until they were gone.

Each child was given a pinch of tinsel and a few glass balls to hang on the tree along with their popcorn chain. As we hung decorations, we chanted a song. A dog-eared book of Hank Williams music rested on the piano, and somehow one song had caught our fancy. We sang—not the complete song, but lyrics that echoed through our heads. *Jambalaya, cowfish pie, and a filly gumbo, son-of-a-gun we'll have big fun in the bayou for tonight I'm gonna see my ma cher amio.* I smile today at how we bastardized the lyrics with cow pies and horse gumbo. That's what the words sounded like—maybe I was the only one who used those words. I picked up music from the others. That night I remember glancing up toward the black window, into the night. Barb's reflection nodded in approval. I sang loudest. Christmas Eve night, I lay listening for noises. Of course I knew there wasn't a Santa, but we all played the game, keeping the myth alive for Randy and Laurel.

Christmas morning after chores was a day for sitting near the woodstove, eating peanut brittle and shelling handfuls of peanuts: pop them into the mouth with a piece of fruit-syrup-filled hard candy and crunch it up, swallow—then start over. I don't recall ever running out or being scolded for taking too much, but we gorged ourselves, worried about getting our share.

Whenever I heard Chris hum or sing "Bill Grogan's Goat," I knew I was in trouble. Throughout the year, Barb rehashed my shortcomings as an object lesson of how a child should not treat his Mommy Darling. "Bill Grogan's Goat" was to me what "El Deguello" must have been to the defenders of the Alamo. It's the tune Santa Anna's band played to the Alamo defenders—translated, it means "No mercy; no quarter."

But that Christmas morning we gathered in the front room to open presents. Mine was wrapped in a large box. It wasn't the shape of a bicycle but I convinced myself it had to be assembled. "We Three Kings" ended on the Victrola. I listened to the needle scratch at the center of the record. It was my turn to open. Chris started humming "Bill Grogan's Goat." I was secure in the knowledge I had my Schwinn. Inside the box was a smaller one. I opened it and found another, yet smaller. Eventually I unwrapped a shoe box that rattled. It was a wind-up stagecoach pulled by four horses with a little man perched on the coach seat. Chris and Tim thought it hilarious. When I wound up the toy, I discovered the spring was broken.

With *Best Wishes*
for CHRISTMAS
and the NEW YEAR

Herman, Linda Barbara & Family

Almost three years after they were married, Herman still thought Barb's name was Linda. Over the next decade his correspondence with Elsie triggered many arguments.

Excerpt from my grandmother's 1939 diary:

Monday, September 25, 1939: Barbara and I set out early to see about school for her. She wanted to try Brearley [School] so we went there; very nearby but there were no ways of making the curriculum fit her past work. Then to Juilliard [School of Music] and after to Bernard [College]. Juilliard seems to be the only possibility. Poor Barb feels like a lost soul.

Thursday, September 28, 1939: B and I went to the New York Hospital Clinic. I think it best for her to have a general overhauling as she doesn't feel at all well. We had to wait and wait and then only given an appointment for tomorrow.

Sunday, October 1, 1939: A very rainy Sunday and not very pleasant. We all went to St. Bartholomew. Dr. Sargent was marvelous as usual. I find such peace there with such beautiful music. Barb made a Frenchie little luncheon—then after an argument went to Gerta's to Tea. Barb had a wonderful time playing their Steinway which they sold this afternoon.

Monday, October 2, 1939: Barb walked all the way from Juilliard. Her piano didn't come. We are furious with them. In the aft we went to the "Y" to see about reducing exercises for B. She is very unhappy about being weighty.

Monday. October 16, 1939: I cleaned the whole house and did a big washing. Then to the New York Hospital to see Dr. Russell. He thinks Barb is definitely a psychiatric case. She is to see Dr. Henry next week. I hope they get at it.

1953
Battle Lines

On rare occasions, Herman pulled his gray .50 caliber machine gun ammo box out from under a hinged step. Setting the steel box on the floor in front of his tattered chair, he sat down and pulled the clamp that sealed the lid and removed the top. The box opened a mysterious world to me. Herman stared silently at the yellowed papers, newspaper clippings, and pictures as if unsure of what to pick up first.

Slowly he began to remove items—the papers and clippings first with a cursory glance. Next, black and white photos showing young uniformed men, desert in the background, or in front of exotic domed buildings or armored tanks, or as a group holding rifles. There was a picture of him standing near a jeep with a dark skinned, kinky-haired woman standing to the side and behind him. In another, Herman was standing in front of the farm house in his uniform looking very proud.

He handled these pictures gently, refused to let anybody touch them, only allowed us to look while he held. He never spoke of the men in the pictures. Gently he placed the pictures back into the envelope and continued exploring the box. Near the bottom were medals and ribbons and official certificates. Pushing those aside he pulled out a wrinkled black piece of cloth not much larger than a cotton handkerchief. Masking his face like an Arab woman, he seductively swayed the scrap back and forth playfully as he chanted a ditty:

"Dirty Gertie from Bizerte,

Hid a mousetrap 'neath her skirtie

Strapped it to her knee-cap purty

Made her boyfriends' fingers hurty"

We witnessed the following scene many times. I wonder if Herman knew he would get a rise.

"Don't sing about your nigger whore to me," Barb said.

"She's more woman than you'll ever be," Herman replied.

"You bastard." Barb yanked a chair out from the table and stepped up. The table was round with linoleum glued to the top. It was oak with a center pedestal base. When Barb jumped from chair to table she must have been aware enough to stay in the center, otherwise the table would have capsized.

Barefoot on the unwashed table, she hiked her dress up around her hips, naked beneath, and twirled a few times. "Is this what your nigger whore did? I'm a sophisticated lady from New York. Why don't you go back to your nigger whore and rut?"

"Get down, you dumb bitch. Have you no shame?"

She glared in silence, lowered her dress, and stepped from table to chair to floor. "We need culture in this whorehouse." With that she marched into the living room, sat down at the piano and slammed out Mozart or Bach or Beethoven, punishing the keys, stamping the pedals in an attempt to drown out Herman.

I witnessed the aftermath many times. Herman silently replaced the contents in the box, veins pulsing on top of his bald head. The box was relocked and returned to its resting place.

Among the medals at the bottom of the box was one that fascinated me. It had a blue background with a flintlock muzzleloader etched onto the face of it. It was a CIB, a Combat Infantryman Badge, awarded only to those who had seen combat in the Army. Not until many years later did I understand the significance of it; not until I had one of my own when I was awarded a Combat Action Ribbon from the Navy for service in Vietnam.

The Korean War ended on July 23, 1953. Many of us have read narratives about the nightmarish fighting during the Battle of the Chosin Reservoir, when 120,000 communist Chinese soldiers encircled and attacked 30,000 from the United Nations —mostly U.S. troops—and battled in temperatures that plunged below -35°.

"Peace in Korea," Elsie wrote in her diary on July 27, 1953. For us on the farm it meant nothing. A few neighbor men came home, but nobody talked about it. They just went back to farming.

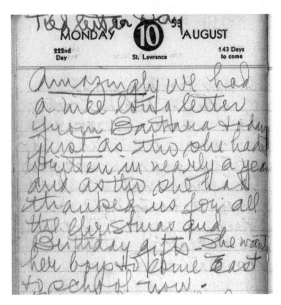

Two weeks later, August 10, Elsie wrote, *Amazingly we had a nice long letter from Barbara today just as tho she hadn't written in nearly a year and as tho she had thanked us for all the Christmas and Birthday gifts. She wants her boys to come East to school now.*

So Barb was scheming to escape again. As I reflected on the old documents, I tried to imagine how miserable she must have been, trapped on the farm. However, that was not the facade the world saw. As I mentioned earlier, in 1950, Elsie had connected with the regional Episcopalian church leaders. I found this letter in the chickenhouse.

The Diocese of Minnesota
1409 WILLOW STREET
MINNEAPOLIS 3, MINNESOTA

ARCHDEACON FOR THE INDIAN FIELD
THE VEN. FREDERICK K. SMYITHE
305 PLEASANT AVENUE
PARK RAPIDS, MINNESOTA

TELEPHONE
PARK RAPIDS 398

October 7, 1953

Mrs. Henry O. Philips
316 East 58th Street
New York 22, New York

Dear Mrs. Philips:-

On Monday, September 28th, my wife and I drove to Nebish and fortunately found your daughter and family home. We had a very nice visit with her and with Mr. Affield. She spoke as if she had written you recently so perhaps you have heard from her by this time.

The family is well - the children look very healthy. They have a nice farm and have just built a new barn.

There is an Episcopal Church just eight miles north of them (at Redby) and they said they would start going to Church there. The next time I am in Redby, they want me to Baptize their youngest. The children have been going to a Sunday School at Nebish but it is a fundamentalistic group and they are not satisfied with the Church. Mr. Affield is a former Lutheran, and so he doesn't care for that Church either. I will let them know when I am in Redby next, and will Baptize the xxxxxxx child if they can get in. The Church is in charge of a layman and I go there monthly for a Communion service. *missionary*

Thank you too for the $5.00; I have placed it in my Discretionary Fund. It was very good of you to send it.

If I can be of further assistance, do not hesitate to write.

With all good wishes.

Faithfully,

Frederick K. Smyithe

We sounded like a model Midwest farm family.

Chris was six years old in 1949 when we left New York so he remembered our grandparents. In the chickenhouse I discovered a letter he wrote to our grandfather on November 11, 1953. *Dear Grandpa, Thank you very much for the dark blue pants and striped shirt and jackets and toys. We like them very much. Now would you like to know about our farm? We have eleven cows and a Farm all [sic] tractor and four sheep and 50 chickens. I'm in the 5th grade. We have a workshop and like to make stuff out of wood. Our teacher's name is Mrs. Madison. Tim and I like to go hunting with the 22 rifle. I have my own 22 short bullets. I have my own BB gun and bike. It is a Schwinn. We have a Surge milking machine and De Laval separator. I tripped the bundles of grain on the binder last summer and that's how I earned my BB gun. I drove a Case tractor 24 miles in high gear to help thrash grain with the thrashing machine. Tim and I helped put up hay with our new hayloader. Love to Grandma and Polly and you.*

Yours Truly, Christopher

Two developments impacted my grandparents in 1953. First, Elsie's mother, Idalia, won a lawsuit against Robinson Lumber in Everett, Washington. In the 1920s, Idalia's late husband had been an executive with Robinson and had invested with them. During the Great Depression of the 1930s, Robinson had maneuvered to swindle Idalia out of the investment. From what I can gather, fraud was committed by the company

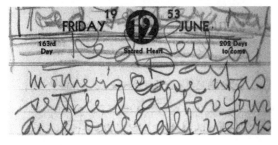 under the Securities Exchange Act of 1934. By 1951 the case had reached the U.S. Court of Appeals for the Ninth Circuit. On

June 12, the case was settled. I don't know what the award was, but for the previous two decades Idalia had been dependent on her children. When she died in 1955 her estate was valued at $75,000. The last few years of Idalia's life, Elsie spent hundreds of hours writing letters, telephoning, and doing research into the old case. Elsie was bitter about the whole thing because her brother took credit for winning the case. She felt she deserved something out of the settlement.

The second development for my grandmother was on November 7, 1953 when Elsie received $1,000 from Idalia to come and visit her. On November 13 Elsie flew to Seattle, spent three weeks with her mother and then flew to Minneapolis from where she took a Greyhound bus to Bemidji. It was the first time she had seen Barb and us children since the summer of 1949.

Here are Elsie's diary entries about her visit.

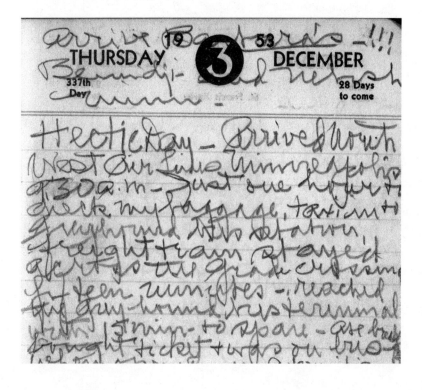

Thursday, December 3, 1953. Arrive Barbara's!!!Bemidji and Nebish, Minn.

Hectic Day—arrived Northwest Airlines Minneapolis 9:30am. Just one hour to check my luggage, taxi in to Greyhound bus station. Freight train stayed across the grade crossing fifteen minutes—reached the Greyhound bus terminal with 15 minutes to spare. Ate breakfast, bought ticket, and was on bus. When countryside opened up, a terrific snowstorm began immediately. North at 70 all the way, arrived Bemidji 5pm promptly. Herman there to meet me. We drove on through the storm north to their farm where Barbara and dear Timmy, Chris, Windy, Laurel, and Randy greeted me warmly. They have a good big 400 acre farm [actually 160 acres] *with good farmhouse on it. Only bad feature—no bathroom. Barbara had a delicious dinner ready. After the dinner Timmy demonstrated the Surge Milker. After the children were in bed B. and I talked until 2am.*

Friday, December 4. Barbara's, Nebish, Minn.

I slept well with two pills to overcome the strange surroundings, the lumpy mattress, and the freezing cold, and Timmy and Chris and Windy also sleeping in my room. Timmy and Chris got off to school before I awakened. Herman, Bobbie [Barb], *Windy, and Laurel had a good breakfast together and then set out on an all day Christmas shopping tour in Bemidji. Amazing how well we went through the deep snow* [Herman always put chains on the car tires]. *Large road plows out—Bemidji is a sweet town. We had luncheon at a nice little place on Lake Bemidji and right next to Paul and Babe his blue ox. We got a lot of shopping done and back home at dusk. Timmy and Chris seemed a little cold. We had a pleasant evening visiting. B. doesn't like me to talk to Herman. She and I talked until 2am.*

Saturday, December 5. We all arose in good season. Had a good breakfast and started on an all day shopping tour in Bemidji. Must have been so tiring for the children but they were so thrilled to buy so many new things which they wanted that they were all good. We had luncheon in our same favorite place again.

December 6 is blank and December 7, Elsie wrote, *Nebish, Bemidji, and Minneapolis.*

On Christmas Day, 1953, Elsie wrote to her mother, Idalia,

Dear little Barbara and her many children we sent a lovely package to and said many things were from Dear Gram, good warm jackets for dear Chris, Timmy, and Windy—warm things for Barbara, Herman, Laurel, and Junior (Randy). She still seems to wish to remain separate from the family tho I have written her that you are ill and that she should be kind and write to you. I do think this husband is a very fine man—Herman Affield. He writes me quite frequently and seems to be able to understand Barbara's idiosyncrasy. They live on a farm in northern Minnesota. This is Barbara's fourth Christmas there...

Elsie's comment, "...he writes me quite frequently" is curious because I didn't find any of Herman's letters in the chickenhouse from the early 1950s to Elsie.

Racial overtones wove into the family. First from Barb, about "dirty nigger whores." She discovered trigger words that angered Herman. He was a Nazi and a "stupid German immigrant" (immigrant being synonymous with inferior), a coward and a stormtrooper. She began to pit Chris and Tim against him. Over the years, as the chasm widened between Herman and the two boys, he began referring to them as Mexican meat hounds because he felt they ate more than their share.

My biological father was euphemistically referred to as the "nigger-in-the-woodpile," implying that Barb didn't know who he was. Chris and Tim had dark complexions with dark hair. I was fair skinned with straight brown hair. The older boys latched onto the slur about my father and repeated it, teasing me, calling me "nigger-lips."

In 2015 I had an ethnicity DNA test done. Almost one third of my genetic make-up originates in the Iberian Peninsula. I wonder if my ancestors might be traced to black Phoenician merchants who settled in Cadiz before Jesus was born. Maybe Herman was closer to the mark than he realized.

After our return from Chelan, the hard years began. Barb and Herman grew increasingly antagonistic toward each other. I don't know if spousal rape is too strong a term, but every so often, in the dark of night, his voice echoed in the stairwell, "Get down here and be a wife."

Over the next six years, she birthed four children and her animosity toward Herman evolved to hatred. I think Herman suffered most psychologically from her verbal assaults, but Barb definitely suffered most physically. The outhouse was one source of contention—Barb felt it was below her dignity to use such a crude accommodation.

When the outhouse was originally built, it had a layer of tarpaper nailed to the rough cut boards that sealed out forty below zero drafts and offered a thin sense of privacy. By the time we moved to the farm the laths holding the tarpaper had rotted or popped loose when the outhouse settled and the boards cured and shrank. Near the peak, black paper remnants flapped in the breeze as garter snake skin-sheds shifted on the top plate of the little building.

The gable ends were vented beneath the eaves. The door had a half moon carved into it and a bent wire latch for privacy. In the summer Chris and Tim spent hours locked inside comparing Sears and Roebuck catalogue models. Randy and I sometimes climbed silently up onto the low roofed woodshed that the outhouse leaned against, snuck up to the vent, peeked in and listened silently until we lost interest.

Stench wafted across the surrounding area during the summer. Inside the outhouse, sluggish flies buzzed around the holes. Bees often made their nests under the seats and garter snakes slithered across the floor.

Sometimes we captured a fat snake and held her over the hole. Grasping the snake just behind her head, we wrapped our fingers around her torso and slid them down, milking her babies out as she writhed and hissed in fury. Dim light filtered through the back of the outhouse beneath the seats and revealed the pencil-sized baby snakes as they oozed from her fat body, dropped into the hole and slithered across slimy, paper-littered piles and into damp shadows along the walls of the pit.

I hated the outhouse. Chris and Tim often threatened to stuff me down the hole if I didn't stop following them. I knew I'd fit, and at night, drifting off to sleep, I imagined being sunk to the neck with tiny snakes slithering about my face, Chris and Tim sitting on the holes above, laughing.

Winter brought frozen cheeks and crusty butts. When I was punished for stealing toilet paper from the house, I started bringing it home from school—Herman wondered where the small squares came from. By spring the two brown stalagmites neared the open holes, but spring thaw always seemed to beat the race.

More than a decade later, while patrolling the rivers in Vietnam, that same smell wafted from rice paddies and flashed me back to the outhouse. We had no toilets on our boats so we—our boat crew—squatted our bare butts over the stern and did our business into the Mekong River while sampans chugged past, mamasan, papasan, and kids, shouting and gesturing at us.

Success is subjective. I guess I've come a long way from an outhouse that serviced seven people and an open-air boat toilet. Today I have four bathrooms—inside the house—for two people.

Basement

The musty basement was a magnet. When we first moved to the farm in 1949 there were still implements from when the farm was homesteaded: beer bottles and a capper, a cabbage grater, a two-gallon butter churn, and several earthenware crocks for sauerkraut and pickled meats. When Herman was out of the house we often went down to play, especially in the winter.

In the unlit cellarway—the small landing at the top of the stairs—a set of shelves sagged with junk. One item that I found irresistible, even though it creeped me out, was Tim's tonsils, preserved in a pint jar of formaldehyde. Why Barb had saved them was a mystery. I'd shake the jar like a snow globe and create a tissue flake blizzard. In the early 1950s, Tim injured his hand in the buzz saw while helping with firewood. Thank goodness it wasn't severed. A pickled hand waving back at me would have really been scary.

Rough-cut two inch thick steps with no banister went from cellarway down to the dirt floor. Not long after we arrived at the farm, I fell down the steps and snagged my neck on a protruding spike. To this day I have a faint scar. When we played hide-and-seek in the house, I was sometimes tricked into going down to hide. Chris or Tim then flipped the switch in the cellarway and left me screaming in the dark. In 1957 the world learned about Ed Gein, the Wisconsin psychopath who butchered and canned humans. My brothers had a new boogeyman to terrorize me. Even though I was afraid down in the basement, I often volunteered to fetch potatoes, canned goods, and whatever was needed in the dead of winter because I could pee in the dim back corner rather than go outside. When I squirted onto the cracked concrete wall, a salamander sometimes shot out—a moving target.

During the 1950s Barb organized basement digging expeditions in search of Hoganson. We older siblings have our theories on who the mysterious delusion was; an old lover, a Bemidji doctor Barb was infatuated with, or, Chris thinks, maybe it was a cover story and we were searching for money Herman had buried.

I remember one search—I was about six or seven. Barb, Chris, Tim, Laurel, and I, were in the basement. Barb handed me a tarnished, bent dinner fork. "Crawl under that table and see what you can find," she told me, pointing at a low homemade bench leaning against the concrete wall adjacent to the potato bin.

I crawled between the bracing, through cobwebs, back into the shadow cast by the overhead bare bulb, and began scratching the moist black dirt with the dull fork. I may have unearthed a bottle cap or two, but no Hoganson.

As I've mentioned, I found no letters in the chickenhouse from Barb to Elsie during the 1950s, but Elsie must have continually worried about Barb even as her other daughter was in the VA hospital receiving electro and insulin shock treatments. In Elsie's "Mental Health Journal" I found this entry:

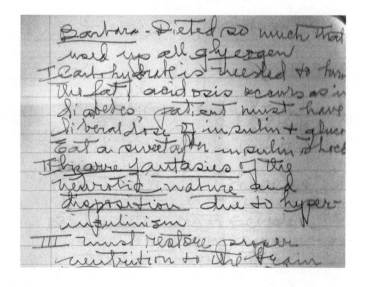

Barbara (underlined) Dieted so much that used up all the glycogen. Carbohydrate is needed to burn the fat, acidosis occurs as in diabetes, patient must have liberal dose of insulin and glucose. Eat a sweet after insulin shock. Bizarre fantasies of the neurotic nature and disposition due to hyperinsulinisum. Must restore proper neutrition [sic] to the brain.

In the 1950s, over the course of nine years, Barb birthed five children. Pictures from that time reveal that her weight fluctuated wildly. For nine years she breast-fed babies nonstop—at times she was nursing two babies. Our daily diet and nutrition was sketchy at best—certainly not sufficient for a woman who was breast feeding and often pregnant with the next child. Did Barb's nutritional deficiency manifest psychologically?

Did Barb send Elsie some delusional letters? It was during these years she had us digging for Hoganson. Recall earlier that Elsie mentioned Herman sent her letters. Did he write about Barb's erratic behavior?

Author's fifth birthday *(left to right)* Chris holding Randy on his Schwinn bike, Wendell holding birthday cake, Laurel, Barb behind them, and Tim, perched on his Schwinn.

Excerpt from my grandmother's 1939 diary:

Wednesday, October 18, 1939: Barb went riding in Central Park, beautiful morning. I got a nice luncheon for her which she ate. Then went shopping for books for her. Went to Barnes and Noble—18th and Fifth and sold some music books for her and bought some. Barb went to the "6" exercise group at 4:30. Pol met B at St. Bartholomew for choir.

Wednesday, October 25, 1939: Such a rush day. Went to the hospital with Barb, took all a.m. on her diet. This time she is going to try to stick to it. After getting her luncheon at home I went to the Vassar Club.

Wednesday, November 1, 1939: Went to the hospital at nine with B. Waited until 11:30 to see Dr. Russell, then had only brief talk with him. He was still busy with B. I wonder if he will prove to be any good.

Friday, November 3, 1939: Finished Barb's things. Took her bags to meet her at 125th St. station to go to Stamford to meet Dr. Slaughter, drive to Ithaca to spend weekend with Dr. Slaughter and go to Cornell-Columbia game.

Saturday, November 11, 1939: Armistice Day. How ridiculous to celebrate the quiet guns this year when they are booming away harder than ever. At 1, Barb and I went to Stouffer's for luncheon on Park Avenue then to see "Tobacco Road," the play, before it went off after its six-year run. Such a horrible grubby thing. It depresses one. Went to Maxwell House for coffee.

1954
Stew

By 1954 Herman knew that Barb wasn't the "wonderful cook and housekeeper who knows how to farm or ranch" as described in *Cupid's Columns* five years earlier. He reverted to many of his bachelor habits. For example, Barb wouldn't sew his clothing, so he used "bachelor buttons"—metal two-piece buttons that locked together. He shared them with Chris, Tim, and me, even though we knew how to sew on our own buttons. I don't recall if my brothers used them, but I did.

Naturally, having to provide three meals a day put stress on the family. It became a collective effort as we children grew into jobs. Stew was a staple—Herman called it Mulligan stew. During the Depression he and our Uncle Charlie had traveled out west, probably spent time in hobo jungles, and that's where he picked up the name. Our stew generally consisted of about six pounds of meat—usually beef, but pork, raccoon, or squirrel could be substituted. (Allow two hours extra cook time for adult raccoon.) We started it early in the day and after adding water, salt, and pepper, the concoction simmered until suppertime.

A typical stew day went something like this. A halved beef carcass hung in the granary, a cull cow that wouldn't have survived the winter. After morning chores Herman brushed mouse and sparrow droppings from the dehydrated blackened surface, took the ax or Swede saw and hacked out two brick-sized pieces from the frozen carcass. He didn't pay any attention to basic beef cuts. The bricks might be suet or prime rib— actually the cows we butchered rarely had any fat cover so bricks of suet is an exaggeration—more likely grisly flank and shoulder cuts. He carried them into the house and dropped them onto the table.

"Today we make Mulligan stew," he shouted over the tune coming from the piano where Barb sat, Chris on one side, Tim on the other. Laurel, Randy, and I, sat on the floor nearby, playing marbles. The tune drifted off as Barb paused and twisted irritably, awkward in her fifth month of pregnancy.

"You boys," Herman nodded toward Chris, Tim, and me, "go to the basement and get vegetables."

"Make them do it, Daddy," I complained. "They'll shut the light off and lock the door. The boogeyman will get me."

"If I hear him screaming again, you two will spend the whole day down there with the light off," Herman said, as he pulled the stew pot out from under the sink. "Jesus Christ, why wasn't this washed after the last time it was used?" he yelled at Barb.

"I'm giving my sons piano lessons." Belly protruding, Barb rose from the bench and shuffled toward the kitchen. "Get your own vegetables and make your own swill."

"They eat, they can help cook. Chris, scrub this pot." Herman set the dented aluminum container in the sink and turned the faucet on. "Tim, take Windy and get the vegetables."

"I won't have my sons doing your nigger work." Barb grabbed the crusted pot and slammed it against the sink. Water splashed on the floor. "You think you're still in the army giving orders? That's probably what you were—a cook." She swished a washcloth around, dumped the water, and threw the pot on the table. "Here's your damn stewpot. Now leave my boys alone. Make that ignorant Irish stew yourself."

Herman spit his snuice wad in the garbage. "You better settle down. I'm not going to take much more."

Barb grabbed Chris by the hand and stomped across the room toward the piano. Chords from Mozart's "The Marriage of Figaro" echoed through the house as she slammed keys and stamped pedals. "Don't spit your filthy tobacco in my house. Culture—we need culture in this hell hole," she screamed.

Herman shook his head as he scrubbed the stew pot. "You boys go get the vegetables."

Tim and I collected a few pounds of potatoes, two handfuls of carrots, several onions and rutabagas from dirt floor bins and stacked them in a pail. Heading for the stairs, Tim took the lead. Two carrots fell from the bucket and I bent over to pick them up—Tim shot up the stairs, shut the light off, and slammed the door.

I screamed in the blackness. No words—curdling, primordial screams. Finally, "Daaaaaddy," came out of my six-year-old mouth.

"Damn, I told you not to scare him. Damn!" shouted Herman from above. "You're getting the belt."

In the darkness I went silent and listened.

"You're not belting my sons, you bastard," Barb shouted.

"Get the hell out of my way," Herman yelled. "I warned him."

I listened to the belt slap flesh.

Tim howled, "I'm sorry, Daddy. I won't ever do it again. Don't let him hit me Mommy—help me."

The floor echoed as feet raced.

"Don't you hit him again, you bald bastard."

The belt slapped flesh. "You'd hit a pregnant lady—that takes a real man."

"That damn kid better start listening. Tim, go down and get your brother."

I listened to feet cross the floor.

The light went on and Tim came down the steps. "You're going to get it when he goes out to milk the cows. Mommy is mad and you made me get strapped."

Between sobs, I sniffled out Tim's threat. Herman grabbed Tim by the arm, "You touch him and you'll get the buckle end next time. Now peel those damn spuds."

Barb sat in the front room looking across the field toward Maple Lake, humming a tune, hands on her belly.

Snuff

It was mid-February. Two Arctic Clippers had swept south, one behind the other, paralyzing northern Minnesota. School was cancelled for several days. Chris, Tim, and I loved it and dug tunnel mazes in the mountainous snowdrifts on the hillside near the unplowed road.

Barb, six months pregnant, sat in the front room holding Randy, silently staring into the storm, across the field toward Maple Lake.

Herman ran out of Copenhagen by the fourth day. He sat near the heat stove, reading. Most of the cows were dried up, so chores didn't take as long.

The driveway was drifted shut, no letup in sight.

"Where do you think you're going?" Barb asked me. "I want you to stay in and play with Randy. I have work to do," she said, and set Randy on the floor and stood up.

"I'm walking to the store with Daddy," I told her as I struggled into my coat and boots.

Barb grabbed me by the arm, "You're not going anywhere. He'll get lost in the storm. Let him go."

"I'm going too," I said, jerking out of her grasp. She glared at me in silence.

The wind, coming from the north, cut into our faces. In my rush out of the house, I had left my scarf behind. Steam clouds puffed from my chapped lips and disappeared in the wind as I followed Herman's footsteps across the field to Maple Lake. A fifteen foot drift had formed on the lee side of the bluff above the lake. Herman sat at the upper lip, gave himself a push, and slid down on his butt. He looked up at me and laughed.

"I used to slide on this bank when I was your age," he said.

I sat, pushed off, and shot down the bank, "That was fun, Daddy. Let's do it again."

"No, we got to get my snuice. You and Randy can slide tomorrow."

Snow was fluffed on the spongy bog surrounding the lake. I watched it break and settle as Herman broke trail. Cattails poked above the snow near the shoreline. I broke several off, then twisted each one in my mittened hand. Brown spores whisked away in the wind. Out onto the ice it was easy walking because the wind had blown the ice clear. I tossed the bare cattail stems and they whisked across the ice. Near the center of the lake, in a shallow spot, a wild rice bed still released chaff to the wind.

"Look," Herman said. "There's a turtle swimming under the ice."

I could see him, stirring a mucky wake as he paddled along the bottom. "How does he breathe?" I asked.

"There must be an open spring somewhere," Herman said. "We need to steer clear of the island."

It wasn't really an island any more. It had sunk. Herman often told the story of how, when he was a little boy, it had been an island with Norway pines growing on it. Now it was just a wild rice bed, but he still called it an island.

On the far side of the lake we struggled through spongy bog and up a bluff. At the top, Herman dropped heavily onto a fallen tree, sweat pouring down his cheeks, breathing rapidly.

"I'll break trail for a while," I offered.

"Okay, go ahead. I'll catch up."

I pushed into the snow—waist high in the low places. At times I used my fists to break the crust before lifting my boot to crunch forward another step. Sweat soon poured down my face. Herman caught up and followed. Half an hour later, Herman in the lead, we climbed through the ditch onto the drifted road near Nebish Store.

The wood heat and smoke smell blasted my face when I opened the door.

"Give me a can of snuice," Herman told Pearl, the gray-haired lady behind the counter.

"Sorry, we're out until the supply truck comes. It should have been here yesterday but the storm…," she trailed off.

"Damn, we walked all this way for nothing," Herman muttered in disgust.

"Look, there goes the snowplow," I shouted. "Can we walk on the road going home, Daddy?"

"Yeah, sure," Herman replied. "I put the flag out for the plow—hope he sees it. Put your coat back on. By the time we get home it'll be time to feed the cows."

On the way home, I ran ahead a few steps and slid in the ice tracks left by the heavy plow. At the driveway, we discovered the flag had blown down and was buried under a drift.

"Guess I'll have to start shoveling in the morning," Herman grunted as he climbed over the newly plowed drift. "I got to get my snuice."

Through the 1950s, the following was a typical winter situation: Our driveway was drifted shut again. There was a low spot west of the new barn and granary that, with a west wind and loose snow, drifted three to four feet deep and packed so that it had to be sliced out by block. After every storm, Herman doggedly set forth with his grain shovel, sliced downward on three sides of the drift, forming a cube. He'd then slip the shovel blade two feet down in the cube, lift and toss over his shoulder. On deep drifts, he might repeat this maneuver three times before he reached the frozen, ice-covered ground.

Herman did morning chores, ate breakfast, shoveled until dinner, ate, and spent the afternoon slowly, methodically, digging his way toward the distant road. After a bad storm, it took him four days to dig out. At the road he was greeted by a frozen, crusted bank left by the county snowplow. If he came down with a severe cold or if a storm was too wicked, he might relent and place a red flag at the end of the driveway, signaling the county snowplow. It took the big truck about twenty minutes to clear the driveway and yard with the ten foot blade. As I recall, it cost three or four dollars.

Herman's first daughter, Bonita Rosalinda, was born in May. For many years it was a source of humor for us children how Barb incorporated the name "Linda" into all three of her daughter's names—one Linda and two Rosalindas. In one of my interviews I asked Barb why she liked that name so much. She told me that she had attended an operetta in France—couldn't remember the name of it or the composer—but she had considered one of the characters, Rosalinde, to be a sophisticated, clever lady.

I did a bit of research and discovered that the character Barb venerated was from "Die Fledermaus" (The Bat). It was originally written as a farce by German playwright Julius Rodrich Benedix in 1851. The operetta was composed by Johann Strauss II in 1874. I wonder if what impressed Barb most was how Rosalinde was so successful at manipulating men.

City Slicker Clothes, Baseball Uniforms, and Slingshots

(Autumn 1954, *left to right*) Chris, Tim, Laurel, Randy, Wendell, and
Barb holding baby sister, Bonny. Chris and Tim were terribly embarrassed
about the baseball uniforms that Barb ordered from Sears and Roebuck.
She forced them to wear the hateful outfits to school.

At some point in the mid-1950s we started receiving boxes of clothing
from our Seattle cousins. The clothes were very baggy on us. We went
to Nebish School, sporting letter sweaters from Notre Dame, Princeton,
and Purdue, with a military surplus web belt holding our four-inch-too-
big-waist trousers up.

It may have been the winter I was eight and in second grade. Because
I was always cold at home, I learned to layer my clothes. Rather than

changing a dirty shirt, I put another one on over it. At school, the big room kids held me down and counted them. As I recall, six was my record. But I was warm.

We created our entertainment. We spent hours out in the woods searching for the perfect forked maple sapling for a slingshot. When discovered, the tree was chopped down, the fork rough cut with a hatchet, and then trimmed with a jackknife. Some of our favorite targets were mud swallows perched on the power line and at their mud nests built on the underside of the barn peak.

One of Chris's prize possessions was a jackknife he'd gotten for his birthday. It had a large and small blade which he kept razor sharp. It also had a bottle cap opener, corkscrew, screwdriver, awl, and can opener. One autumn day I talked him into letting me borrow it so I could carve a slingshot. Knife in pocket, hand wrapped around it for additional security, I shuffled through deep, crisp maple, oak, and basswood leaves. In a draw north of the house, I discovered the perfect forked maple but realized in my haste I'd forgotten the hatchet. Pulling the small tree over, I straddled the trunk, cut it, and whittled the two forked branches off. I carved notches near the top of each fork to tie the sling onto.

Removing the firing mechanism from my pocket—a strip of rubber cut from an abandoned inner-tube—I attached the ends to the notched fork. I pulled a round stone from my pocket, cupped it in the pouch at the center of the rubber strip and pulled back, aiming at a nearby tree. Satisfied, I began stalking through the deep leaves in search of a worthy foe—a gray squirrel high in an oak tree. I drew back and sighted carefully. I missed and the squirrel moved up a branch, his twitching tail taunting me as he chattered.

I blamed the miss on a small burr on the handle. I began whittling. The knife slipped and the two-inch blade pierced my wrist to hilt. I yanked the blade out and a fountain of blood shot from the wound. I panicked and ran for home. The faster I ran the harder the little fountain spurted. By the time I burst into the house I was convinced I was dying. Barb drenched it with iodine, covered my wound with a plastic coated pad, wrapped it with gauze tied down with rag strips, and sent me back out to play.

Chris asked where his knife was. In my panic I had dropped it and the slingshot out in the woods. Chris demanded that I find it or he would beat me to a pulp. I spent the rest of the day searching—found the slingshot, but the knife is still lying out there.

Marriage Proposal

Just as the short cold winter days may have affected Barb's frame of mind, I wonder if the heat and humidity and long days of summer with no other adult to share her burdens influenced her mood. I'm still trying to make sense of this next incident.

On an overcast summer afternoon, Herman, Barb, and all of us children climbed into the car and drove over to a neighbor's farm. When we arrived, the man was near his barn, off-loading his hayrack by hand. Barb got out of the car, went over, and talked to him. He stopped pitching and listened. Suddenly he stabbed his fork into the hay, jumped off the wagon, and stormed over to Herman, who by then had gotten out of the car. We children sat in the car, windows down, and listened in amazement.

"Herman, get this crazy woman off my property," Lee shouted. Herman didn't reply. "She wants to move in with me and you can take my wife home with you." Barb didn't say anything. "Get her out of here. You and the kids are welcome to come back, but I never want her on my property again."

Barb got in the car. Herman followed suit and drove away. I remember looking back, watching Lee climb back up onto his hayrack as storm clouds gathered in the west. I don't remember Herman saying a word.

A few years ago, I visited with Laurel about that incident, and we wondered what prompted Barb to be attracted to Lee. I mentioned an event that had happened a few years earlier, when the loft trusses were erected on the new barn. The construction crew, including Lee, was in the house having noon dinner when one of the kids came in and reported that

I, four years old at the time, had climbed to the top of the barn—about thirty feet up. The men scrambled out of the house. Sixty years later during an interview with me, Barb said, "There you were, sitting on the peak."

Lee ran to the barn, climbed to the peak, and carried me down. Is it possible that in Barb's mind, Lee became her hero archetype—the "prince" to save her from Herman? Was Herman a willing participant? Otherwise, why would he have driven Barb over to Lee's farm?

How desperate was Barb to escape? After I cleaned out the chickenhouse in 2010, I started on the old farmhouse. Upstairs, beneath loose floorboards in the room at the top of the landing, I discovered mouse skeletons, fossilized sanitary pads, and a page remnant from an undated letter.

The letter was obviously one Barb received in response to a lonely hearts club advertisement, because the author specifically speaks of his love for children—a prerequisite for her interest in a man. In those earlier advertisements, Barb used the name Linda Curry. This writer addressed her as Miss Stanley, an alias Barb used in 1952.

Here is the end of the single page I found, followed by the full transcription.

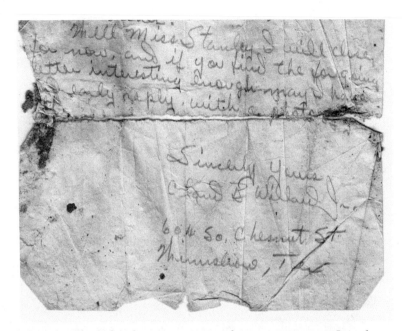

...fact that the kids take every minute of my spare time, as I am home with them at night and week-ends. I love them very much as they are two wonderful children. My mother comes in and cares for them days while I work. Mother tries to get me to live with her and dad but I have my own place to live, and that's the way I like it. By the way, I'm a pretty good cook too. I like to cook when I'm not too tired but I've never felt well enough to like to wash dishes.

Well Miss Stanley I will close for now, and if you find the foregoing letter interesting enough may I have an early reply with a picture. Sincerely Yours, Claude B. Willard Jr. 604 So. Chestnut St. Winnsboro, Texas.

I found a headstone for Claude B. Willard, Jr. at Fort Bliss National Cemetery, El Paso, Texas. Like Herman, he had been a private first class (PFC) in WWII. Willard died a single man in 1989.

Not long after we moved to the farm in 1949, Barb found a beautician named Flossie—an older white-haired lady who worked from her home in Bemidji. I recall boring hours of waiting in Flossie's little house, bitter ammonia smell stinging my eyes and nose, Barb chatting as Flossie formed tight little curls in her black hair. Flossie shouted replies while Barb's head was in the drying dome.

In 1950 there was no rural mail delivery service at the farm. Depending on the weather, Herman hiked or drove into Nebish—two miles from the farm—to pick up our mail. I wonder if Barb induced Flossie to accept her mail so Herman wouldn't intercept it.

After Herman and Barb were married, did she communicate with other men, using Flossie's address? Did she keep the list of men who had contacted her earlier? When Herman did not live up to her expectations, did she begin reaching out to them with a new identity? Is it possible that Barb purchased another lonely hearts advertisement after moving to the farm and used the last name "Stanley" with Flossie's address? In Elko and Chelan she had registered Chris and Tim for school with that last name.

The Cold War

By 1954 we had a gas cook stove in the kitchen. A bottle of propane lasted about twenty-five days. Barb quickly learned to open the oven door and turn the oven temperature dial on high as soon as Herman went out to do chores. It wasn't long before he came in and discovered what she was doing.

On one particular day, he came into the house on a winter afternoon for supper and discovered nothing had been prepared. Barb had lost track of time listening to an opera on the radio and forgot to cook supper. Herman yanked the radio plug out of the socket, pulled his jackknife from his pocket, opened the blade, and cut the radio cord in half. He must have been furious because *he* liked to listen to the radio, too.

Tensions ratcheted up. As Chris and Tim grew, Herman expected more work from them. Barb felt menial labor was below her sons' dignity. The confrontations often happened at mealtime when Herman told the boys of a chore he had for them. It was almost like the lines we children rehearsed for the Christmas play at school each December. Barb and Herman memorized their squabble lines.

"Chris, Tim, fill the wood box this afternoon," Herman said over his coffee.

"Fill your own damn wood box. They're not your slaves," Barb said.

"They live here, they can help," Herman replied as he stood up, tapped his Copenhagen can lid, and placed a pinch under his lip.

Barb jumped up and marched across the kitchen. "You Nazi bastard, they're my sons. I tell them what to do." She goose-stepped to Herman's end of the table, pivoted 180 degrees, thudded her bare heels together, shot her right hand high into the air, and shouted, "Heil, Hitler."

"Be careful, bitch," Herman said, as he donned his sweat-stained cap and walked out, the spring-loaded screen door slamming behind him.

Fighter aircraft buzzed the house several times a month—Hellcats, Corsairs, and Avengers, on training exercises out of Duluth. First, training for the Korean War; then it continued as the Cold War intensified. The planes rattled windows and made us jump—especially Herman. Apparently the barn, with the shiny new steel roof, was a visual marker. They swung north and dropped bomb loads on peat bogs and deep in the forests of the Red Lake Nation.

On still nights and days when the air was heavy, low rumbles of the detonating bombs could be heard miles away. Forty years later, Red Lake Nation received a financial settlement from the federal government for the damaged timber because shrapnel imbedded in the trees by the exploding bombs made the logs unfit for lumber.

At times, high altitude formations glittered in the sun. Some of the glitter was aluminum foil strips released from the aircraft to confuse radar. Air Force training missions were realistic as fighter craft flew below, guarding the bombers. In the forests we picked up strips of aluminum that looked like Christmas tree tinsel. We also shot at the planes. First with BB guns, later with .22 caliber rifles. Everybody laughed when Randy talked about flying an airplane when he grew up. The nearest we got to high flight was WWII stories and comic strip heroes like Buzz Sawyer.

We didn't know it then, but in the very early 1950s, secret flights of high altitude B-36 bombers originating as far away as New Mexico flew mock attacks using Mark III and Mark IV atomic bombs without the nuclear core. The bombs detonated 3,000 feet above Upper Red Lake.

Nebish School had two classrooms; first through fourth grade were in the "little room" while fifth through eighth were in the "big room." The Cold War was taken seriously. Our little room teacher, Mrs. Madison, worried about the communists taking over the world. She said they had failed in Korea. The spring of 1954, the commies had defeated the French in a battle at Dien Bien Phu, in a little country called Vietnam in Southeast Asia. Our teacher said the commies were doing the same thing as the Japs had done twenty-five years earlier—conquering Southeast Asia and forcing their way down the Malay Archipelago to Australia. "President Eisenhower called it the Domino Theory," she told us. I remember thinking that dominos and commies kind of rhymed.

Each school day began with Dewey, the rotund WWII veteran janitor, and a student assistant raising the flag. We stood at our desks, faced the flag pole beyond the large windows, hand on heart, and recited the Pledge of Allegiance as the flag rose. We studied *Current Events*, a weekly student newspaper. World domination by devious communists was instilled; the ever-present fear of atomic bombs reaching Nebish first over the North Pole warranted bomb shelter drills.

When the fire alarm sounded we tucked text books into our desks—I suppose it wasn't patriotic to get vaporized with a cluttered desk—and marched single file down the stairs into the basement where we sat in class groups along the walls, bent forward, hands locked over our heads in anticipation of our little school being at the epicenter of an imminent commie attack.

More than sixty years later, white-haired seniors reminisce about our childhood days of "duck and cover."

Town Day

After chores and breakfast, Herman loaded the full cream cans into the trunk and changed from his dungarees into green trousers and a fresh denim shirt. My siblings and I were always ready to go. Barb, who struggled to get the little ones bundled up and herself ready, was always late. We kids sat with Herman in the car, waiting, as he impatiently honked the horn. Eventually Barb came out carrying the newest baby and scurried toward the car. She always rode in back.

As she approached, Herman put the car in gear and eased forward.

"Come on, Mommy. Come on, Mommy," the kids in the back seat shouted, as one held the door open. Just as she reached the door, Herman would speed up a bit, leaving her behind, then slow down and wait for her to catch up. After several tries he'd let her climb in as he eased forward.

By then she was disheveled and winded. Herman seldom drove faster than forty or forty-five miles per hour. In the summer, the windows were down, kids piled on top of each other, as air and arguments whipped past our ears. Winters, the arguments ricocheted off ice-covered windows as we etched intricate designs in the frost.

Along with the AFDC checks came free medical care. With free medical care came hours of waiting at the clinic in Bemidji. In winter we fidgeted in the waiting room. In the summer we stayed outside and played on the north side—the shaded side—of the clinic. Until I outgrew my harness, Barb controlled my every move. I learned not to tug forward too hard because she'd jerk the leash and I'd fall backwards. I vividly recall hours tied to a maple tree outside the clinic, watching Chris and Tim play. As the sun moved, I moved around the tree, staying in the shade as much as possible.

Herman usually did the grocery shopping. When Barb did go with him, she'd place items in the cart and he'd throw them out. Eventually she learned to use her own cart, spending some of the AFDC money on food. Once home, her food was horded upstairs, only to be eaten when Herman was not in the house. When we got big enough to climb in and out of dumpsters, we began digging behind Red Owl and Super John's, searching for fruit, dented cans, and soup bones.

A decade later, when I was in the Navy, our ship spent a few days in Hong Kong, secured to a buoy in Victoria Harbor. Boat people were allowed to come aboard and wait on the mess deck. When all of the sailors were done with our food trays, the Chinese women—always it was women—salvaged our leftovers. After each meal, they'd pack up their containers and return with them to their sampans.

When Herman drove to town alone, it was our time to explore— mainly the blacksmith shop and the garage loft. He padlocked the blacksmith shop but we tunneled a hole beneath the locked door.

In the center of the shop's dirt floor, an anvil perched on the butt end of a three-foot-wide oak log. Along the north wall, below the only window in the building, a workbench constructed of two-by-six rough cut oak boards had a vise bolted to it. A wall-mounted drill press hung just beyond the bench. At the other end, tucked in the corner, a forge with a hand-crank bellows rested below a smoke hood mounted in the roof. There were pails of used, rusty nails that we spent hours with the ball peen hammer on the anvil, straightening for tree houses and other projects.

More than sixty years later when I close my eyes and remember, I can still taste the heavy coal smoke fumes and hear the ping, ping, ping, as Herman tapped glowing steel against the anvil. While he straightened bent orange-hot mower sickle bars and other damaged parts from his machinery, I cranked the forge blower, keeping the little coal pile glowing. Today that forge sits down by my shop in the ferns.

Originally, the garage housed two horse carriages, tack, and other stored items in the loft. After the horses were sold in the mid-1930s, the shed was converted to a garage. By the time we moved to the farm in 1949, nails protruded from the sway-backed cedar shingled roof. The back side was built into the hill with the eaves only three feet from the ground. When Herman wasn't around, we'd climb to the peak and slide down. After gouged butt cheeks and spools of thread to repair ripped pants, we learned to use sleds.

We didn't know it then, but the distinctive odor in the garage was from generations of guano built up between the ceiling and the loft floor. The bats, curled in dim cool recesses of the old building, were easy to catch and provided hours of entertainment.

Two sets of double doors swung from loose hinges at the front of the garage. A peeled oak post set on a flat stone stood between the two stalls and propped the sagging loft floor. A stuffed pheasant and several antler mounts lay on the cluttered workbench against the front wall. Chris said that when we arrived from New York, the mounts decorated the living room, but the beady-eyed bird gave him nightmares, and Barb felt the antlers were uncivilized so Herman removed them. Over the years, mice destroyed the antlers and the bird.

I remember a particular rainy afternoon when Herman was nailing a heel back onto my shoe. He had it fitted over the small cast iron shoe anvil mounted on the bench. I was spinning a homemade top he'd carved for me out of an empty thread spool and I got a sliver in my finger. Herman traced his hand over the old adz scars in the workbench from which I'd caught the sliver.

He said something like, "I was about your age when my dad made those cuts while he was repairing horse harnesses. I must have been about six, then." That's the only time I recall Herman talking about his father.

Above the benches, open cabinets and cubbyholes still held tarnished buckles and brass rivets once used for traces, reins, and homemade horse collars. My brothers and I didn't care about those things. It was the forbidden fruit in the loft that attracted us.

Entrance to the loft was gained through a trapdoor at the top of a two-by-four ladder nailed to the wall. Bats sometimes nestled behind the rungs and flew away when we climbed the ladder. Pushing the trapdoor open revealed a dim scene, shaded by decades of fly scat on the only window. Once in the loft, peering toward that opaque light, I felt a knot in my stomach, certain that ghosts lurked in the shadows. I imagined that Bruno's spirit still played up here. Bruno was Herman's little brother who had been killed in 1916 when horses bolted and he was thrown from the buckboard.

Behind the top step of the ladder, just above the trapdoor, was the bayonet Herman brought home from WWII. We ran our fingers gingerly across the rust stains and blunt stabbing tip, thrilled at the stories we conjured. To us, the rust became dried Nazi blood. Years later, I somehow ended up with that bayonet, and it's still rusty and mysterious.

I don't know why Herman never locked the loft even though I don't remember him ever going up there. Just above the ladder a small door hinged out, allowing light and fresh air to drive the ghosts away. There were two boxes filled with carpentry tools. Over the years, piece by piece, the tools disappeared as we built tree houses and forts and left the tools in the woods.

Dry-rotted tack lay wedged beneath the sloping roof trusses. Acorn shells from chipmunk stashes covered them in places. Salty sweat stains permeated the old leather, attracting little rodents who chewed for the salt. Holding the collars to our noses, we could still detect faint horse scent. By the time we played in the loft, we knew the "Herman stabbed the horse story." When Herman was a child, he had thrown a pitchfork at a stallion he couldn't catch. The fork pierced the horse's stomach, and Herman's father had to kill it. I wonder if some of those old harnesses belonged to that stallion.

Another treasure in the loft was the explosives—remnants left from clearing the land in the early 1900s. Tucked in a dark corner behind the old harnesses were four wooden boxes with stenciled images of explosions and flying men—a warning to careless handlers. Two of the boxes were empty. The third had a coil of fuse; the fourth had a cigar box full of copper blasting caps. We were devastated to be denied the opportunity to blow things up, but the blasting caps proved a satisfactory substitute. In westerns and war movies, we'd witnessed Hollywood's masterful use of dynamite. Again, when Herman went to town, we experimented.

Our escapades went something like this. Chris pulled a small coil of gray fuse from the box and Tim picked out several blasting caps.

"Windy, if you tell, we'll lock you in the basement with the light off," Tim warned.

"I won't tell. I want to see them blow up."

The first time we set one off, we went behind the barn, out of Barb's view from the house window. Tim cut a short section of fuse, inserted it in the open end of the dynamite cap, stuck it in the manure pile, and lit the fuse with a wooden match—"Lucifers," we called them.

"Stand back. Hide behind the wall. It's going to blow," Chris announced. We peeked around the corner of the barn and watched the fuse smolder. With a sharp clap and tiny puff of smoke, the blasting cap exploded and left a smoldering grapefruit-sized hole in the manure pile.

"Put a can over it," Tim said. With the next blast, the can leapt ten feet into the air. We were impressed by how it had shredded the metal rim.

"Let's play chicken," Chris said. He cut three fuses the same length, inserted them into the caps and laid them on the ground. Handing a Lucifer to me and one to Tim, he grinned. "We all light our fuse when I say go, then see who dares to hold the cap longest."

"I don't want to. Look what it did to the can," I said.

"You chicken, you're just a baby," Tim said.

"I am not. I'm six years old."

"Then stop whining and pick up your fuse."

I pinched the wooden match between thumb and forefinger and raked the head across the small rock Tim and Chris had used. I held the fused blasting cap in one hand, burning Lucifer in the other.

"When I say go, we all light our fuses. The last one holding is the winner," Chris said. "Ready? On three—one, two, three—go."

I held my match to the fuse while Chris and Tim watched for a moment, then they lit theirs. The three fuses sputtered toward the copper caps. I threw mine toward the barn, Tim and Chris close behind. "You chicken," Tim said. "We win."

Shotgun

The guns Herman had tucked in the garage loft enthralled us. I vaguely remember the 40-65 Winchester rifle with a pitted octagon barrel. We never found ammunition for it. There was also a single shot 12-gauge shotgun. For perhaps two years we played with the guns. Finally, Chris, about twelve that summer, worked up the courage to shoot the shotgun.

We'd never seen or heard a 12-gauge fired—only the .22 rifle when Herman took us squirrel hunting or shot a pig or an old cow for butchering—but we had heard rumors from school kids about the vicious recoil that left a bruised, sometimes broken, shoulder.

Because of the heat and high milk volume from the cows during the summer, Herman made a cream run into town twice a week. Before the old Chevy's dust settled in the driveway, Chris was in the loft and passed the shotgun down to Tim.

"Let's go on patrol," Chris said, shouldering the gun. Ammo bearer Tim followed him. "Windy, you're rear guard—no talking." And he made me swear to secrecy.

We were Hawkeye, Green Mountain Boys, Lewis and Clark, Rangers patrolling Pork Chop Hill. We were General Patton at the Battle of the Bulge. Beyond the muck-filled pothole behind the barn, beyond the fence near the sumac maze, beyond the glacial gullies that connected several small lakes during spring melt, we set out to guard our front.

"I see a Kraut," Tim whispered. Herman had been on the European front so we usually battled Germans.

Dropping to the forest floor, Chris looked back to where Tim and I were lying. "Give me a bullet—where did you see him?"

"Behind that stump—see that big stump?" Tim said. "I saw something move—the top of his helmet I think."

I squinted and peeked over Tim's back but couldn't see anything.

I don't know whether the shotgun loads were birdshot, slugs, or double-ought buckshot. Chris loaded the gun and whispered, "You two stay here. I'll crawl around the side and flank him."

We lay silent. Tim began twitching and looked back at me. "I think we're on an ant nest but we can't move—the Nazi might see us and shoot. What's taking Chris so long?"

Chris jumped up by the stump. "He's gone—you guys scared him away making so much noise."

"You chicken—you're afraid to shoot the gun," Tim said, brushing a mosquito from behind his glasses lens.

"I am not. You shoot it," Chris held the gun toward Tim. "Prove you ain't."

"You first," Tim dared him.

"I know what we'll do," Chris said. "Let's set it on the stump, cock it, and then pull the trigger with a stick."

That seemed like a genius plan. Chris balanced the loaded, cocked gun on top of the stump while Tim found a long stick. We lay flat in the damp leaves as Chris reached up, worked the stick into the trigger guard and touched the trigger. The gun leapt into the air, did a cartwheel and landed about ten feet from us.

Wide-eyed, Tim stood up and said, "That would have for sure broke our shoulder if we shot it."

"No, I don't think so. I want to shoot the other round into the stump. I want to see the hole it makes. It can't hurt too much or people wouldn't shoot them," Chris reasoned. "Give me the other bullet."

Tim handed him the shotgun shell. "Well, at least hold it away from your shoulder—that way it won't hurt as much."

Chris loaded the gun while Tim scratched a crude circle on the side of the stump. "Inside the circle is the Kraut's head—go for a head shot."

Chris held the gun a few inches from his shoulder, closed his eyes, and fired. Immediately he dropped the gun, grabbed his shoulder and howled in pain. "It broke my arm—it's numb—I can't feel it."

Tim picked at the hole in the stump with his jackknife.

That evening, while slopping skim milk to the hogs, Chris carried one bucket at a time.

"Take one in each hand," Herman told him. "It's easier to carry if you're balanced."

"We were playing war while you were in town today and I got wounded in the shoulder. I can only use one arm," Chris explained.

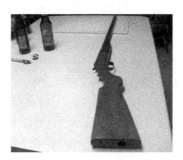

The old 12 gauge; after I purchased it at Barb's estate auction in 2010 I gave it to my nephew, Nathan, hoping it will remain in the family for another hundred years.

I learned squirrel hunting by tagging along with Herman, Chris, and Tim. Herman encouraged us to hunt—free meat. Within a few years I began bringing wild game home with the .22 rifle. I don't remember Chris and Tim doing a lot of hunting— I'm sure they did, but as they grew older, cars became their passion.

Excerpt from my grandmother's 1939 diary:

Tuesday, November 14, 1939: I had to go to the hospital with Barb—a headache. After, we went to a terribly realistic French movie, "That They May Live." The Dead of Verdun 1918 come to life in 1939. Barb enjoyed speaking French with Gabby.

Wednesday, November 22, 1939: Spent all a.m. in the hospital with B. I like the new Dr. Brown on the case very much. Hope she will get somewhere. After three years Barb seems not the least bit better to me. Yes. I suppose she is some in some ways. No violent scenes now. Just silence. Dr. Brown has her on nine pills per day. Henry bought a beautiful turkey.

Thursday, November 23, 1939: "Thanksgiving." Will we ever be through with this man (President Franklin D. Roosevelt) and his mad cheating the people? His egoism and selfish ideals to gain more power. The whole world is wrecked by the four of them – Franklin, Stalin, Hitler, and Mussolini. Dottie and Nick drove in late in the afternoon. Connecticut didn't celebrate today. Henry bought a huge turkey and we had a delicious meal and a very good time. Dottie asked Barb to play for her which she did very beautifully but didn't feel well; couldn't eat her dinner.

Wednesday, December 13, 1939: Went to the hospital as usual with B. I can't see a great deal of progress. Dr. Brown is in too much of a hurry. Barb and I had a nice luncheon together.

1955
The Dip

It was the winter Randy peed on the pork. After butchering a hog, rather than hanging the two sides in the granary, Herman brought them in and laid them across broken chairs on the porch. One afternoon during a blizzard, Randy, almost four years old, didn't want to stand outside on the steps. Chris caught him peeing on the hog carcass. We rinsed it off and ate it. "Put mustard on it," Herman told us.

By early spring 1955, Chris and Tim were again trying to ditch me, so I followed Herman like a puppy. I was seven and chores were still a game—pitching hay to the cows, washing manure off teats before the Surge milking machine was connected, scooping manure out of the gutter with my little broken-handled shovel. The barn smell is still vivid sixty years later. Another odor that transports me back to those days and makes me gag is Copenhagen.

It was a typical Saturday. Morning chores were done. We had eaten our breakfast of hot farina. Late in the morning, Herman loaded silage onto a high-sided homemade sled. Randy rode and I helped to pull it. We scooped silage to the cows and then cleaned the barn gutters while the cows were busy eating. The odor of silage mixed with manure smell was ripe; the fermented corn passed through the cows and created manure as soupy as the first few days of lush spring grass.

After lunch, a man came to the farm to purchase some cows. For me it was great excitement to have a stranger in the barn. I showed him my BB gun and the empty Copenhagen snuff can Randy and I used for a target. He challenged me to take a shot and seemed surprised when I hit the target. He was also impressed when I opened the target and proudly showed him how I saved the BB. He laughed when I put it back in the gun.

Abrahamson, the cattle buyer, haggled with Herman over the price of two cull cows. I imagine the conversation went something like this.

"They're thin—I can't give you more than twenty cents a pound for them."

"For Christ sake, by the time I pay trucking and yardage, I'll be sending them a check," Herman argued.

"Oh, you'll get something for them. There's just so many being shipped right now with this hay shortage. Last summer's drought hurt a lot of farmers. At least it'll be two less to feed." Abrahamson pulled a Copenhagen box from his bib overall breast pocket, rapped his knuckles twice on the metal lid, and twisted it open. Extending the snuff—we called it "snuice"— he said, "Here, have a dip." Herman took a generous pinch and tucked it in his lip.

"Can I have a dip?" I asked. Abrahamson looked, Herman nodded, and I reached into the round waxed box, seized a fistful and put it in my mouth. I chewed and swallowed.

Nausea rose in my throat. I felt dizzy instantly, as if I had gone too fast on the little merry-go-round on the playground at school. I grabbed for the nearest steel beam, missed, and dropped to my hands and knees, face near the gutter. The two men roared with laughter. Vomit spewed— bitter, brown, peppery. As I write this, I again feel the burning in my nose as snotty snuice juice dripped out. I grabbed the steel pipe and pulled myself up, shivering with dry heaves. The two men howled.

"That's the best show I've seen in a long time," Abrahamson said, handing me a dollar. "Want another dip?"

A dollar bought ten rides on the electric pony at Ben Franklin or two banana splits across the street at Woolworth's.

Inheritance

Barb received an inheritance from her grandmother, Idalia's estate. She spent the money to improve the farm, which was surprising because she still harbored the dream of escape. Maybe, now that she had six children, she realized that there was nowhere to go. By then, during arguments, she told Herman that Chris and Tim would inherit the farm when he was dead so perhaps she considered her inheritance an investment.

First came the indoor bathroom. In the dead of winter, twelve feet from the house, a crew dynamited through frozen ground to dig the septic tank. Herman considered the indoor toilet an extravagant waste. Only Laurel and Barb were allowed to use it.

She persuaded Herman to relocate the kitchen from the west end of the house, where it had been for fifty years. The new kitchen wasn't practical because there was no room for a table and little room for cabinets. She hired Herman's brother-in-law, Ben, to cut a huge hole in the east wall of the house and install a picture window. The window did provide a panoramic view across the field to Maple Lake. The kitchen sink was installed below the window. Nine months after the kitchen relocation, Rosalinda was born.

The window was single pane. During the winter, at night, ice built up and water dribbled down when sun hit it each morning. First, the paint peeled. Over the years, the bottom window casing rotted and the heavy window settled. From the beginning, Herman was not happy with the kitchen arrangement.

The first spring after the toilet was installed, after the ground thawed, Herman felt compelled to empty the septic tank. We used buckets on long ropes to dip out the sewage, carry it about forty yards to the edge of a hill, dump the pail, and go back for another. When we reached the bottom of the tank—the last eighteen inches of sludge—and the buckets just flopped on their side and lay, Herman had me strip my clothes off. He lowered me into the tank on a rope. I stood naked in the sludge and scooped the buckets. Later that spring we trenched a line to the edge of the hill and dug a dry hole—a six foot deep hole similar to a septic tank—and filled it with rocks. Beyond the dry hole, sewer water trickled into the pigpen.

That autumn at school I jumped out of a swing and broke my ankle. Because it was difficult to maneuver around on crutches with my cast, Herman allowed me to use the indoor bathroom. By winter we were all using it.

Another improvement Barb made in the house was a central heating system. A crew installed a wood furnace in the basement with ductwork throughout the house. To heat the upstairs was a colossal failure because there was no crawlspace for ventilation and the roof was not insulated between the joists. Heat rose and escaped through the rough cut boards, tarpaper, and shingles. Ice dams formed and the roof leaked.

One evening, in an effort to help Herman, I went down to the basement and packed the furnace for the night. I overfilled it and by late evening, with the draft completely shut off, the furnace got so hot Herman worried about it igniting the wooden floor two feet above. He sprayed water on top of the furnace in an effort to cool it down. He didn't get angry at me but I was told never to fill the stove again.

The following winter we used the old wood stove on the main floor. Barb's dream of central heat lay rusting in the basement until the winter of 1959 when she sold the furnace and all the duct work.

Barb bought a small flock of sheep with some of her money. It was one of the few things she and Herman ever did in agreement. The sheep project was a communal effort. Each child owned a ewe and received the money from wool and the sale of the lambs in the autumn. Barb purchased a small wooden box, the lid secured by a padlock to which *she* held the key. The plan was to store the sheep profits—everyone's share— in the box.

I think Herman was excited about raising sheep. Perhaps the idea brought back memories of a more carefree time. He told us stories of how, during the Great Depression, he and his future brother-in-law Charlie had worked out in Montana on a sheep ranch. In the spring, after lambing, we prepared the flock for pasture just as Herman had learned in the 1930s. It was exciting with the new crop of long-legged, black-nosed lambs bleating in the barnyard.

Late spring, before the sheep and lambs were allowed to go out to pasture, they were sheared and dipped. The itinerate shearer set up in the new barn, and, holding the sheep butt- down between his legs, he took about two minutes to clip her. Once in a while the side tooth of the shaft-driven shear caught a fold of skin and sliced the sheep open. The shearer took a thick sewing needle and a length of waxed twine, sat on the ewe's head and sewed her up as she bleated in pain. After the stitching job was complete he took a cedar chip, scooped a glob from the tar bucket, and rubbed the black goop into the stitched gash.

After the ewes had been sheared, they were dipped in a petroleum-based insecticide—probably laced with DDT— to kill ticks, lice, and discourage flies until the dip wore off midsummer. The sheep left a dripping trail where grass didn't grow that summer.

We docked—amputated—the lambs' tails and castrated the males. It was necessary to remove the tail because the lamb's manure would stick to their fuzzy tail, build up, and create a breeding ground for flies. The docking iron was similar to an old fashioned branding iron, but instead of a heated symbol to sear into the skin, the iron had a sharp blade on the end. Two of us held the lamb securely while Herman stretched the lamb's tail over an oak block. He pressed down with the glowing hot blade, severed the tail, and cauterized the wiggly stump. I can still smell burning wool and cooking flesh. The twitching tail was cast aside for the chickens to fight over.

After the tail was removed, we checked the lamb's sex. Males were held upside-down, front and hind legs held together and spread apart, exposing their groin area. Herman, using his jackknife, severed the tip of the scrotum and pushed the sack's skin down against the bleating lamb's body until two slippery pink testicles popped out of the hole. He leaned down, took a tiny testicle between his teeth and pulled. The lamb screamed as it was ripped from his urinary tract. After the second one was removed, hot tar was rubbed into the empty scrotum to discourage flies and infection. Herman spit the testicles into the dust for the chickens.

"Out west they fry them up between docking irons and eat those—Rocky Mountain oysters," he told us with a grin. "I never tried them." The bleating lamb was then bathed in the tick-dip and ready for pasture. By midsummer, the pasture was grazed down to stubble. It was the only paddock with woven wire so we couldn't rotate the flock to fresh grass.

We belonged to the local 4-H chapter and brought lambs to the county fair—never won a ribbon. Looking back, I realize we never had a chance. Because of the pasture situation, we had to take our project lamb away from its mother and tie it to a stake in the yard in lush grass. In retrospect, the lamb probably would have done better on the "ball diamond" as Herman called the pasture, because the poor lamb frequently had no shade, was often out of water, and suddenly wasn't able to nurse.

When the buyer came for the lambs, Barb cashed the check, and with great ceremony, placed each child's share in a separate envelope with our name on it, and locked them in the wooden box. That was the last I ever saw of my share. I don't know about my siblings. Chris told me that he once suggested savings accounts be opened for each of us. Barb slapped him and the wooden box remained locked. Eventually the sheep flock dwindled. Here's a chilling event that twelve-year-old Randy shared with our grandmother seven years later, the spring of 1962.

This morning one of our sheep had a lamb and the pigs ate it all up bones and everything not a piece of blood left.

Sheep are very susceptible to internal parasites that deplete nutrients, including blood. My wife and I raised sheep for several years on our farm. Each spring after lambing, we vaccinated the lambs and the ewes for disease and treated them for parasites. Over the course of the grazing season, I'd rotate the pasture each week and continue a preventative worming maintenance schedule. As I look back on the crude husbandry practices we used on the farm in the 1950s, I'm amazed that any animals survived.

It was the year that an Encyclopedia Britannica salesman sat in the front room. Midsummer sweat dampened his shirt armpits as he closed the sale on the deluxe, gold letter embossed edition. The twenty-four elegant volumes came jacketed in faux leather with a dark mahogany case to store them in. I remember the salesman returning to the farm several times seeking payment. Eventually, he quit. I don't know if he just gave up trying to collect or got fired.

Barb was very proud of the new set, often reading the volume about New York. She tried to monitor our use of the encyclopedias. The bookcase was the first casualty. Within two years, the volumes were scattered across the house, pages colored, ripped out, and dog-eared. Today, more than sixty years later, I have the fourteen surviving volumes stored in the steamer trunk that Barb took from Chelan. We all used the encyclopedias through our school years. It was perhaps the greatest tangible gift Barb acquired for us. Today, I think those books were my gateway into a love for history.

I recently pulled one of the old encyclopedias out—it happened to be #24, *Text Index Atlas/Atlas Index*. The old volume fell open to a yellow index card near the center. I tucked my nose down into the spine and smelled again my childhood and the stuffy upstairs of the old farmhouse. Then I noticed a note, written in the margin with an arrow pointing to Yokosuka, Japan.

Fifty-two years earlier, when I was eighteen and in the Navy, Barb had written, *Where Windy is—May 8th, Mother's Day 1966*

Strawberries and Randy

Randy and I spent countless hours together. I recall it as a carefree time, before I was old enough to work full days. I was seven the summer of 1955 and Randy was going on five. Whippoorwills called in the night, the garden was planted, and purple lilac petals lay shriveled among mint leaves. Randy and I had finished breakfast. We headed north from the house, ready to conquer the world—at least our little corner of it.

"Let's check the wren eggs," Randy suggested. Dew on the oats binder steamed in the morning sun as we approached it. The tiny brown bird flitted from the hole in the twine box as we crept forward.

"Open it," Randy said.

I pried the hinged top up and peeked. Inside were three hairless baby wrens.

"Let me see, let me see," Randy begged.

I lifted him up and he stuck his finger down and touched them. Their heads shot up, eyes closed, mouths open wide with little chirps.

"They think my finger is a worm," he laughed. "Let's go catch frogs." We slammed the lid on the twine box, walked back over the hill past the pothole, and down to the bog surrounding Maple Lake. The legal name of our little lake was Smyth Lake. Why it came to be called Maple Lake is a mystery—maybe it was the autumn-time crimson maples bordering the north side.

But that long ago summer morning, flies rose lazily as our bare feet squished cow pies along the edge of the swamp. Water-filled divots—deep holes made by cow hooves the summer before—swarmed with tadpoles.

The new growth grass was short and stood out against the burned over black stubble. Soot puffed up between our toes with the smell of burnt grass.

Earlier in the spring we had set the old swamp grass ablaze with our Cracker Jack magnifying glass. It may have been the same spring I taught Randy how to angle the glass until a tiny dot of sunlight focused on the brown tinder-dry pile I had bunched together. In previous years, I'd watched Herman start swamp fires, so I knew he wouldn't mind. It was great fun to watch sheets of flame race across the swamp and up into the woods. As in past years, the fire died out when it reached the still-damp tree line.

"Let's bring some tadpoles home and put them in jars, like the goldfish at Ben Franklin," I said. Randy scooped his cupped hands into a hole and came up with several squiggly critters. The water quickly leaked out.

"We'll never get them home alive," he said, and cast them into the swamp.

We walked around the bog to a small creek that flowed between Maple Lake and Round Lake in early spring. Mayflowers were gone and yellow swamp flowers had not yet bloomed. Sliding down the bank into the creek, Randy fell into the knee-deep water.

"It's cold," he said, scampering out.

Instead of wading, we lay on our stomachs and raced sticks in the flowing stream.

"Look, there's a real minnow," I said. "We could make them goldfish."

"We need a bucket to catch them. My stick is beating yours," Randy laughed. "Let's go find the cows."

Stopping at the bog again, we shed our shirts in the warm sun and splashed swamp water from the tadpole holes at each other. Tiring of that, dripping wet, we grabbed our shirts, crossed the alfalfa field, and crawled under the electric fence onto the lane.

"I got to pee," Randy said.

"I dare you to pee on the fence."

Randy unzipped his jeans, stood tip-toed, and squirted onto the wire. He jumped back with a squeal when he got zapped. "I'm going to tell Daddy on you."

I doubled over laughing. "He won't do anything. He dared me when I was your age."

We followed the lane out into the pasture. Cows grazed in the late morning sun. A constant, low, tearing sound accompanied the herd as we approached them. We stood watching as the Holsteins ripped grass, dandelions, and young weeds up by the mouthful, trailing the smell of fresh manure.

"Let's climb trees," I said, looking over toward the edge of the pasture. "Race you!" I took off running, Randy far behind. At the tree line I selected a young maple and shinnied up. Randy picked one nearby, wrapped his hands around the trunk, jumped up as he pulled, then wrapped his legs around the trunk as he reached for a higher hand hold. Soon he was fifteen feet off the ground, looking across at me.

"Swing yourself down. That's the fun part," I said. "Watch this." Holding tightly, I swung my legs out away from the tree and the young sapling swayed over, lowering me slowly toward the ground. I let go and dropped the last four feet. "Okay, your turn."

Randy swung out. The tree quivered, but stayed upright. He tried again, casting his feet out on the other side of the tree. Slowly it bent over, leaving Randy eight feet above the ground.

"Hold on tight. I'll get you." Climbing onto a nearby boulder, I jumped toward him, caught his foot, and pulled him down. We hit the soft ground and lay laughing.

"Daddy thinks Rosie might have her calf today. Let's go find her." We started walking and I got quieter. "Mommy sure got mad when Daddy named her Rosie," I said.

"I don't like when they fight. It scares me."

I nodded. "You know he did that so Mommy wouldn't name our new sister Rosalinda," I said.

We walked toward the back of the pasture where forest had been bulldozed into windrows a few years earlier. Rosie stood on the south slope, her tail twitching.

"I think she's getting ready to have her calf. Let's watch," I said. "Hey, look at all the strawberries."

Thumb nail-sized wild strawberries dotted the hillside. We gathered handfuls and stuffed them in our mouths. It became another race. Pick a handful, gobble them down. We giggled as we raced. Rosie stood watching in the warm sun. I flopped onto my back and looked into the sky.

"Look at that cloud. It looks like a smoke puff."

Randy lay down beside me and looked up. "Look at those eagles floating. They don't even flap their wings."

I watched them spiraling below a small cloud.

"Someday I want to fly like that," Randy said. "But fast, like those jets over the house."

I looked over at Randy and snickered.

"What's so funny?" he asked. "I can fly a plane someday."

"Your face is red with strawberry juice. It looks like somebody hit you."

Rosie's face was suddenly above mine, her huge nostrils woofing fermented grass smell.

"You stink, old girl. Get away," I said, pushing at her jaw. She slowly ambled off.

"It's cold when that cloud goes in front of the sun," Randy said. An anvil shaped cloud covered the sun, lightening flickering high in the sky.

"That's weird. Just that one dark cloud—look how fast it's moving." A few rain drops splattered down as the cloud thundered past. Five minutes later, the sun was out, steam rising from the squall.

"Hey, look, Rosie's laying down," Randy whispered, peeking through an opening in the tree windrow. "Let's sneak around behind her and watch."

We got on our hands and knees and, what we called Indian-style, crawled through the opening to where we could see Rosie's rear end. A small black nose and two hooves peeked out as Rosie grunted and strained. We watched in silence. Rosie was breathing fast. She stood up, pawed the ground, turned in a circle, and lay back down. Suddenly she gasped, became rigid and pushed. Out popped the calf's head and front feet. Rosie lay panting. We remained silent. The cow squeezed. The calf's neck slipped out. Rosie took a deep breath and pushed. Shoulders, body, and back legs slid out. Rosie lay moaning. The calf was on the ground, gasping muffled bleats. Rosie stumbled to her feet, turned, and began licking.

"Yuck, how can she eat that stuff?" Randy asked.

"I don't know. I sure wouldn't if I was a cow," I said. "Let's go get some more strawberries."

"I'm not hungry anymore."

In 1978 Randy's Navy P-3 Orion, a four-engine turboprop, went down off the coast of Africa while on an anti-submarine surveillance exercise. He never had the chance to tell our stories to his young daughter and infant son. A few years ago, I spent a spring morning walking the path Randy and I had taken more than sixty years earlier. As I walked, I scribbled images that popped up in my memory of that morning so long ago.

The ditch between the two lakes was still there. The bog has crept farther out into Maple Lake—climatologists predict that in another thousand years the lake will become a hundred acre bog. The windrow opening—where we'd watched Rosie—was overgrown, but flowering strawberry plants flourished at the tree line. The large stone—the boulder that I stood on to reach Randy when he dangled in the tree—was still there, lichen covered and shaded by hazel brush. No cows have been in the pasture for many years. I lay down in a warm, grassy dandelion patch and watched an aircraft pass high overhead, eagles soaring beneath the vapor trails.

(Late summer, 1955) Calves and lambs. *(Left to right)* Laurel holding Bonny, Wendell, Tim holding a lamb, Randy, and Chris. We are behind the new barn, the dried up pothole and treeline in the background. Note all the stumps. Late in the winter when we ran out of firewood, Herman cut trees close to the buildings and we hand-carried logs up to the house through deep snow.

By the summer of 1955 Chelan was a distant memory. Chris was twelve years old, Tim was ten— both old enough to work long days through the summer and do chores morning and evening. Herman became more demanding, expecting them to perform a day's work equal to his.

I was assigned the hateful job of washing the separator and milking machines that summer. I had to scrub them in the kitchen sink, which meant that I also had to do last night's supper dishes and the breakfast cereal bowls before I could take the scummy separator and the manure-crusted machines apart. Barb was usually in the shaded front room playing with the younger kids.

In the summer, after breakfast Herman took the hoe and worked the dirt around the potato hills in the garden while he watched Chris and Tim weed their assigned vegetable rows. Herman seemed to have eyes of a hawk and watched for seedlings pulled accidentally with a weed.

War Games

In the mid-1950s, Herman began bringing us up to Redby, a small town north of the farm on the Red Lake Nation, to the movie theater as a reward for our work—tickets were about thirty-five cents. I remember the movie *Chief Crazy Horse*. I was surprised by the Native children who cheered when a cowboy or soldier was killed and how they booed when an Indian was shot off his horse. It was confusing. The Indians were the bad guys, weren't they?

Barb claimed that James Fenimore Cooper was one of our ancestors. In searching Cooper genealogy, I discovered that Anthony and Thomas Cooper emigrated to North America in the 1630s, the same decade as my ancestors, Richard Olmsted III, his younger brother, John, and their sister, Rebecca. There weren't many Europeans in North America at that time, so it's certainly possible there was a connection through marriage. Barb had grown up with Cooper's *Leather Stocking* tales. She passed them along to us, so we were well-versed in Hawkeye's exploits and the heroic Uncas in *The Last of the Mohicans*.

We became Crazy Horse, Cochise, Uncas, and Geronimo. For bows, ironwood was best; it was tough, flexible, and it bent but didn't break. A supple stick about four feet long was cut and notched at the ends to hold the twine string. We used hazel brush for arrows, trimming several pencil-thick sticks, sharpened to a point, and packed in our quiver. We cut a target from a cardboard box. The arrows wobbled thirty feet and skidded into the dust.

Chris gave us Mohawk haircuts with the cow clippers. Tim, a year and a half younger, sheared Chris's black curls off. We scratched our wrists bloody with jackknives, and pressed them against one another.

Barb was furious. "You boys are from New York City. Your ancestors came over on the *Mayflower*. You are not filthy redskins. Don't be surprised if you get blood poisoning."

Herman was pleased, no doubt because it angered Barb. With his hands resting on Randy and me, he ruffled our Mohawk strips that arced from forehead to nape of neck. "You hunyuks ought to dance in the powwow." Hunyuk was a term of endearment.

Sunday morning, we tuned to the local station broadcasting church services in the Ojibwe language. We listened intently, not understanding a word they preached to our blood brothers, but we chanted prayers with them.

Wendell in front with a Mohawk, Tim on left, and Chris. I wonder if by the time this picture was taken they felt too mature for such antics.

One summer day, Randy and I rode into Bemidji with Herman when he made the cream run. We delivered to Land O' Lakes Creamery, then went downtown on some forgotten errand. Randy, about four that summer, and I got bored and wandered outside. We must have crossed Second Street, heading north, past Gene's Tap or The Flame. Two heavy-set Native women sat on the sidewalk outside the bar.

"You're cute little shits," one of them said. "I'm taking you home to be my boys." I think Randy's blond Mohawk had grabbed her attention. We scampered back to the Co-op store.

Chris convinced Barb to buy him a bow and arrow set for his birthday. The new professional arrows only had blunt tips. Chris filed the head off a three inch nail and taped it to the blunt end, nocked the arrow, and told Tim to set up the target. Anxious to try the new arrow, Chris released it while Tim was still near the target. The arrow whizzed through the air and into Tim's head, the nail embedded between his ear and skull. I don't recall any repercussions. I don't think Tim went to the doctor.

We each had a jackknife by then—just like Herman—and, when bored, we pulled them out to whittle, trim finger and toe nails, or just flip and stick into the ground. The latter usually evolved to a game of stab: we stood an arm's length apart, spread our legs so our feet were about two to three feet apart, and took turns flipping the knife at each other's bare feet, seeing how close we dared come, and knowing that our opponent would soon have his turn.

BB guns added a dimension to playing war. We could shoot each other, but only below the waist. If we wore long pants, the pellet would not penetrate our skin and only left a red welt. Randy got a new BB gun. He and I declared open season on anything that moved. Airplanes, cats, birds of any kind, dogs that were tied up, cows—nothing was safe. When a cow was hit, she jumped like a bee had stung her.

When we played war, it seemed like I was always the Nazi, the Jap, or the Indian, depending on the movie we had most recently seen or which comic my older brothers were reading. They'd give me a count of one hundred to escape, before hunting me—I never got very far before they began tracking me.

As a Jap, I learned early that it was a losing proposition to mount a one man banzai charge against two grenade-wielding American soldiers. We used rotten chicken and goose eggs in the spring; fist-size rocks after the eggs were expended. Usually, I'd hide behind the chickenhouse. As time went by, I realized that the squawking hens betrayed me. I'd charge out; Chris and Tim (Patton and Eisenhower) would drop to one knee, level their Tommy guns and fire. I couldn't feign a hit because they'd examine my corpse for red welts. If I got within range, the grenades were thrown. A close rock was considered lethal; like the old cliché, "Close only counts in horseshoes and hand grenades."

Rotten goose eggs were contact weapons, and it took days for the smell to wear off. Just grabbing the eggs was hazardous duty. After the goslings hatched, the female goose still guarded her nest. With a warning hiss, she'd dart forward pecking, clawing and beating us with her wings. It took three of us—two decoys for her to chase—and a third person to streak in, grab still-warm eggs, and rush back. Once I was hit on the side of the head with a goose egg. They were heavy and had a hard shell. It stunned me, exploded into my ear, my hair, down inside my coat, and ran down to my belly button. By evening it was dry, but I wiped it off the best I could. Our baths were often two weeks apart. At school the kids called me "Stinky" for the rest of the week.

Being a Nazi wasn't as suicidal as a banzaiing Jap. I was allowed to ambush the Americans. I remember one summer after the eggs were gone, I had fist-sized rocks for close-in combat. It was haying season and the big door on the new barn was open for hoisting bundles into the loft. When Chris began the count, I raced for the barn, climbed into the haymow and up a ladder to the big door, about twenty feet above the ground. Peeking around the corner, I watched them advance. Chris flanked me, around the side of the barn, in the back door. Tim crept forward, rushing from cover to cover—brooder house, to chickenhouse, to corn crib, to hay wagon. He didn't see me as he crouched below the lip of the hay wagon. Hanging onto the ladder with one hand, I positioned myself and, like my hero, Audie Murphy, lobbed a grenade and struck him in the head. He flipped over and quivered like a beached bullhead. A thrill shot through me—for once I won, no question. Then I realized he might be dead. I yelled to Chris; he ran out to inspect Tim as I looked out from the big haymow door. When Chris raised bloody hands, I knew I was in trouble. I don't remember my punishment for that victory, but it was no doubt worth the beating. Again, I don't think Tim went to the doctor.

Being Indian was my favorite. I raced to the bull thistles and cockle burrs where the straw pile was blown each fall during threshing. By late summer the weeds stood four feet tall—jungle thick. I'd hunch low, still and silent, as BBs *phh 'ted* past, often followed by grenades. In the early summer we used the sumac patch north of the sheep pasture. Sumac must be poison because sheep wouldn't touch them, unlike the high browse line they created on other bushes. I raced ahead, circled in from the forest behind, and lying flat, I'd creep through the sumac patch, often escaping unscathed.

One time I was hit in the back with a rock grenade. It left a welt that took weeks to heal. Tim said he saw the tops of the bushes moving. A decade later I remembered that childhood incident as I crawled toward a medevac chopper through jungle foliage along a riverbank.

Grandparents Visit

I didn't find any correspondence in the chickenhouse from the farm to our grandparents in the mid-1950s. They had their own problems. In January of 1955, my grandfather Henry traveled to Seattle for five weeks and left Elsie alone with Polly. That was two years after Polly had disappeared for several months in 1952-53. A few months after Henry returned from Seattle, Elsie's diary entries indicated that Pol was acting out again:

May 6, 1955. What a wearing afternoon at the V.A. the answer is always a stonewall and I did get a colored social worker after all—very dumb! How he had the nerve to say he had never seen a schizo cured!!

July 4, 1955. Henry and I had an early appointment with Dr. Wesley Culver [Elsie often refers to him as W.C.]. *He thinks dear Pol should be hospitalized.*

July 6, 1955. If Pol Dol [Polly] continues to miss the good of the summer we realize something must be done. Now that all my winter activities are over which requires her typing she is really slipping. Henry had luncheon with General Maxwell to see if we can't pull some influence for dear Polly. I must write to Nubs [Elsie's brother in Seattle] to raise some money if we succeed.

July 29, 1955. I met Henry at 2pm at the V.A. We saw Dr. after Dr. All seemed hopeless until finally just at the last the Dr. that seemed the most so suggested that South Oaks, Amityville, private, was approved by them for women.

July 31, 1955. Henry and I drove to Amityville to look at South Oaks. A beautiful place—Miss Browell, charming—is quite sure everything can be arranged. I hope it's the miracle it seems to be. Here ended the hottest July in history—didn't once get Polly to the beach.

August 1. Dear Henry spent all day at the V.A doing a miracle getting legal matters signed, etc. About five we drove down to see Miss Browell and stayed until nearly midnight making arrangements.

August 3, 1955. Red Letter Day. The dear Lord was with us on this day. Dear Pol came home at noon. I had her luncheon ready-- then told her I had to move the car if the ticket man came. She went right out [to move the car]. The limousine from South Oaks was right there, followed her a short distance and picked her up easily. The dear thing really needed hospitalization and I am glad for her tho of course she won't be glad for a long time. Thank goodness for ourselves and the Veterans it went so smoothly.

By 1955 Henry had been handling his cousin Eloise's funds for several years. I can only imagine the financial pressure he must have been under. The following letter from the chickenhouse was badly damaged. I spent several hours reconstructing it because I believe it reveals just how much Henry had deviated from the original agreement. Here's an example of the letter.

From Eloise Garstin at the Hotel de Palais 8'Orsay, Paris, France.

March 25, 1955

Dear Henry, Your long letter of March 16 was received a few days before I crossed the Channel and it will require a lot of answering, but today I *will try to clear up just one point as you appear to be under a fantastic misconception.*

This is not the first time you have alluded to my "desire to help" you, but on previous occasions I have let it pass. Now, however, the idea seems to have become ingrained in your mind

Let me say at once, definitely and finally, that it was Estelle and Julia Thomas I desired and still desire to help, and no one else. Everything else is pure wishful thinking on your part.

It is true I told you to recompense yourself for trouble taken in investing the money for the Cousins, but by that I meant, and you very well know that I meant, nothing more than paying yourself a fair and just commission on such transactions. A business commission, not helping to support you out of my money.

As you are unable to furnish me with any financial statement of account whatsoever, showing how you have invested the money or what Commissions you have paid yourself for your trouble, the inference is only too plain. But this subject I will reserve for another letter.

For the moment I want to make it once more perfectly plain that never in my life have I entertained the idea of helping to support you—it is a fantastic idea that I, a woman, and single, should wish to part with my money to help you, a capable business man of 60, in full health.

But the point is (and let us be realistic) just what "assistance" do you expect me to compensate you for? Once a year I asked you to be kind enough to ask the Socie'te' Ge'ne'rale to send me some of my own money to Paris or Rome. This has taken up maybe half an hour or one hour of your time once a year to oblige a cousin. The other "assistance" was to "stand in" in the place of Fred Pierce, on my Trust, which no doubt involved you in signing one form and returning it to the Bank of California. Never did they ask your advice about my investments or trouble you in any way whatever except when you signed one more form at my request, relieving yourself of this onerous task. So please let us be realistic and stick to the truth.

I bitterly regret ever having asked even this slight amount of assistance from you, and I never dreamed you would expect money for so slight a service other than negligible out of pocket expenses involved. The signing of a form, the sending of a draft once a year to someone of your own blood.

You still have money from the thousand pounds I sent you some five years ago and I now ask you to send the equivalent of 100 pounds to me before April 20.

C/O La Socie'te' Ge'ne'rale, 29 Boulevard Haussman, Paris

Thank you for writing me about Harriet—Eloise

On August 18, 1955, Henry and Elsie left New York on a trip to our farm. Elsie's diary detailed their escape from Hurricane Diane on August 19, the drive on the Ohio Turnpike, a stay at the Palmer House in Chicago, and a short stop in Racine, Wisconsin, where Elsie's father, Charles Diller Fratt had been born in 1862.

I discovered this picture in Elsie's 1955 diary. Barb must have given it to her mother during the visit. The back of the picture is signed,

"Summer 1951" and inserted among the August 1955 entries.

Elsie's diary continued:

August 25, 1955. Stillwater, Minnesota to Bemidji. We arose at eight after a good night's sleep at the adorable Lowell Inn. Charming breakfast there and set out in the rain on the last lap of our long journey to see the children. We had written ahead for a cottage at Shorecrest Resort on Lake Bemidji. It is really lovely—all white with green shutters in the birches on a high point overlooking Lake Bemidji. The shops were just closing and we had great fun shopping and getting our first home dinner after a strenuous week of traveling, driving, and visiting.

(August 1955, *left to right*) Tim, our grandfather Henry, Laurel, Chris, Herman holding Randy, Barb, 7 months pregnant, holding Bonny, and Wendell.

Friday, August 26, 1955. Bemidji, Minnesota. We set out about noon to purchase "sugar and spice and everything nice" for the children and Barb. Arrived at the farm about two. Barb was even worse than I had anticipated. She is gross with another child. She reviled me, almost couldn't have been worse, but the children helped us. They are darling—the farm looks well. The children took us over to see Herman in a corn field. They are devoted to him. We left after a while—returned to the resort for dinner. Then Judy Reese, owner—Harry just killed, invited us down—we stayed until 3 a.m. Probably good after the way B.A. [Barbara Ann] acted.

(August 1955, *left to right*) Elsie in back, Wendell, Laurel, Randy, Barb holding Bonny, and Chris.

I remember when the blue Buick New Yorker convertible pulled up near the house. Two distinguished gray-haired people climbed out as we clustered around the car. Barb ran forward, "Stay away from me and my children," she screamed. Bonny tucked under one arm, Barb paused in mid stride, leaned down, and, according to Chris, pulled her shoe off, and threw it at Elsie. When I asked Laurel about what Barb threw, she said, "rocks." That's what I recall, too. When Barb bent down, she picked up rocks and threw them at her mother.

Elsie's diary continued:

August 26, 1955. We arrived at the farm at noon. The dear children ran to meet us. Timmy is so dear. Barb served quite a good luncheon and we set out for Bemidji to get a fishing boat but couldn't get any that would take all of us, so all four boys and Laurel went out in paddle boats. They enjoyed it. Henry, Barb, Bonny, Herman, and I watched. Then we all had "picnic supper" on outdoor tables at the "Red Onion." It really was a very good day subsequent to yesterday.

August 28, 1955. Again we went to the farm about noon. Again the dear children ran to meet us. B served a good dinner. They have a big picture window in the kitchen. Everything to make life easy—a new bathroom— we polished everything white. Then drove to Redby on Red Lake to the fisheries—Indian Reservation. Very interesting. The Catholics are there in a big way. Hatcheries wonderful—we bought two gorgeous smoked whitefish but we hardly saw them again. B didn't really save us a bite. Then we all went to Deer Lake for supper—all ten of us.

August 29, 1955. We did not go to B and children today. We thought they needed a rest—so did we. I wrote a lot outside in the birches overlooking the beautiful lake. Judy kept asking us down. Henry and I went for a good swim— first, and only—on the trip. Lake swimming not invigorating. To Judy's for tea—then to Bemidji to shop a bit. Then back for dinner but it was one of the worst evenings. Just when we were starting to relax for the first time up came Judy. Upset dear H and we were both up half the night. Such is life.

August 30, 1955. On account of no sleep, we didn't get to the children until late in the afternoon. Then we went over to call on Herman's sister and family.

Wednesday, August 31, 1955

243rd day — 122 days follow

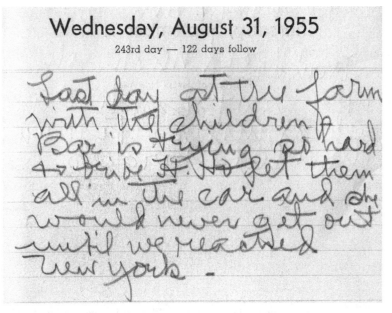

August 31, 1955. Last day at the farm with the children. Bar is trying so hard to bribe Henry to let them all in the car and she would never get out until we reached New York.

That August visit was the last time Barb saw her father. I don't have any letters from Barb to Elsie, but here is a letter draft that Elsie wrote fourteen months after the visit.

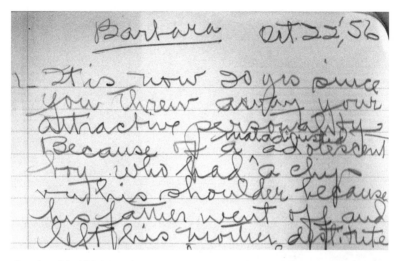

October 22, 1956. Barbara, It is now twenty years since you threw away your attractive personality because of a maladjusted adolescent boy who had a chip on his shoulder because his father went off and left his mother destitute with two little boys to bring up, you withdrew from people. You changed your whole personality from loving people to hating people when you were just sixteen—just three years older than Chris is now. Hating people has never done anybody any good, but most especially it hurts the person who hates.

In our two-room, eight-grade school, the teachers assembled the student body downstairs in the lunchroom for a surprise. I didn't know that my grandparents had sent two huge boxes of gifts and treats, something for each child. Elsie recorded it in her diary:

Thursday, December 8, 1955

342nd day — 23 days follow

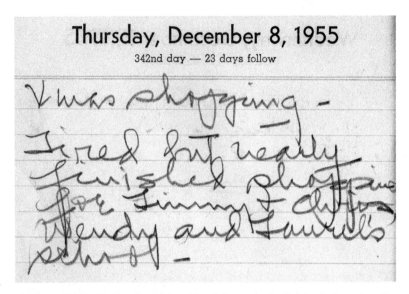

Dec 8, 1955. Xmas shopping—Tired but nearly finished shopping for Timmy and Chris, Wendy and Laurel's school.

Dec 10, 1955. Our Anniversary. Made getting the Christmas boxes off to the children's school in Nebish our anniversary present to each other. It really was thrilling. It looked so beautiful, bright red snappers on top.

Dec 19, 1955. I'm too tired. Certainly [was] a terrific job getting those big boxes off to our grandchildren's school, c/o Mrs. Katherine Cheney, Nebish, Minn.

Mrs. Cheney sent our grandmother a thank you letter:

Nebish, Minnesota, December 23, 1955,

My Dear Mrs. Philips, I want to tell you how very much the children enjoyed your party. They were so surprised and thrilled. Christopher, Timothy, and Wendell were hosts. They gave out the gifts, taking out a package they named the child they wished to have it. The children really made some clever Santas with the apples. I have asked that each one write you and am sending their notes along. For my part I want to thank you for the lovely candle holders. I do think you're doing such a kind thing is an example of true unselfishness. I marvel at the time spent in planning and preparing so nice a party. I'm sure the children will all remember it all of their lives. Thanking you again I am sincerely yours, Katherine Cheney

I remember being terribly embarrassed, handing the little gifts out. Several years ago a neighbor and I drove over to a farm near Duluth to purchase some sheep. During the drive, while visiting, Andy recalled that Christmas party more than fifty years earlier. "Your grandparents must have been wealthy," he said. At the time, we certainly thought so.

Excerpt from a letter Barbara sent to her grandfather, Calvin Philips:

Tuesday, March 14, 1944,

Dear Grandfather: John has completely deserted me and my two children, Yes, I am going to have another child in a few months. I wrote a letter to his draft board and asked them to please examine him again and take him into some branch of the Service if possible. He saw me write that letter and was really scared to go in the Army, for fear of being killed. Because it was the very next morning that he deserted me without a penny.

You can imagine how such a frightful shock has affected my nerves. It is a terrible awful thing that has happened to my brain and I might even fear a nervous breakdown the way I have felt so weak and shaky the last few days. You must not judge me too harshly, Grandfather. If you read your psychology books you will find that in the old days the parents had the power of life and death over their children. It is still the same today. If the child grows up unhappy and a misfit in society, you must not blame the child. It is the fault of the parents.

What does the future hold for me? Right now, less than nothing. I can only live from day to day and wonder what bitter blow tomorrow will bring.

I'm truly sorry Grandfather, that I disappointed you so. I hope you think better of me now. And don't think that I don't appreciate greatly what you've done for me.

Love, Barbara

1956
School Shots and Springtime

Author's 4th grade Achievement Award from Nebish School.

I attribute my above average attendance to three school enticements—
escape from the farm, lunch, and the warm classroom. Over the course of
the years I spent at Nebish, I read almost every book in the little library.
Every few months District Superintendent Stapleton would visit and
bring new books, rotating them from school to school.

February crept into March. The sun tracked north, snowbanks settled, and the snow tunnels Randy and I dug during the past winter collapsed. Snow melt trickled the first hot March day. By late afternoon, rivulets carved trenches in tire tracks and froze over after the sun set. Morning hikes from the house to the school bus meant treading on crusted ruts. More than once, I slipped and fell, skinning my knuckles on jagged ice. Flowing water danced beneath the ice panes, squiggling, bubbling, transporting tiny seeds. We'd break the rivulets open and dam the flow with our booted feet. By afternoon, snow and ice turned to slush in the driveway—great for hard-packed bruising snowballs.

Adults called it spring fever. At school, the first bare patches of brown grass peeked through and we stared out windows, oblivious to multiplication tables, state capitols, and proper nouns. Marbles were packed away. We dug out last season's softball, along with frayed mitts and scarred bats. I was a terrible player—usually the last one picked when choosing teams. At recess, the first games of the season were played, and the ball was often hit into a snowbank. There was a mad scramble to dig it out before the bell rang; otherwise it might be lost until the snowbank melted. The scrambles usually ended in finding the ball and a snowball fight between the opposing teams.

At home, melt water meandered across the yard. Rivulets straddled the new barn and pooled in the low spot behind it. We watched the pothole pond grow each day.

"Race you to the barn," Tim said to Chris as the afternoon bus pulled away. Tim's straight brown hair hung in his eyes.

Chris flipped his head, tossing his black curls, revealing a pimple-covered forehead. Each night he rubbed Noxzema on, hoping to get rid of them. Every morning he slicked his hair back with Brylcreem as he chanted, "A little dab'll do ya."

Chris glanced over at Tim and said, "It's too muddy to run." Suddenly he sprinted forward, laughing as he flipped a finger at Tim.

Tim took off after him. "What's that, your age or IQ?" he shouted.

Laurel and I raced behind them.

The icy ruts had melted, leaving a squishy driveway and yard. Not just mud, but clay-mud that stuck to our boots, layer upon layer until they felt like a deep-sea diver's lead-soled boots. An iron boot-scraper was mounted in the concrete steps leading into the house, but it didn't help much. Each day we had to pull Laurel's muddy boots off and clean them.

One afternoon while walking up the driveway, Tim spotted the old mama barn cat searching tufts of brown grass for field mice.

"Kitty, kitty, kitty," he called.

Tim picked her up and carried her to the edge of the pothole. Holding kitty by the tail, he swung her over his head and released her out over the pond. The cat, in a beautiful arc, sailed high over the surface, and splashed down ten feet from an ancient white pine stump sticking above the water. The cat paddled to the stump and clawed her way up out of the water. For the next three days we checked morning and evening as the water level rose on the stump. The cat sat silently. On the afternoon of the third day, we rushed from the school bus to the pothole. It had been a warm day and snowbanks were shrinking fast. Water flowed across the yard. The stump was submerged. That evening, the old cat slunk into the barn for a pan of skim milk.

Spring temperatures fluctuated wildly. Barb ordered spring jackets for us. It was the early days of "Made in Japan" clothing. Plastic technology was primitive. My unlined Roy Rogers jacket arrived with a cold front that brought sleeting rain. As I stood waiting for the bus, I started to shiver and swung my arms to warm up. The sleeves cracked and the fringes snapped like brown icicles. By the time the bus pulled up, both of the arms had snapped off.

Rain poured one night. In the morning, the bus was late because frost was coming out of the ground and the clay-based roadbed became mire. By afternoon when the bus dropped us off, the wheels spun and the bus couldn't climb the hill. Mud days had arrived.

Spring also brought childhood inoculations. Ivy Bud, the school district nurse, was a name that conjured terror over several decades for hundreds of school kids. Nurse Bud was a tiny woman in a crisp white uniform. Children in outlying country schools were bused to a central location—we went to Northern School, about seven miles north of Bemidji. We stood in line, watching the person in front as the formation inched forward.

Inoculations varied from year to year depending on the student's age. For the most part, it went something like this: First shot was for small pox; dab fluid on the upper arm, then puncture the skin with several pin pricks. Next the polio shot to the arm; it burned like a docking iron against the skin—many kids cried out like a lamb getting his tail burned off. Tetanus next. Tetanus shots left the shoulder sore for a week but were mandatory because so many kids ran barefoot all summer, and the threat of lockjaw from stepping on rusted nails was great. On the trip from the inoculation clinic back to Nebish School, lockjaw was discussed each year, building to more and more horrific dimensions.

I didn't think that tetanus shots were necessary. In the past, when I stepped on a nail, Herman had taken me to the barn and made me wade in the gutter. The gutter wasn't cleaned very often during the summer because the cows were only in their stanchions long enough to be milked. It was a living mass of urine manure swarming with fly larvae, flies, and once in a while, a dead cat or bird. A light mist of DDT each evening didn't help much. Herman said that when he was a child, wading in manure was the standard treatment for foot injuries to avoid infection. The bacteria in the gutter killed the bacteria in the injury.

Later in the spring, as the school year wound down, families looked forward to the school picnic. Barb, five months pregnant, embarrassed us by dolling up our pre-school sisters and bringing them in for free food. Today I'm thankful she did, otherwise I wouldn't have these pictures.

On back, Barb wrote, *May 29, 1957, Nebish School Picnic. Christopher age 14, grade 8, Mrs. Katherine Cheney, [big room] upper grade teacher, Timothy, age 12, grade 7.*

On back, Barb wrote, *May 29, 1957. Nebish School Picnic. Laurel, age 8, grade 2, Mrs. Bessie Madison, [little room teacher] Wendell, age 9, grade 3.* Note my baggy "city slicker" trousers, three sizes too big—hand-me-downs from my plump Seattle cousins. Chris and Tim wouldn't wear them so I was forced to.

Puppy Love

Herman and I were at the Park Rapids Sales Barn. We'd taken the back seat out of the Chevy and crowded seven one-week-old bull calves in. Calf shit oozed down the windows where their little rumps had been squished against the glass. The calves sold for six dollars each and Herman was in an expansive mood. Earlier in the spring, young bull calves had been worth nothing, and Herman had sledgehammered the new-born males in the head and thrown them behind the barn on the manure pile.

I was nine years old and stood beside Herman in the line as he waited for the calf check. A little brown mutt's head and her white-socked front feet peeked out of my open coat. Her ears drooped like the box flap she had been hiding under. She was the runt of the litter, the last give-away, and I fell in love the moment she peed in my arms. I felt certain she was as excited as me.

"Can I have her? Can I have her? I'll buy food with my trapping money. I'll teach her how to hunt and round up cows."

"I suppose, now that Shep's gone," Herman answered.

"That'll be my dog's name, too. Shep."

Herman always named his dogs Shep.

Hugging my new puppy, I recalled the last Shep. That dog had no protection from bitter arctic winds—just a shallow depression burrowed under the corncrib by an earlier dog in an attempt to escape summer flies and mosquitoes and winter storms. Like earlier generations, he had been held by a bare steel chain bolted tightly around his neck. At the top of his neck the chain had chafed through flesh to bone. The bone was constantly irritated when the dog lunged forward for milk separator scum. The residue left in the separator bowl was the dog's main source of nourishment. The scum was about the size and texture of a small Dairy Queen soft-serve cone. Skim milk, gut piles at butchering time, and meager meal scraps were his only food. A dog rarely survived a second winter at our farm.

On a forty-below night, the previous Shep froze to death, his chain wrapped tightly around the corncrib pillar it was secured to. He must have struggled to get loose. The chain was snagged high on the post, tight against the dog's neck. Shep was forced to stand or he would have choked himself. He had frozen in the standing position.

"Look at him—standing at attention." Herman joked, "Won't have to feed him anymore."

That evening while doing chores after school, I saw the empty chain under the corncrib. Later, I spotted the dog's tail sticking out from beneath a mound of still steaming manure on the pile wheeled out of the barn that day.

"I won't let that happen to you," I whispered in the puppy's ear. I'll teach you to listen and do tricks," I said louder.

"Only trick he needs to know is how to bark when Indians come up the driveway," Herman said.

"She. She's a girl Shep."

That winter I spent some of my trapping money on dog food.

"That mutt can eat milk and gut piles," Herman said. "You're wasting money."

"It's my money. I earned it," I argued back.

"You want to pee it away, you can buy your own shoes. Watch your mouth."

Herman was mostly good to me. By the time I was eight, he considered Chris and Tim to be firmly in Barb's camp. I was his greatest ally, but he was still generous with the belt; for playing with Shep and not carrying in enough firewood at night when it was my turn; for talking back when I felt wronged; for slipping and falling on an icy path with buckets of skim milk sloshing against my legs on the way to feed the hogs; for sneaking whole milk to Shep.

At first, my puppy lived in the barn with the cats and the cows but as snow melted and days lengthened and warmed, she started running outdoors.

One afternoon I came home from school to find her chained under the corncrib. I released her, and the little dog yelped in joy.

"Chain that damn mutt up," Herman shouted from the blacksmith shop. "He's not a puppy anymore."

"I don't want to chain her. She hasn't done anything wrong," I yelled back.

"I said chain him up. Dogs are always chained. That's where they belong."

"No. She listens to me. She won't do anything wrong. I feed her and take care of her. She's my dog."

"You don't talk back to me," he said, striding toward me, unbuckling his belt.

I stood frozen, held by the invisible force of obedience. The belt came down across my back, the end whiplashing—snapping—on my fingers; schoolbooks dropped to the mud.

"You don't talk back to me. I said that damn dog will be chained—I want him chained." The belt came down twice more.

"No. She's my dog. I don't want her to freeze like the last one. I like to play with her."

Barb came out of the house and stood with Chris and Tim, watching.

Herman glanced at her, then looked down at me. "You can let him loose to play, but otherwise he stays chained," he conceded, with a final slap across my legs.

"Can I build her a little house under the corncrib?" I begged, sensing victory. More than sixty years later, I realize that Herman didn't want to give Barb the satisfaction of seeing a wedge between him and me.

"Don't let me catch you using good lumber or new nails—he stays hooked when you're not playing with him," he relented as he re-looped his belt. He rumpled my hair and kicked playfully at the bouncing dog.

For our building projects, we always used lumber scraps and sawlog slabs and spent hours straightening used rusty nails. I could use scrap lumber to build a house for Shep. "Thank you, Daddy, thank you. I'll take good care of her—you'll see."

Evenings and weekends that spring I ran in the woods with Shep. I buried her in leaves until she barked and jumped out and up at me. I let her knock me down and lick my face. I hugged her close and rolled down the glacier-carved gully. Landing at the bottom I'd lie on my back, looking up through the trees as she hopped back and forth over me, yipping happily.

One night Herman approached me, "How come the wood box isn't filled? Tim said it's your night to fill it."

"I was playing with Shep and forgot," I admitted.

"I've about had it with that mutt," he growled.

"She's not a mutt. She's a nice puppy."

"It's dark now and the stove's low—get that damn wood carried in and no more back talk or you'll get the belt. Is she hooked up for the night?"

"It's going to rain so I put her in the barn."

"Damn it. I told you she goes under the corncrib." He unbuckled his belt, jerked it through the loops, and lashed me across the back and legs. "Hook her under the corncrib. Don't make me come out," he ordered.

I cried my way to the barn, got Shep and tied her under the corncrib while she licked my tears. Herman was done with chores, so I took Shep's dish and squirted it full of milk from one of the cows, then carried the wood in.

In mid-April the mailman delivered boxes containing 150 day-old, yellow peeping chicks. They were released in the brooder house with a heatlamp to keep them warm. It was my job to make sure they always had fresh water and feed.

At school I found a book in the little library about a boy and his dog, Mesu. The boy taught Mesu to fetch a stick, to roll over, to stay, to come; I wanted to teach Shep those tricks, too.

The garden flourished—especially the weeds. The chicks grew; yellow fuzz changed to white feathers, and they were allowed outside to eat insects and scratch in the dirt. After school each day, I released Shep and we ran out in the woods. She had an eye for spotting gray squirrels on the ground or in the tree. She'd sit barking while I shot at them with my BB gun. I taught her to retrieve sticks from the pond behind the barn.

When school was over for the summer, I played with Shep every morning.

"Watch," I told Herman as we walked from the barn to the house.

"Shep, sit," I commanded. I pulled a short willow stick from my pocket. Shep's eyes locked on it. I drew my arm back and threw the stick over the chickenhouse. "Shep, fetch." The little dog shot around the building and returned moments later, tail wagging, stick in her mouth. "Shep, sit." I smiled and put it back in my pocket. "See how smart she is."

"Will he bark at Indians when they come up the driveway?"

"She's smart. She will," I said with confidence as we walked into the house for breakfast, Shep was left bouncing outside the screen door.

After breakfast, Chris, Tim, and I were weeding our assigned garden rows while Shep romped beneath the crabapple trees at garden's edge. Concentrating on young carrot tops and emerging pig weeds, I didn't notice her disappear. I could hear Randy laughing as he slopped water onto the rasping whetstone while Herman sharpened a mower blade.

Suddenly, the peace was broken. In the still clear morning, Herman shouted, "Randy, get in the house. Chris, get the gun. I've had it with this damn dog."

I jumped up from my carrot row and ran. There stood Shep, tail wagging, proud of the dead chicken at her feet.

"I warned you to keep her hooked up," Herman growled.

"I'll hook her up. I'll keep her hooked up from now on. I forgot this morning." I explained, panicked.

"You forgot once too often," Herman said, pulling a length of baling twine from his pocket. "Shep, come."

She came, tail wagging.

He slip-knotted the twine around the little dog's neck and dragged her toward a post in front of the barn. Shep, sensing something was wrong, pulled against the rope, tightening the noose, choking herself. "Come on," he yelled, jerking the rope. Shep growled and lay down as she was dragged toward the post.

He kicked the little dog, "Get the hell up." She snarled and snapped at his boot. Furious, he kicked her again. "You're getting it now," he said with another kick. The little dog yipped.

I grabbed the rope and pulled at it so Shep wouldn't choke. Herman cuffed me on the side of the head, knocking me to the ground. I jumped up and tried to pick her up. He jerked the little dog away.

"Please don't, Daddy. Please don't hurt Shep. I'll get another chicken."

"No mutt snaps at me, damn."

He tied Shep to the post. Chris handed him the .22 rifle. Tim stood watching. Chords of Mozart drifted from the open living room window and across the yard in the still morning. Fluffy clouds passed high overhead. Early summer flies buzzed the thawing manure pile.

I knelt and hugged Shep to me as Herman approached, rifle in hand, barrel near the little dog's head. "Please don't do it," I begged.

"Chris, get your brother the hell out of my way."

Chris pulled me, screaming, away from my little dog. "Shep, Shep—don't!"

Herman held the loaded rifle to the dog's forehead and pulled the trigger.

The sound was drowned out by my scream. "No! Please don't."

The little dog went to her knees, whined, then stood up, blood oozing from her forehead. An eyeball dangled on her cheek from a shattered socket. She snapped at the bloody eye until it was in her mouth. She began to chew. Herman cursed and went to the garage for another bullet. He used .22 caliber short rounds— cheaper, but not as lethal as .22 caliber long-rifle rounds.

"You hold him, I don't want that damn mutt untied," he told Chris.

"No, please don't hurt her again. I'll never untie her again," I screamed, trying to pull loose from Chris.

Herman looked at me.

Returning, he lowered the angle of the shot so it went through the dog's head and into her neck. I screamed in shared agony with the dog. Shep leaped into the air, quivered on all four feet and snarled at Herman. Furious that the dog was not dead, he retrieved a heavy sledgehammer. The maul-head swung like a pendulum near his heavy boot as he strode toward the post. Stepping up to the dog, he lifted the sledge up over his head and finished Shep off.

I'd seen him kill many new-born bull calves. One smash to the forehead and they dropped, quivering, eyes rolled back in their heads.

I began screaming again. "No, don't! I love Shep. Hit me."

"Chris, if he don't shut the hell up, get him out of here."

I watched—we all watched—gripped by the horror.

I untied the rope, picked up my puppy and—cradling her in my arms like the day I'd gotten her at the livestock sales barn—carried her out into the forest where we'd played together. Her limp body felt so tiny beneath the bloody fur. I don't remember carrying the shovel with me, but I must have. I dug the hole, slashing viciously at roots in the humusy earth until I reached clay; I didn't want scavengers to further ravage her. I tried to straighten her little head—laid her on the side that still had an eye—smoothed her matted hair. I nestled her tail over her face, the way she liked to sleep, and slipped the willow stick down between her paws. Maybe Bruno, the little boy buried up in the cemetery, could play fetch with Shep in heaven. Cradling her in my hands, I gently lay the little bundle in the hole on the hillside, then shoveled dirt over her. Later that summer I placed an empty coffee can on her grave for a marker.

Natives from Red Lake Nation stopped by every few weeks, selling iced walleye fillets out of their car trunk. We got a new Shep from them later that summer.

In late autumn of 1968—eleven years after Herman killed my puppy, I returned to the farm on convalescent leave while recuperating from wounds I received in Vietnam. I wrote in my memoir, *Muddy Jungle Rivers*:

I wandered north one sleeting afternoon, beyond the barn, over a fence, into the woods—stopped to check the twine box on the oats binder—yes, the wrens had used it again this past season. My feet carried me back, beyond the thickets of the sumac maze we'd played in, down through a gully carved by glaciers, up the far side where I shuffled through dank leaves until I found the Hills Brothers coffee can. I sat against a birch tree and sobbed the racking cries of the little boy whose puppy had been murdered; for everybody—the pilot in the Gulf of Tonkin, the crew of Tango 7, the Marines at Cua Viet, the Army troops in the Delta, the Sailors, the Viet Cong soldier, the little dog. I wept as I stared at the rusted can I'd used as a headstone that morning so many years ago when I buried the puppy.

Livestock Forage Harvest

It was the summer I chopped the washing machine drinking tank and Herman struck Barb in the knee with his belt buckle. No more needs to be said about that. I didn't realize it then, in my child mind, but as I axed the tank I wanted to hurt Herman—hurt him the way he had hurt me when he'd sledgehammered my puppy to death a few months earlier for killing a chicken.

When Herman purchased the farm from his father in 1946 the sale included some horse-drawn farm implements which were used into the late 1960s. Herman shortened the drawbar on the grain drill, the grain binder, and the dump rake. The drawbar on the two-row corn planter remained full length—perhaps for easier maneuvering. We took turns riding the planter. At the end of each row, upon a nod from Herman, who was driving the tractor, the rider pulled the lever back and raised the chisel blades from the earth and stopped the seed corn from dropping onto the ground. Herman turned the tractor to start a new row and then paused for a moment and looked back again to make sure the rider had dropped the planter heads back into the harrowed soil.

He drove slowly—about four miles per hour. Many times I nodded off. The low hum of the Farmall engine, the sweet scent of moist spring earth and the gentle sway of the rusted corn planter seat as we moved across the field lulled me to sleep. I'd jerk awake and grab the lever as I tilted toward a wide flat wheel which at the worse would have scratched my face or arm.

(circa 1964) Randy, thirteen years old, sitting on the corn planter. It was the summer the author left home and rode the rails out west. The old garage stands in the background.

In 2010, after Barb died and I was settling her estate, I went through the attic of the old farmhouse and discovered that our childhood photo albums had been pulled apart. Several pages had a photo clipped from them; other full pages were cut out. A few times in the process of clipping out an individual picture, the person had cut the photo on the backside of the page in half.

Whichever siblings took the pictures, they overlooked the real treasure—thousands of negatives left bundled beside the vandalized albums. I've spent countless hours with a magnifying glass poring over a light box, studying our shadowed past. This photo of Randy is one of the many treasures I discovered.

By mid-August the corn planter was parked back in the weeds for the season and the corn—if there had been sufficient rainfall—was at least four feet high and developing cobs. The cows usually had the pastures chewed down by then. I don't remember Herman ever attempting to regenerate pastures through rotational grazing or frost seeding. Rotational grazing is a management strategy where livestock are periodically moved from one pasture to the next, allowing the grasses to regrow before the forage gets chewed down too low. Frost seeding—broadcasting grass seed on existing pastures—is done in the early spring when ground freezes at night and thaws during the day, working the seed into soil contact.

After the pastures were exhausted in late summer we fed the cows corn stalks. Herman drove the tractor, pulling a single axle trailer along the edge of the corn rows while Chris, Tim, and I harvested corn stalks. With two-foot-long homemade machetes, we swung the tip of the blade at the base of the corn stalks. Chris enjoyed hacking the stalks. On one occasion, a rock deflected the blade and it cut into his shin. Blood leaked down his leg, across the top of his foot, and seeped into the parched gray dirt as it trickled between his toes. The tractor never stopped. Chris limped along, chopping corn.

The trailer, piled high, was towed into the yard behind the barn. We walked along the sides pulling stalks off as Herman drove slowly, leaving a trail of corn for the cows to eat. One time, as I wrestled a stalk from the pile near the front of the trailer, the wheel rolled over my bare foot. It was a solid wooden wheel and the earth was packed hard. I screamed in pain as I fell to the ground. The trailer continued on. I was left crying and cradling my foot. I sat among the stalks, foot throbbing, cows nosing me. One began pushing her forehead against the back of my head. Then I felt the bull's steel nose ring rubbing my back as I watched the tractor in the distance. I froze and held my breath. Eventually, he wandered away chewing a corn stalk. That summer I limped for weeks. I never went to the doctor.

In late autumn, we chopped cobs from the corn stalks for the hogs. The days were often rainy or mixed with early winter snow. We walked along with our machetes and hacked off cobs and left the stalks to be chopped for silage. We had to move fast to keep up with the trailer, yet not miss any cobs. Chris, alone on one side of the trailer, was very fast. In one motion he could pull the ear away from the stalk and, with a sharp downward swing, sever it. Tall weeds and bent corn stalks often deflected his aim and on two occasions he chopped terrible gashes in his hand. The trailer didn't stop. We kept chopping.

Sixty years later, the scars are visible on Chris's hand and leg. My foot still bothers me—perhaps it's just old age, but I believe that bones were broken when the trailer rolled over it.

The harvest of hay—winter forage for the cows—was a summer-long project. The first cutting, if the weather cooperated, was done and the hay stored in the loft by mid-July; the second cutting, by late August.

Preparation for the harvest was an annual ritual. Herman attached the John Deere sickle mower to the Farmall and pulled it out of the weeds and dead grass. The seven-foot sickle bar was removed, rivets pounded tight on the cutting sections, and while one of us cranked the whetstone and dribbled water, Herman angled each section against the turning stone and sharpened it. The guards on the cutter bar were tightened and oiled, the sickle bar replaced, and the pitman stick that connected to the blade was checked for wear. The mower was greased and the tractor gas topped off. By then dew had evaporated from the hay fields and Herman set out. Even today as I drive through the countryside early in the summer, the smell of fresh-mown hay carries me back.

After the hay was cut, it lay drying and curing for two or three days. In perfect weather, on the third day, Herman connected the side rake to the tractor and windrowed the hay in late morning. When raked, the thick windrows—a mix of grass, alfalfa, and red clover— almost braided themselves into quarter-mile long, three-foot-thick hawsers. The clover never dried properly because air couldn't circulate through the moisture in the thick stems the way they were woven when raked.

The windrows had to be turned so the sun could dry the underside before we picked them up. Herman usually did it with the side rake, but I recall times when we did it by hand—especially after it had been rained on. Forking the snarled ropes was hateful. We didn't have gloves and after walking a quarter mile, constantly flipping the underside of the damp hay, using hips and upper legs as fulcrums to pivot the loaded pitchforks, we had bruised legs and blisters from the fork handle. When the blisters ruptured, the fork handle got slick as it chafed raw flesh. Along the tree lines at field's edge, poison ivy often blended with the hay.

One summer while Herman greased and tightened bolts on the hayloader, he was lowering the pan at the top, and the steel finger on the bracket that held it in position went completely through his hand. He seldom cursed, but that morning he pushed the pan up, pulled his hand off the bracket, cradled it, and cursed in pain.

Herman refused to go to the doctor. He went up to the house trailing blood, washed it, poured peroxide on both sides of the wound, rubbing the liquid in as it foamed. Barb wrapped gauze around his hand, secured it with rag strips, and he went back to work. The hand didn't heal properly and from then on his fingers wouldn't straighten completely.

The summer I was going on twelve was the third season I worked with Chris and Tim. After lunch we'd hook up the hayrack to the tractor. When we reached the field, we connected the hayloader behind the rack and laid the sling rope out. The sling consisted of three ropes secured at one end by a metal connector; at the other end each rope had an individual connector. With the first sling rope laid out on the wooden bed, Herman drove slowly, straddling the windrow of raked hay, as the hayloader lifted the hay up and dumped it at the rear of the hayrack.

Chris, Tim, and I struggled to keep up, pulling the braided clover/alfalfa mix apart and spreading it evenly around the rack, over the sling rope.

Working on the hayrack was a hateful job—fighting the chaff, dust, poison ivy, and sharp stubble. When Herman determined the sling held enough, we laid out the second one and continued until it, too, was about four feet deep with hay. By the time the wagon was full, we were coated with dust and chaff. Sweat streaks laced from our foreheads down to the waistband on our pants. While on the hayrack we seldom wore shirts because they trapped bees and horse flies and deer flies. By mid-July our bare torsos had darkened to acorn brown. Hayrack loaded, we'd disconnect the hayloader, put our shirts on, and collapse in the wagon of hay as we rode from the field to the barn where Herman centered the hayrack beneath the barn peak that I had climbed to when I was four years old.

A steel track ran the length of the loft, a wheeled trolley with ropes connected for lifting the hay from the rack up into the barn. One end of the trolley connected to the tractor to pull the hay up; the other end was connected by a thinner rope called the trip rope. We always fought about who got to pull the trip rope.

(Summer 1959) Wendell, eleven, connecting sling ropes on the hayrack
to hoist cured hay up into the dairy barn loft. Chris and Tim delighted in
calling him names. On the back of this picture one of them wrote "Bongo."

The sling of hay was pulled through a series of pulleys up into the haymow, along a rail, and tripped—released. The load dropped into a one ton mass. By evening the sun had heated the steel-roofed barn to well over one hundred degrees. We climbed into the hayloft with pitchforks and pulled those masses apart, spreading the heating hay out so it would cool. That job done, we ate supper, milked the cows, ran the milk through the separator, cooled the cream, and fed the skim milk to the hogs. By twilight we were free to clean up. With Lava soap and bundles of fresh clothes tucked under our arms, we biked to Nebish Lake.

Stripped naked, we dove in and rinsed the loose dirt and sweat off, soaped down, jumped back in and paddled around, too tired to enjoy it. Climbing out of the water, we inspected each other for wood ticks and blood suckers, usually finding a few. In the late dusk, mosquitoes attacked in droves. With the swipe of a hand down a bare leg you could expect to squash at least five. We quickly dressed and rode home, hands swinging about our heads, often inhaling a mosquito. Nine years later, deep in the U Minh Forest near the southern tip of Vietnam, the mosquitoes were much worse.

Upstairs, our bedrooms were hot and stuffy, not much better than the hayloft. Our windows were always open to catch any hint of breeze, but the thirty-year-old rusty screens had long ago been damaged beyond repair. We kids didn't help. I remember pushing my head against the screen, shouting to Randy down below in the yard.

Eventually we'd doze off, scratching the day's bites and old poison ivy bumps as we brushed at the ever present, nocturnal hum. The mournful cry of a whippoorwill and the random midnight calls of a loon drifted through our fatigue.

Autumn brought the grain harvest. First the McCormick binder was pulled out of the weeds which had grown up around it since the last season. It took several days to make it field-ready. The grease zerks had to be pumped until grease oozed out around gears and shafts. The wooden slated canvas conveyor belts, which were stored in the granary, had to be cleaned and repaired of mouse damage caused since last year's harvest. It was always fun to unfurl the conveyer belts out in the yard and watch the mice scurry for shelter. We would stand by with our cats and release them. Pink, hairless wiggly babies were kitty hors d'oeuvres.

The canvas belts were mounted and the rollers tightened on the binder. We slipped the sickle out from the end of the cutting bar, checked the knives, tightened loose rivets, and replaced worn blades with new ones. Just as with the mower, Herman spent a morning sharpening each cutting blade while one of us cranked the whetstone and trickled water onto the turning wheel. The eight-foot wooden-paddled reel that pushed the oats onto the conveyor was greased, belt tightened, and any broken paddles were replaced. The wren nest, fledglings long gone, was cleaned out, and the twine box was filled with four rolls of hemp rope. The twine was threaded through small guide-eyes leading to the knotter, a tying mechanism which resembled a bird's beak.

By the autumn of 1956 I was almost nine, old enough to ride the binder. Chris, Tim, and I took turns—it was an important job—watching that the canvases stayed centered on the rollers, not chafing the sides. They could catch and snap the wooden slats riveted to them which held the stalks of grain as they passed up through the machine.

The twine had to be watched, a new roll tied to the old one as it was consumed. The knotter was constantly under observation, as each click was checked to make sure the sheaf it had ejected was tied. Every eight sheaves, whoever was riding the binder stepped on a pedal and dropped the steel basket that collected the sheaves, dumping the cluster in a pile on the fresh-cut stubble.

After the field was cut, we shocked the oats. A sheaf of oats was grasped by the twine, pressed seed head up on the stubble, and other sheaves leaned against it. The last bundle was laid across the top of the shock to protect the exposed seed heads from dew and rain.

The purpose of shocking the grain was to allow it to cure—finish ripening if there was moisture in the seeds. Oat fields were often infested with thistles and weeds. These also had to be dried before the sheaves were threshed because moist weed seeds would make the grain mold once stored in the granary.

We owned a threshing machine in partnership with a family north of the farm. Threshing season was an exciting time because the neighbor brought his boys along. His wife, Ruth, worked right along with the men, something that infuriated Barb, who considered the woman vulgar. Out in the field, with a long-handled, three-tine hayfork, Ruth could pitch sheaves of oats up onto the wagon faster than the men.

When the loaded wagon was pulled alongside the threshing machine, she was the acknowledged expert at flipping the sheaves on top of the conveyor belt, seed head forward each time. That was important because as the sheaf approached the jaw of the machine, six steel-knifed scythes swung up and down, pulling inward. Grain seeds were flailed loose in this initial assault, and, if the sheaf was on the conveyer backwards, the grain would trickle down onto the ground.

The first season I was allowed to help toss sheaves onto the conveyer, my fork stuck into a bundle and slipped from my sweat-soaked hands and onto the conveyer. Ruth jumped onto the moving conveyer, grabbed the fork from the sheaf, and jumped back to the wagon. She silently handed it back to me with a grin and a wink.

By the end of threshing season there was a mountain of bright yellow straw in the sheep pen next to the barn. This was used for bedding during the winter for the cattle and hogs. Once crusted by ice and snow, it made an excellent slide.

I think it was the summer of 1957. Pastures burned off from the drought, alfalfa and clover withered, and corn stalks wilted in the fields. By mid-August, boggy swamps were dry enough to harvest the grass. Herman mowed one swamp, weaving around willows and low clumps of brush with the Farmall. The ground was too rough for the side rake, so he attached the dump rake to the John Deere. He drove the tractor and I rode the rake. We bounced across the dry swamp, gathering grass against long curved tines dragging the ground. I stepped on the pedal every forty feet which lifted the tines and released the trapped grass. By late afternoon jagged rows of dried grass snaked through the swamp.

At one point, suddenly Herman threw the clutch into neutral, jerked the throttle back on the tractor, leapt off and ran. He looked back over his shoulder as he sprinted, yelling and waving at me. I couldn't hear him because the engine was still sputtering to a stop. I thought he had lost it until, from all sides, I was surrounded by buzzing hornets up under my pant cuffs, stinging my arms, face, and bare feet. Herman had driven over one of the small brush clumps and destroyed a nest. The tractor was sitting directly on it. That night after dark we snuck down, restarted the tractor and drove it off the nest.

Almost sixty years later, the old dump rake rests in the orchard with trees growing up through the tines and wheels.

Excerpts from my grandmother's 1945 diary:

June 1, 1945: Barb called for me to send her a little money. She says she is out. I had to cash a check at the Vassar Club and send it special delivery.

August 11, 1945: Barb's Birthday. The first birthday I've had with Bar since she was fifteen years old. Took all birthday things with me. She's living on 94th St, here in New York City with her two sons.

August 14, 1945: Japan accepts the Potsdam Declaration. World War II ends—claim the atomic bomb did it. I happened to be in the government district at 2 p.m. when it was announced—went there to shop at Macy's. Suddenly the whole sky was filled with little pieces of material as all the workers in all of those tremendous buildings threw their scraps out of the window, making the whole sky black with tiny pieces of material and what a tremendous loud cheering!! I'll never forget it.

Barbara's sister, Polly, wrote,

August 20, 1945: Dear Mother, I got your nice letter today thank you so much. I imagine you must have celebrated a good deal. Peace is something we haven't heard about in so long. I think it's too good to be true. It's nice you and Dad got a chance to listen to Truman's speech. How is Barbara? It's too bad she didn't get in the spirit of things. But then for her I guess this war has lasted longer than for most. So you must have been glad to see her. It must have been an awful crowd on Times Square.
Lots of love, Polly

1957
Doctor Visit

I have a particular incident that sticks in my mind. It started with hurting to swallow. Quickly, my neck stiffened, my throat swelled, and my ears throbbed. Chris and Tim teased me because I was losing my balance and I couldn't turn my head to look when they spoke—I had to turn my whole body. One stood in front, the other behind me and both talked low. At first I didn't catch on and turned in circles as they roared with laughter.

"Ben Tungg is clumsy as a pig shot in the head," Chris whispered to Tim, alluding to a hog that didn't instantly drop, but wandered incoherently after being wounded.

I turned toward Chris, stumbled over my feet and fell.

"More like a bullhead flopping on the dock," Tim laughed.

"He dances like a drunken sailor," Chris mocked, nudging me with his toe. "Come on, Ben Tungg. Get up and do a jig."

"You boys shut the hell up and fill the woodbox," Herman said.

For the night, I was allowed to sleep downstairs on the lumpy couch because it was warmer. Ears throbbing, I cried in pain.

Herman listened for several minutes in the bedroom before he shouted, "Shut the hell up out there. People are trying to sleep."

"Ohhh, it hurts," I moaned, slowly building to a full cry. "It hurts too bad. Ohhh."

"Shut the hell up before I come in with the belt," Herman shouted after several wails. His threat had the desired effect—I lowered my cries to a soft moan.

I lay in the darkness, silent, sweating. "I'm thirsty. I want water."

"Shut the hell up before I belt you."

Barb slept through it, upstairs.

When morning came, I could only hear voices from a great distance. Herman ordered me up. A rough hand that smelled like cows caressed my forehead. "He's burning up."

I dreamt that I fell into the cow's icy water trough. I struggled to the surface and discovered I was getting an ice-water bath.

Sunshine moved from the front window to the side window as I dozed. Voices penetrated.

"I've been shoveling all morning. Why the hell isn't dinner ready? I got to get the driveway open." The cow-shit-smelling hand rested on my forehead again. "For Christ sake, he's burning up. Why the hell ain't you bathing him? Turn that damn opera shit off and do something around here."

"He's my son. I'll take care of him as I see fit. I don't need an ignorant German immigrant telling me what to do."

"Make some damn dinner and shut up. Tim, fill that pail with cold water and bring it in here."

The smelly hands gently swabbed ice water across my shivering body.

"Damn wind keeps drifting my shoveling closed. I put the flag up out by the road so the snowplow swings in."

I listened through a haze. My swollen jaw throbbed—the toothache speared into my ear. I stopped eating.

I spent another night crying. The throbbing pain was interspersed with ice baths and belting threats. I dreamt that I was up in heaven, sitting at Jesus' feet, just like the pictures at KYB (Know Your Bible) church class.

Next morning, the snowplow opened the drifted driveway, and I was driven to a doctor's office in Bemidji. Barb grabbed my hand and pulled me along, up to the second floor. I stumbled up the stairs into the office where we were checked in.

"Send the bill to Social Services," Barb told the receptionist.

The woman wrinkled her nose and nodded.

The doctor seemed disgusted, too. "How long has he been like this?"

Barb shrugged, "A few days, I'm not sure."

"You're his mother and you're not sure?" he asked. "How old is he?"

"He'll be ten in October," Barb countered defensively.

"I'm going to take a rectal. Take his clothes off."

I stood lethargically as Barb undressed me.

"When is the last time he was bathed? Look at the gray filth on his neck and wrists and ankles."

"I've been giving him ice water baths for two days," Barb replied.

"Well, why didn't you get him in sooner? Look at those scales of filth. It took months for them to build. Ice water won't remove them."

Barb glared at me through her black horn-rimmed glasses. I'd seen that look before.

"Hold him down on his stomach so I can insert the thermometer. My God, his rear end is filthy. Look at his underwear," the doctor said, nodding toward the wad of clothes on the floor. "Doesn't he know how to wipe? When is the last time he sat in a bathtub?"

I squirmed and mentally cursed the slick catalogue pages as the cold thermometer penetrated.

Moments later it was removed. "One-oh-four-point-six. He should have been brought in sooner."

Barb's lips tightened. "Our driveway was drifted shut and we couldn't get out."

"Why didn't you call somebody for help?"

"We don't have a telephone." Her responses grew shorter with each question.

"Sit him up so I can examine him."

A new shivering fit seized me as the cold stethoscope moved across my bare back.

"Why didn't you give him a bath before you brought him in? He stinks."

Naked, trembling, I cringed.

The doctor was outraged. "It appears he has mumps, but because he was neglected, it caused infections in both ears and tonsils and spread to his gums, by the looks of the way they're swollen. Does he own a toothbrush? Has he ever been to a dentist? One tooth is abscessed. His ears are so filthy I'm going to have my nurse peroxide them. This is neglect. I will file a report with Social Services. Why doesn't he have decent winter clothes? That coat smells like a manure pile— it's not even insulated and the zipper looks broken. It's five below out there and he's walking out of those tennis shoes. Why is he dressed that way? Hold him still while I give him this penicillin shot."

I whimpered as the serum burned into my butt.

The nurse cleaned my ears. The Q-tip felt like a hot needle on an abscessed sliver. I jerked away.

"Hold his head still," the nurse told Barb.

I heard a low hiss and felt the fluid bubbling inside my ears as she swabbed them. I screamed in pain as she scrubbed.

"Hold him still," the nurse reiterated as the Q-tips poked. "I've never seen such filth." She wiped my cheeks with cotton balls while she talked. "The doctor wants to see him again in one week—I'd suggest you clean him up before you return. Get him dressed. I'll have an antibiotic prescription for you."

Barb snatched the prescription from the nurse and grabbed my hand. "You need to clean that shitty little ass of yours," she said and dragged me toward the office door.

"Doesn't he have a hat?" called the nurse. "Those ears won't heal if he doesn't keep his head covered." We didn't return for the appointment seven days later.

Years later, after I'd left the farm, a rather humorous incident happened—I heard the story from my younger siblings. Barb's youngest daughter passed a worm. Barb picked the worm out and brought it to the doctor.

"I don't want to see the worm," the doctor told Barb. "I want to see the girl who passed the worm." The girl acquired a new nickname: Worm.

When I heard the story I wondered if it was the same doctor who had taken care of me.

Pig Check

On a hot July day in 1957, we all, including Barb, gathered for a baptism ceremony at Our Redeemer Lutheran Church. A neighbor couple stood as our godparents. (Sixty years later the godparents' daughter and I do volunteer work together at our local Food Shelf.) That hot July day when we were little kids, Randy and I had the giggles and just couldn't stop. Later we took pictures at the farm.

(July1957) after our communal Baptism. *(left to right, standing)* Wendell, Herman, Chris, Tim. *(sitting)* Laurel, Linda, Bonny, and Randy. This is one of the few surviving pictures of Herman from the 1950s.

The following week, Herman, Randy, and I came home from town and discovered that a hog buyer had been out to the farm and purchased several feeder pigs—piglets that weighed forty pounds, weaned, and ready to be grain fed until they reached slaughter weight. Barb refused to give up the pig check, and a vicious fight ensued.

The next evening while Laurel and I were upstairs playing, I discovered the check tucked in a book of Michelangelo paintings that Barb had brought to the farm with her eight years earlier. The pictures fascinated and terrified me—the naked people and the horror of being condemned to hell. At night, I sometimes lay awake worrying about the Last Judgment and how I might sneak across the River Styx without the devil spearing me. After listening to the minister on Sunday, I was pretty sure I'd go to hell. I tucked the check in my pocket and brought it out to the barn.

"Look, Daddy. Look what I found."

Herman smiled, took the check, and gave me a gruff hug. "Good boy. Does she know you found it?"

"No, but Laurel does."

"You better steer clear of her for a day or two. Run up to the house and get that box of milk-strainer filters we bought yesterday."

The moment the screen door slammed behind me, Barb asked, "Where is the check, honey?"

I knew from past experience that I was in for a severe beating. A sit-on-my-head-suffocating-type-of-pounding while Barb demanded an undying declaration of love. "Mommy Darling I'm very, very sorry I made you mad. I love you more than the world," was the expected response.

Chris played a melody on the piano and sang: *"Bill Grogan's goat was feeling fine. Ate three red shirts right off the line. Bill took a stick, gave him a whack, and tied him to the railroad track. The whistle blew; the train drew nigh, Bill Grogan's goat was doomed to die. He gave three groans of awful pain, coughed up the shirts and flagged the train."*

Unlike Bill Grogan's goat, I had no red shirts to cough up. Barb blocked my escape route toward the door.

"I'm sorry, Mommy Darling," I said, beginning the ritual as I moved around the table, the door to upstairs behind me, Barb on the far side of the table.

"I'm going to teach you 'sorry,' you little bastard. Why do you love him and not me? I'm your mother."

"I'm sorry, Mommy Darling. I do love you—not him."

"You lying little bastard. I'm going to teach you love." She pushed the table against the wall, blocking me from the front door. Trapped, I raced upstairs.

I ran ahead, into a bedroom, slammed the door, and braced a chair under the knob. I heard the hall floor creak as Barb approached.

The door knob turned slowly, "Open the door, honey. I'm your mother. I won't hurt you. I love you." Her voice sounded strange—guttural. I felt like a trapped raccoon. They'd chew a leg off to escape.

Barb kicked at the door and the chair began to move. "If you don't let me in this instant you *will* be sorry. Now open this door." Kick. The chair rung that was wedged beneath the knob cracked and the door opened an inch. She felt it give. "Now I've got you, you little bastard. Now you'll be sorry."

I ran to the window, pushed the rusted screen off, threw pillows and blankets to the ground, then eased myself out feet first. Hanging by my fingertips, terrified of the long fall, I heard Barb burst into the room.

"You can't hide from me. Come out from under that bed. Now." I heard her drop to her knees as she looked under the bed—the only possible hiding place in the little room. "Where are you?" she screamed. I let go of the window ledge and plummeted to earth. When I landed, my chin hit my knees and I bit my tongue.

"You little bastard, now he'll belt you for breaking the screen." I looked up to see Barb leaning out the window, spit-flecked mouth working silently.

I ran to the barn, blood dribbling down my chin and blubbered my story to Herman. He removed the milking machines from the cows, turned off the air compressor which ran the machines, and stalked toward the house. I hid down by the hog house and listened to the screams.

Later, after he finished milking the cows and separating the milk, he found me hiding in the pig weeds, shivering in the night dew. "You go up to the house—she won't bother you."

After Barb died in 2010, one winter day while I was going through her treasures upstairs in the old farmhouse, I took a break and went back into that bedroom, pushed the curtain aside, and looked out the window. It was still a long way down. I tried to imagine just how frightened that little boy must have been fifty-three years earlier.

I didn't find any 1957 letters from Herman or Barb to our grandmother, but in Elsie's "Mental Health Journal," I discovered a newspaper clipping about mental illness dated March 3, 1957. Across the top, Elsie scrawled, "Maladjusted emotions, Barbara."

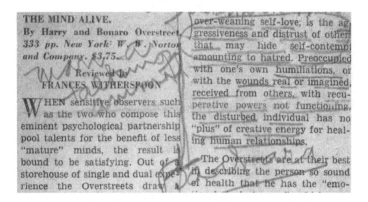

THE MIND ALIVE.
By Harry and Bonaro Overstreet.
333 pp. New York: W. W. Norton and Company. $3.75.

Reviewed by
FRANCES WITHERSPOON

WHEN sensitive observers such as the two who compose this eminent psychological partnership pool talents for the benefit of less "mature" minds, the result is bound to be satisfying. Out of a storehouse of single and dual experience the Overstreets draw a

over-weaning self-love; is the aggressiveness and distrust of others that may hide self-contempt amounting to hatred. Preoccupied with one's own humiliations, or with the wounds real or imagined, received from others, with recuperative powers not functioning, the disturbed individual has no "plus" of creative energy for healing human relationships.

The Overstreets are at their best in describing the person so sound of health that he has the "emo-

Herman's second son, Lawrence Roswald, was born in August, 1957. Why such an unusual middle name? I discovered that the Old German origin of the name Rosalinda is a compound of horse and snake. Roswald—again Old German origin, means mighty horse. I wonder how long Barb searched for a boy's name that she could bend to a derivative of Rosalinda.

It's impossible to know what motivated Herman and Barb's arguments. Herman didn't like the name Barb had selected for her youngest daughter. He named cows Rosalinda—Rosie for short—and Marie, often talking about those two cows by name. Just over a year after Rosalinda was born, Barb went into the courthouse and changed the little girl's name.

Pulpwood and Dump Rakes

Chris was thirteen and wanted to earn money for school clothes. He was forbidden from working for the neighbors because he was needed on our farm. In his spare time, he cut a truck load of pulp wood. Herman said he could have the trees. With ax, Swede saw, and a one hundred inch measuring stick, Chris and Tim went to the edge of a pasture and began dropping trees and cutting them into lengths. I peeled the bark from the logs with vague promises of future riches.

When we weren't helping with hay or weeding the garden that summer, we were logging. The larger the tree, the more grueling to cut it down, but the shouted *timberrrr* and the rewarding crash made the extra effort worth it. We weren't allowed to use the tractor to drag the trees from the forest and pile them, so we did it by hand. Chris on one end, Tim on the other, and me, grunting in the middle—we lugged each log to the growing stack. Many of the butt end cuts were just too heavy to lift so we flipped them end over end to the pile.

One heavy log in particular slipped and hit Chris on the shin. The next day he limped but continued logging. The following day his leg was swollen and purple, and oozing pus. Barb insisted that he go to the clinic and have the injury x-rayed. His shin bone was chipped and the doctor said he had blood poisoning. Later, Chris told us about the doctor cleaning his injury. He sounded quite proud. The purple-red boil was puffed and shining with yellow-white puss, and it glowed beneath the bright light over the operating table. The doctor lanced the swollen wound and bloody puss sprayed into the air. The doctor squeezed it between his thumbs. Chris said he clenched his teeth like a cowboy getting an arrow pulled out.

It took several weeks to heal but Chris continued working the heavy logs as he favored the sore leg. By late August an eight-cord load of naked logs was neatly stacked at pasture's edge. A neighbor came with his logging truck, loaded it and hauled it away. Barb insisted the check be made out to her, and she would store our shares in the little wooden box that only she had a key to. As with the lamb money, I never saw a cent of the logging money—I don't know if Chris and Tim received any.

Over the years at family gatherings, my older brothers and I talk about how we worked when we were children. Our family was like two generations—the four Barb brought to the farm in 1949, and the later kids, Herman's biological children. Symbolic of the different generations is an old cream can I found in the woods at the farm. To my older brothers and me, that container represented countless hours we worked harvesting hay, milking, cleaning the barn, and doing the chores that went with the dairy business. Herman sold the cattle in the late 1960s. When I found the cream can in the junk pile and showed it to my youngest brother Danny, he told me that in the 1970s he had welded legs, installed a chimney, and cut vent holes. It was a fishhouse stove.

Those evenings when I was a child in the 1950s keep pulling me back. Memory delineates late summer twilight and early winter darkness. Today we have light-emitting diode (LED) lights, computers and flat screens. iPhones, streaming, DVDs, and cable, to ward off the darkness.

In the 1950s, after supper, after chores, we children did our homework beneath the flickering fluorescent lights and then played games around the kitchen table. Card games—Hearts and Whist, Old Maid, and Poker for toothpicks. Barb attempted to teach us how to play Bridge but to no avail. Randy and I often played spoons or checkers—regular and Chinese. We all spent whole evenings playing jacks and pick-up-sticks. On most evenings, a stony silence hung in the air between our parents.

Barb sometimes talked about her past, trying to get a rise out of Herman, who sat near the stove, reading.

(December 1957, *left to right*) Randy, Wendell holding a fox he'd trapped, Laurel holding Larry, Linda with muff, and Bonny. Standing alongside the corn crib that our dogs were chained to.

Cats, Coons, and Chicks

One of my early memories with Herman—back to the first winter at the farm—was when he lifted me up to feel for sparrows cuddled together against the winter night cold in the eaves of the old barn. I'd wrap my child fingers gently around a drowsy little bird and Herman would carry me back into the warm barn where he taught me how to pluck the wing feathers and throw the sparrow to the half-starved cats mewling at my feet. It was great fun watching them play with the terrified bird. We continued that practice throughout our childhood, passing the game down to the younger kids.

Cat life was cheap. At night they'd nestle between stanchioned cows for warmth. The cows would shift position while lying down as their large paunches digested hay and grain. It was not unusual to find a smothered cat in the morning. We'd take the hoe that we used to clean manure around the cow's back feet and pull the cat into the gutter. By afternoon, the carcass was freezing into the manure pile behind the barn. The following summer as we hand-loaded the manure spreader, we'd shout out when we found a cat carcass—kind of like discovering the prize in a Cracker Jack box.

One time when I was about five—it was before we got an indoor toilet—I was sitting in the sunshine between the woodshed and the house playing with a kitten and she scratched me. I hit her with a stick and broke her back. Frightened by her high-pitched mewling, I panicked. I grabbed her by the tail, ran to the outhouse, and dropped her down the hole. Terrified yet fascinated, I stared down and watched her squirm as she tried to claw up the slick, catalogue-page-embedded stalagmite. Eventually she bubbled down beneath the brown liquid surrounding the island. It was no doubt a cruel thing to do, beyond what a child could comprehend.

Each spring a raccoon birthed a litter in a dry culvert west of the barn. Herman let us capture the kits and raise them as pets. As the summer progressed and the young coons grew, they became vicious. The top of the mesh cage hinged open so we could drop food in. They ate fish heads and guts, frogs, and tops from vegetables harvested from the garden. The little beasts lashed out with sharp claws as their beady eyes searched for a negligent finger they could sink teeth into. By mid-summer, their meat-based feces reeked and going near the cage meant being enveloped in a swarm of flies. By autumn the little critters had worn out their welcome.

One day we came home from a school clothes buying trip and discovered that the raccoons had worked a corner of the mesh loose and escaped. That evening we were in the garden picking supper vegetables when Tim heard noise in the orchard. Moving in to investigate, he spotted a raccoon in one of the crab apple trees. He spotted another curled in the crotch of a wild plum tree, acting strange. Moving closer to the thorned branches, Tim saw what the little critter was gnawing on—its own intestines. A thorn had sliced the coon's soft under-belly like a scalpel, spilling its guts out. Tim shouted out his discovery and Chris and I came running.

"Let's get him down," Chris said. He ran to the woodshed and returned with a length of slab wood and poked at the raccoon until it fell from the tree. The little coon bounced, curled into a ball and continued eating. We watched for several minutes as the furry animal slowly chewed; slower and slower until it nodded off to sleep. Tim pulled out his jackknife, opened the blade and gingerly probed the unconscious animal. No response. Chris turned the coon on her back and held her back feet apart. The stomach was slit open from sternum to hind legs. Tim pushed the remaining intestines aside with his knife and we watched the coon's diaphragm expand and contract.

"Want to see her heart beat?" Tim asked.

"Yeah, yeah," we said.

"Okay. I saw her. I get to be surgeon," Tim announced. I grabbed the front feet and held them wide while Tim reached forward and punctured one side of the pale pink diaphragm, then the other. Lungs rose and fell as the heart beat erratically. We watched as the little heart slowed to a stop.

"That'll teach the little shit to escape," Tim said, pricking the heart impatiently with the tip of the blade, trying to make it beat again.

A few years ago while I was visiting with Chris, he talked about the old pumpjack—an electric-powered well pump mounted directly over the well. It had a vertical frame that was about four feet tall and went up and down while pumping. As I think back, it's amazing none of us were seriously injured because we often played with it. We'd climb on the frame and ride up and down, kind of like a stationary merry-go-round. Two large gears with big cogs turned continuously, pumping the water. Chris recalled how he and Tim would catch frogs and lizards and run them through the gears.

A game that Randy and I perfected (I don't recall seeing Tim and Chris play it) was a chicken swimming contest. When Herman was gone to town, we'd each catch a chicken and throw it in the cattle water tank. The winner was whichever chicken stayed afloat longest. It was the most fun with young chicks because they sank faster.

Crows and KYB

Just after the turn of the century, after the big white pine log-off of the North Country, many Lutheran loggers homesteaded the Nebish area. During the same decades, several Croatians also homesteaded in the area. The Croatians were a tight-knit Catholic community. I think in the very early days, the two groups socialized a bit. For example, the story goes that in 1916, when Herman's brother Bruno was thrown off the buckboard and killed, Herman's mother, a Lutheran, and Mrs. Ruzicka, a Catholic neighbor lady, were traveling together to visit an ailing neighbor.

By the second generation, an invisible line delineating neighbors was drawn for first-generation children like Herman. When alluding to the Catholic Croatian community, a slang term evolved—Crows. As the decades passed, the Croatian community developed prosperous farms while many of the—by then—non-denominational community, struggled. I imagine a contributing factor to Croatian success was that they worked together—shared labor and expertise.

When I was ten I fell in love with a little blond-haired girl who rode our school bus. Her family lived about two miles south of our farm. I tried to sit by her on the bus, passed notes to her in school, played with her, maybe even tried to steal a little kiss. Chris and Tim teased me at home about marrying her. Herman just grumbled, "Ain't nobody living in this house going to marry a damn Crow." Today, I wonder if an adult were to ask Herman, just exactly why he disliked our Croatian neighbors, I'm quite sure he would not have been able to give a reason.

In the late 1950s, each Wednesday afternoon during the school year, the Catholic kids walked to their new church on top of a hill for their catechism lessons. The rest of us kids walked in the other direction to a nondenominational chapel for KYB (Know Your Bible). The little church was built near the south edge of a slough, bordered by a dirt trail called Pig Turd Alley. Our Bible classes were taught by two women from Oak Hills Bible College, located a few miles south of Bemidji. After class we'd all return to school, our religious delineation fortified for the week.

I'm sure the Bible College and the teachers had good intentions, but as I look back on the KYB classes I think two things: First, it was an outreach to save souls and recruit for summer Bible camp. But second, I remember the draconian threat preached at us about going to hell—that's why Michelangelo's *Last Judgment* painting gave me nightmares.

Even today I struggle with the theory that all humans are born with original sin. Does that mean that infants and children who have not been "Saved" are committed to an eternity of brimstone? What about the heathens who have never had the benefit of enlightenment? Or the mentally infirm?

I recall the memorial service I attended while in Vietnam for six sailors killed by the mine. In my memoir, *Muddy Jungle Rivers*, I wrote,

Sand swirled around the small congregation as we gathered near the mouth of the Cua Viet River to bid farewell. The memorial service opened with "My Country 'tis of Thee," and I silently mouthed the words and wondered how many hundreds of times I'd sung them as a child after the flag raising and Pledge of Allegiance we all did in the little two room school I had attended. The boys from Tango 7 would never again roam the "woods and templed hills" the chaplain was so joyously belting out. I looked out over the sand dunes, out to the South China Sea, past the homebound fishermen in their low-riding sampans, past the warship silhouette, beyond the horizon and remembered how it was when I was little and terrified of burning in hell.

The summer I was nine and my brother was six we spent a week at a summer Bible camp. We were assigned to a cabin managed by an apprentice preacher. In the evening, the campers gathered in a large, screened gazebo with a bonfire pit in the center and tiered seating around it. We learned of the fires of hell and the certainty of going there if we didn't take Jesus as our personal savior. At home we didn't attend church regularly. When we did, it was Lutheran. This Baptist version was a terrifying revelation. Each night we watched kids go from the bleachers down to the bonfire, kneel near the brim of the pit, and beg forgiveness while flames cast shadows on their sob-racked little bodies as they made their vows in blubbering voices. Afterwards we returned to our cabins for the night. I lay on my upper bunk with the screen window a few inches from my face and watched the moon dance on waves as whippoorwills echoed and a loon called mournfully. I conjured up nine-year-old visions of eternal damnation. By week's end I couldn't sleep, and on Friday evening my brother and I repented our sins and took Jesus as our personal savior.

As I reflect on the religious aspect of my childhood, I think we were torn—torn between what we were led to believe was the satanic Catholic Church, a regimented Lutheran church, and the fire and brimstone dogma of the fundamentalist Bible chapel. If there was love and salvation, how were children to reconcile love in a family torn daily by acrimony?

Sixty years later, that delineation between Croatians and the rest of the community has all but disappeared. I wonder how much of the original biases and prejudices the original settlers carried across the Atlantic with them. I remember how close-knit the Croatian community was, and we all envied that connection.

Perhaps I gained an insight in the 1970s when I was working in Milwaukee in a butcher shop. I sold dozens of lambs to a group for weekend gatherings. They invited my wife and me to visit one weekend.

It was like stepping back a few generations into Old Country Armenia/ Croatia—lambs and goats slow cooked in pit barbeques; curry scented smoke wafting through the park. Croatian music wove with the smoke, and costumed dancers whirled. And now I think this is what the community of my childhood was passing on to their children—it had nothing to do with alienating outsiders.

We Affield children grew beyond the dogma we were taught. Three of us married Catholic girls. My children attended St. Philips Catholic School in Bemidji. My youngest brother, Danny, attends St. John's Catholic Church in Nebish. We watched our classmates hike there in the 1950s from the now-boarded gray stucco Nebish School. I imagine God glances down at my feeble attempt to make sense of the unexplainable and just shakes his unshorn locks.

Excerpts from my grandmother's 1945 diary:

December 2, 1945: [New York City] A great event happened today. Barbara, John, and the 2 boys drove up in their car and spent the afternoon with Henry and me. Henry was very favorably impressed with John. He looked very well in his Naval Petty Officer's outfit. The little boys are so cute—they were very good but rushed into everything. Barb did pretty well but she is not all right yet.

December 8, 1945: Went to Barb's to tell her about Polly's illness. We went riding in the car. What a ride. Barb had Timmy in his go-cart in the back seat. We stopped for gas and lunch which I paid for—then went to park on Riverside. Christopher ran into the street. Barb shrieked, then was very cross. Drove through Central Park—relieved to get home. Got out at N.Y. Hospital—dispensary closed. Barb should take nerve medicine. Dear Henry arrived the same time as I. We decided to celebrate our 28th as Henry is going to Newton D. Baker Hospital Martinsburg, West Virginia tomorrow morning to see dear Pol who has been in the hospital more than a month. (Polly had just been diagnosed with paranoid schizophrenia.)

December 9, 1945: Dear Henry left at 7:15 a.m. for Martinsburg, West Virginia to see Pol who had been in Newton D. Baker Hospital there ill for over a month. I did Xmas things, went for a walk, mailed cards. Sukie came at 5:30. At 6 we went to dinner at Alcoholics Anonymous and stayed to the meeting afterwards. Very interesting—all these AAs are neurotics who have a purpose, in other words have found themselves and now help others—I wish Barb and Pol could.

1958
Hunting, Trapping, and Porcupine Dinner

The Soviet Union launched Sputnik 1 on October 4, 1957. I was in the fifth grade. On January 31, 1958, the U.S. launched Explorer 1. The space race had begun. Cold War tension clicked up a notch. Our bomb drills began to make sense—the Russians would soon be able to drop bombs from space. At the same time, a new Welfare Department worker named Mrs. Hanson began dropping in at the farm.

I purchased a pair of Korean War surplus bunny boots with some of my trapping money. When the snow got too deep to skate around area lakes checking my muskrat traps, I slogged through snow drifts and across crusted banks in my new boots and pretended I was a Korean soldier marching into battle against the hated communists.

In January 1958 President Eisenhower endorsed the bill to grant Alaska statehood. My teacher was excited and said that we were witnessing history, that it was the first territory to be granted statehood since Arizona in 1912. She assigned us to create a project about the soon-to-be state. During the winter of 1958 I spent countless hours on my hand drawn map, marking in cities, mountain ranges, and natural resources. The dozens of natural resources—fishing, timber, gold, oil—are what I remember best. My bunny boots began carrying me across Alaskan mountains in my search for gold.

The draw for manpower to develop those natural resources attracted thousands of men, many from northern Minnesota where the late 1950s agricultural economy was a disaster. Many of those men and women became residents of Alaska, married, raised children, and retired. Jack

London's *Call of the Wild* was a popular book. Stories about hunting and trapping that filtered back from Alaska motivated me to try harder.

Herman didn't hunt or trap but he taught Tim and Chris how to. I tagged along and learned. By the time I was ten I was a proficient squirrel hunter. I stalked silently among the oaks and watched for bushy tails hanging over branches. I'd slowly lift the single-shot .22 caliber rifle to my shoulder, lean against a tree for support, and wait patiently, silently. Eventually the squirrel would peek around the branch to investigate. I'd put the bead on his gray throat and shoot him through the head.

In late autumn as waterfowl migrated, I graduated to the 12 gauge shotgun, mainly because I bought a box of shells. It quickly became my weapon of choice. Early morning—before school—I'd creep through the spongy marsh to the water's edge where mallards were feeding among lily pads and floating roots that looked like pineapple husks. The ducks were just beyond the ice crust bordering the lake. Camouflaged by diamond willows, I'd wait until three to five birds were aligned. I never wasted a round on a single mallard—two-three was the average shot, once in a while four, a few rare times I got five ducks in one shot. I didn't have a duck boat so after school, after the sun had melted the thin ice crust, I'd walk the shoreline and retrieve the ducks.

One drizzly cold morning I returned to the house and set the shotgun on the kitchen table so that I could thaw my fingers by the stove before I unloaded it. Barb, always inquisitive, picked it up.

"Is it loaded?" she asked.

Before I could turn from the stove and answer, Ka-boom! The gun recoiled into Barb's stomach. "I'm shot! I'm shot!" she screamed. Randy and I doubled over in laughter.

Sixty years later, there's still
a hole in the window frame
where Barb's shot left it's mark.

When I learned how to trap, I started with raccoons in autumn. I placed three cobs of husked corn on the ground and surrounded them with steel traps, lightly covered by the corn husks. It was not unusual to catch two or three young raccoons in one night. Herman taught me how to club them on the head, but remembering my puppy, I always shot them. I learned how to skin them out without making holes in the pelts. I nailed the pelts on the east garage wall to dry in the sun and saved the raccoon carcasses for supper.

Everybody was free to gorge themselves without fear of reprimand. By the end of the meal, the little animal carcasses were reduced to piles of greasy, picked-clean bones.

Muskrat pelts were prime well into late winter and plentiful to trap. One late winter, east winds blew snow into my face as I walked the lake edge, carrying my new Stevens .22 pump rifle that I had purchased with my pelt money.

Mud domes of muskrat houses dotted the marshy lakeshore. With my hatchet, I chopped the top of the dome loose, exposing a small platform of woven twigs and lakeweed. I placed an open-jawed trap on the little platform and left the trap chain-end outside the dome. I put the lid back on the dome and packed snow over it to camouflage the broken seal and anchored the trap chain to a stick so the trapped muskrat couldn't escape. In the dark house the muskrat climbed onto his platform, stepped into the trap, and drowned after he jumped off, trying to escape. It was important to check the traps each day, because once the little rodent was caught, the hole froze shut without his body heat. He and the trap would be lost.

The spring-fed lakes had snow-covered weak spots. If I walked or skated into slush under the snow, I quickly changed course. Herman had taught me always to carry a long stick in case I broke through because the pole would cross the hole. One bitter January evening after school, while checking traps, I went through the ice on the far side of Nebish Lake.

It happened so fast I was over my head before I could grab the pole with both hands. Luckily, I wasn't carrying any traps. I was able to pull myself out by getting both hands on the pole and lifting one bunny booted foot to the lip of the hole. I slowly lifted myself out, terrified that the ice would crack more or the pole would break. If it did, I'd sink in my sodden clothes. I gently eased myself out and lay in the snow. I recalled Jack London's "To Build a Fire" and was scared that I would panic like the protagonist in his story. I dropped my pole and headed home. By the time I reached the house, I was walking like a stick man because my coat and coveralls were frozen solid.

Winter was a vicious time. The main source of income—cream from the cows—trickled to a stop as they progressed into the third trimester of gestation. Food was limited to what had been harvested and stored. Cash was conserved for paying the electric bill and buying Copenhagen, coffee, sugar, and flour. Barb refused to share food that she purchased with her AFDC money.

There was no pork and beef left hanging in the granary. Herman decided to bake muskrat carcasses. He talked about the old days when the lumberjacks ate beavers and reasoned that muskrat must taste the same. He seasoned the dark red, bony carcasses and put them in the oven. The kitchen began to smell like mucky lake bottom. When supper was served, the roasting pan of meat looked like blackened shriveled squirrels. The meat was tender—bone slipped out when a leg was tugged. It tasted like lake bottom smelled. Herman thought it tasted great, slathered with mustard.

One Saturday morning I was moving to new muskrat houses, working my way around Maple Lake, three houses at a time. The last trap had been set. I looked across the spongy bog at the cedar swamp on the east side of the lake.

"Daddy will be happy if I shoot some rabbits for supper," I said out loud.

Hatchet swinging in its holster at my side, rifle cradled in my arms, I stepped high through the snow-packed swamp grass. Entering the canopy of the cedar swamp was like entering another world. No snow drifts, sweet cedar smell, and just a one-foot snow cover on the crisp moss. Each tree root system had created its own little island with water visible in the low spots between. I stepped silently from island to island, careful not to slip into the low spots. The past winter I'd slipped into one and sank to my waist. It was a cold walk home.

I found fox tracks, which meant that there wouldn't be any rabbits. Bits of bark rattled down on my head. I looked up into the falling snow and spotted a porcupine. It was the biggest I'd ever seen. Slipping my mittens off, I said, "You're coming home for supper, Porky," as more bark trickled down.

The animal gnawed contentedly at the cedar bark, unaware of me. I moved around the tree but couldn't find a clean shot through the branches. Fingers cold, I shot at his neck. The animal jerked, fell off the branch, caught hold of the next limb down, and clumsily pulled himself up into the crotch where the limb joined the trunk. I found a new position, aimed carefully at the animal's head and fired. The porcupine dropped from one branch to another just below it, unmoving. I aimed and fired again. "You must be dead and stuck on the branch," I said, my voice loud in the still swamp.

I had profound respect for porcupines. The past summer Chris and I had found a dead one and played with it. I had gotten two quills in my hand. They'd broken off with the tips still under my skin, and two days later they were swollen ugly red with gray pus oozing. Barb held me down while Herman heated a heavy leather-sewing needle in candle flame. I watched the needle tip turn orange. I screamed and squirmed as Herman dug until both quill tips were removed. The wounds drained for several days.

Cedar tree limbs started low to the ground, so I took my coat off and began climbing, rifle in hand. I didn't want porky tumbling down on top of me. High in the tree, opposite him, I leaned back and peeked around the trunk. His front claws had sunk into the wood in a death grip. I climbed above and poked with the gun muzzle. No movement. I slid opposite him, and used my gun to pry porky loose. He plummeted through the branches to the ground and thudded on the snow-covered moss.

I realized I couldn't carry him home, so I skinned him in the cedar swamp. Working carefully I rolled him out of his hide, amazed at the thick layer of yellow-white fat. After removing hide, head, and guts, I tied a rope to a still-attached paw and dragged him home, leaving a thin bloody track that faded to clean snow as the carcass froze.

Through the picture window, I saw the little kids playing in the front room as I approached the house. Three-year-old Bonny spotted me and ran to open the door. "Did you shoot a deer?"

Barb came and looked. "Get that stinky raccoon out of here. I'm not eating any more rodents in my house."

I sensed the tension—Barb was searching for a fight. Herman had been sitting in the house all afternoon, and at dinner time they'd been sparring. I ignored Barb.

"Daddy, look what I got for supper," I said, holding the rigid carcass proudly as I stepped into the kitchen.

"That's about the biggest one I've ever seen," Herman said.

"It's a porcupine, not a raccoon," I said to Barb, defending my trophy.

"There ain't a damn thing wrong with eating porkies," Herman said. "We always ate them when I was a kid."

"Well, you immigrants may have eaten them—I am a Daughter of the American Revolution. I'm civilized. I'll be damned if my children and I will eat that."

"Well, damn, you and your children can go hungry."

The carcass was beginning to drip on the floor. Herman rose from his stuffed chair and came over to me.

"I skinned and gutted it across the lake. That's why it's so cold already," I said.

"Cripes sake, how many times did you shoot it?" Herman asked, looking at the bruised body. I told him what had happened.

"Well, he'll still be good eating." Herman carried the dripping porky to the sink and began carving fat off. "It's going to be a long winter, look at the thick layer of fat on this old boy. Dig out the roasting pan, we'll get him baking."

I dug in the cabinet beside the sink and pulled out the black enamel pan. It was crusted with dry muskrat drippings. Barb stood watching.

"Useless bitch. Didn't them pilgrims of yours know how to wash dishes?" Herman grumbled.

"Servants did them," she retorted.

"Start scrubbing," Herman said, "I ain't your damn servant—you want to eat—you got to work."

"You go to hell, you bald bastard. I'm not your servant," she said, as she flipped Larry from one breast to the other.

"Start scrubbing or my belt comes off."

"I'll clean it," I said, hoping to avoid another battle.

"No. She cleans it."

"Go to hell, you bald bastard."

So it began, again. Laurel grabbed baby Larry from Barb, and the little kids raced upstairs and hid. Herman set his knife down as he looked out the window. He wiped grease-covered hands on his pants. Slowly he unbuckled his belt and turned toward Barb.

"You will scrub that roasting pan. I wear the pants in this house. You will do what I say."

"Yes—you wear the pants all right—cow-shit coated. I'm not your nigger to boss around." She stood on the far side of the table from him.

I stood, scrubbing the pan, back to them, watching in the small mirror propped on the ledge. Chris and Tim were outside splitting firewood. The little kids were upstairs, their eyes probably squished closed, hands over their ears.

The belt lashed out—at least it wasn't a buckle-end rage—and flicked like the end of a whip, catching Barb in the stomach. She grabbed the belt and it slipped from his greasy hand.

She reached over to the cabinet and flicked the radio on—Hank Williams twanged across the room. She threw the belt at him. He ducked and it bounced off the wall.

"Turn that shit off," Herman said, as he circled the table. "You are a useless bitch." He flipped the radio off, picked up his belt and re-looped it. He returned to the porky and finished trimming off the fat. "Damn useless battle-axe," he mumbled, veins pulsing on his bald head. "Ain't good for nothing."

"Not good for anything," Barb corrected and returned to the front room.

"This old boy will be good eating," Herman said, as he sprinkled salt and pepper on the dark red meat.

D.A.

By 1958 Barb's rages were out of control; I tried to avoid her. Chris and Tim were by then big enough to defend themselves. A few years ago Tim told me, "I remember the first time Chris knocked her down. I suddenly felt liberated." Eventually we all fought back. We all wrote letters to our grandmother, Elsie, and one of us must have mentioned Barb's rages. I found this note in Elsie's "Mental Health Journal." B.A.P.A. is Barbara Ann Philips Affield.

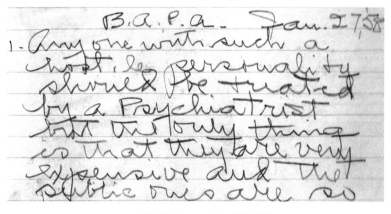

B.A.P.A.   Jan 27, '58

1. Anyone with such a hostile personality should be treated by a psychiatrist but the only thing is that they are very expensive and the public ones are so infiltrated with "anti-parents Freud and the Soviet Socialist World Way" that they might make her even worse.

In the chickenhouse I discovered a letter that Chris, in the tenth grade, wrote to Elsie and Polly.

March 1958. Dear Grandma and Aunt Polly, I was very shocked when I heard about Grandpa's death and hope that you and Aunt Polly are getting along all right. It's been a long time since you were here, we have two more members in the family, Linda 3 and Larry 1 year. We received your Easter cards today and I thought they were very nice. I should have written a long time ago to thank you for the other things but I didn't get around to it. Remember when you sent Tim and me those Swiss watches back in "56"? Well we just found them about a month ago. Ma had them hid all the time. Tim and I are going to Bemidji High School now and I like it pretty well. I am taking four subjects, Shop, Agriculture, History, and English. I don't especially care for History and English though. Our basketball team did good at the Regional but they didn't do too well at the state championship game. Love, Chris. P.S. I have a pig I hope to make a million on.

Writing can be a surprise, taking one into unexpected paths in the labyrinth of life experience. As I studied Chris's letter, layers of our childhood took me into mazes that had been evading me. I was pulled back to how, one Saturday each month, Herman cut our hair with his electric cow clippers.

The Stewart Clipmaster Model 51 shears was eleven inches long and had a three-inch cutting head. Herman had one hair style available; white walls, clipped short to the skin on the sides of the head with a round top-knot. By 1958, Chris and Tim were in high school and exposed to new ideas including Elvis Presley's Duck Tail, or, as most called it "duck's ass," euphemistically referred to as a D.A. It symbolized rebellion.

I naturally followed in their footsteps and discovered that with enough Brylcreem I could comb most of my hair up over the top of my head where it was safe from the clipper. With five boys to shear, Herman didn't get technical.

One spring morning as my brothers and I waited our turns, we began to roughhouse. When it was my turn, much to my horror, I discovered my hair was hanging loose. In short order, my prized D.A. and self-esteem lay on the floor. I begged Herman not to cut it, but he lopped it off like the shitty end of a cow's tail.

Sadly, by 1958, Barb had turned Herman against Chris and Tim and they were in open rebellion. Now I think that, in his mind, eliminating my D.A. eliminated all seeds of rebellion.

(1958) Tim, Lutheran Pastor Trueman Daniels, and Chris. Confirmation picture. Over the next two years, the minister became very active with our family.

After our communal baptism the preceding summer, Pastor Daniels began to visit us at the farm. Barb fawned over him as she served him coffee and cookies or cake. She once gave him a bag of cupcakes to take home to his family. The next day Randy and I were walking to Nebish Lake to go fishing and found the bag of hockey-puck cakes lying on the shoulder of the road. As I mentioned earlier, Barb had tried to get a neighbor man to marry her in 1954. I wonder if, in her impulsive way, she became infatuated with Trueman Daniels as well.

Bloated Cows

"Finish your crusts and eat the meat tucked under your plate, then you can go out," Herman told me.

"I'm full—fat makes me want to puke when I chew it," I protested.

"Put mustard on it."

I spread blackstrap on the bread crusts and ate them. After frosting mustard onto the pork fat, I slipped the cold yellow-coated globs into my mouth. I chewed and pretended to swallow then jumped up from the table and ran out with Randy close behind. We ran to the corncrib where the chained dog was panting in the shade. I spit yellow mush on the ground and the dog slurped it up.

"Why are those cows laying there kicking?" Randy asked.

"Let's go look," I said, and we ran across the yard. "Something's wrong—let's tell Daddy."

"I get to tell or I'll tell him you didn't swallow the fat—you spit it to the dog." We raced back to the house, burst in, and Randy shouted, "Three cows are laying in the dirt out by the silo, just kicking."

"Don't make up stories—go out and play."

"No, they really are just kicking."

Herman tapped twice on his Copenhagen can, opened the lid, and placed a pinch under his lip. "Let's see what you're talking about. You boys," nodding toward Chris and Tim, "finish up. We have haying to do." He slipped his faded engineer hat on, tilted it over his left eye, and followed us out.

Standing on the steps, hand shading his eyes, he looked toward the silo. "No! Oh, no!" he shouted, running toward the downed cows.

Bessie, Rosie, and Elsie lay on their sides, eyes rolled back, trying to breathe, their stomachs puffed like sun-warmed road kill.

"They're bloated," Chris said. "I learned it in FFA (Future Farmers of America) class. We watched a movie about cutting a small hole in the cow's side and putting a pipe in to let the gas out. Their gassy stomach squeezes their lungs and they can't breathe."

"There's pipe in the blacksmith shop by the forge. Tim, run grab three pieces. Chris," Herman said, opening his jackknife, "where did they stick them?"

Chris stepped forward and ran his hand gently over Bessie's flank. "Behind the last rib—I can feel it—poke the hole here, where it's bulging."

(Autumn 1958) Chris, in his FFA jacket. Randy, making a face.

The dull blade of the jackknife folded against the tough hide. Herman reopened it, raised his hand, and stabbed downward. Tim ran up with the pipe; Bessie kicked as Herman inserted the pipe into the puncture. Green-tinted mist blew upward. Chris pushed against Bessie's side forcing more gas out. Herman ran to Elsie. He prodded her open, glazed eye—no response. He slowly walked to Rosie—same thing. He walked back to Bessie and kicked her twitching foot as it slowed. He looked up into the clear sky, then toward the pothole behind the barn. "You boys go shag the rest of the cows out of the water."

He reached down and pulled the pipe out of Bessie and kicked her foot in futility. These were prize Holstein cows in their prime—heifers from four purebred cows he had purchased several years earlier and had artificially inseminated—the foundation of a dream when the new barn was built. He examined the pipe. Small flecks of green alfalfa and clover stuck to the threads.

It had been a perfect summer for hay. We had harvested a bumper crop of first cutting. There was enough second cutting in the south fields to fill the haymow, so Herman had decided to let the cows graze some of the lush second cutting south of the buildings. After morning milking, the cows had gorged themselves on dew-covered grass. Late in the morning they'd returned, up the lane, around the barn, and into the pothole where they guzzled mucky, pee-filled water. The fermenting gases had bloated them. Herman watched us walk toward him.

"The rest look okay," Chris said. "They're in the woods behind the barn."

"Look at the blow-flies already laying eggs around their eyes," Tim said.

I brushed them away. "Those turn to maggots."

"You imbecile, everybody knows that," Tim scowled.

"Daddy, Tim called me an imbecile."

"You boys knock it off. Chris, run get the skinning knife—the meat's no good in this heat, but we can salvage the hides."

Four hours later the three fly-infested carcasses lay swelling in the evening sun on blood crusted grass, the black and white hides folded beside them.

"We'll put the hides in the hog scalding barrel and cover them with water to keep the flies away until I can get them to town," Herman said.

The next morning, using the Farmall, he dragged the carcasses out into the woods.

The following day, a black cloud of flies rose from the hides when we lifted the barrel lid. The water had leaked out. We removed the back seat from the car and put the cream cans in, loaded the rancid, dripping hides into the trunk, and drove to town. Herman brought the hides to the junkyard where I sold pelts in the winter.

The owner came out of his shed, wiping his hands on grease-glazed coveralls. He walked up to the car. Wrinkling his nose, he said, "What the hell stinks? You got something dripping from your trunk."

"I got three cow hides—big ones." Herman opened the trunk. We all gagged. During the ride into town, the hot sun had warmed the water-logged hides. Hair had begun to slough off and maggots were hatching. The blue-tinted edges of decaying flesh were moving.

"Shut that trunk! Get them the hell out of here," the junkyard man said, bent over with dry heaves. Herman drove out Fourth Street to the west edge of town and dropped the hides in a swamp.

For the next several days we played with the puffed carcasses in the shade beneath towering maples. The hooves stuck up in the air. We brushed maggots away with sticks and rode the shanks like teeter-totters until our crotches got moist with seeping juices and the smell made us puke. We whittled points on green hazel brush sticks and stabbed the paunches until we were rewarded with misty pink whistles of gas. Randy and I hid upwind and waited for crows and eagles to arrive and then shot at them with our BB guns. Within ten days, the gut cavities collapsed and scavengers feasted on the entrails. The flesh turned crusty black and our interests turned to other games. Over that summer, varmints devoured the carcasses. By autumn, skeletons remained with dried scraps hanging on rib cages. Losing those cows must have been a terrible blow for Herman. As children we didn't understand the significance.

Sixty years later, a few years before the farm was sold, I revisited the slough edge where the carcasses had been left. I found no trace of Bessie, Rosie, and Elsie, but ironically I found an old tire attached to a chain nearby. The other end of the chain had a bolted loop that would fit a yearling steer's neck. The chain was wrapped around a tree, grown in over several decades, and I recalled a story my youngest brother Danny told me about how, after Herman died, he and Larry had bolted an old tire to a chain and then around their calf's neck because it kept getting out of the fence. He recalled how one day the calf had disappeared. The steer had no doubt gotten the chain wrapped around the tree and slowly starved to death.

On November 3, 1958, Elsie wrote in her diary, *Kath (Polly) brought me a notice she received from Hartman, Jarvis, Attorneys, Superior Court State of Washington, County of King, dated 15 Sept '58. Probate proceedings are pending, Grandfather* [Calvin Philips, Henry's father] *left money to Barb and Pol.*

A year later this inheritance would have far-reaching effects for all of us on the farm.

*Hoping you have
the most wonderful
Christmas
you've ever known!
Barbara and family*

This is the Christmas card message Barb sent her mother in 1958. There was no letter enclosed. I like to think it was the only card Barb had available but what a cruel holiday greeting. Elsie was still grieving the loss of her husband. Polly, who now lived with her, was a constant source of worry.

Excerpt from my grandmother's 1945-46 diaries:

December 11, 1945: Beautiful sunny winter day. Went to Bar's to see how John was getting on—he seems to be so well balanced he's managing all right. B. is really awful—nice to John because he's a good money provider. She plays nicely for him. She never plays for us—unwilling to let her father play with the darling children.

December 25, 1945: Christmas Day—Barb and the children didn't come at the last minute—snowstorm. Later Henry and I went to Kay's for cocktails .

December 27, 1945: Barb came down early with Timmy and Chris and spent the day—a postponed Xmas day. They opened their presents under the tree and had a very good time. They all stayed to a delicious turkey luncheon. We all had Tea together in the living room. The boys made quite a bit of havoc in the house.

March 26, 1946: Henry and I had a letter from John Curry saying that he could not go on with Barbara any longer. I can't say I blame him—he really has tried. We all went up to Barb's in the evening but she acted her usual rude self. If she put as much guts into being generous as she does into some things, entertaining, washing, caring for the children, and piano, she'd be a wonderful person.

April 8, 1946: Pol and I took a lot of things to Barb and had a perfectly awful time because I insisted on coming in and seeing the children. Someone told me that's the best thing to do with neurotics. Everybody pussy foots and lets them have their own wrong way and that is bad for them. But she set upon me and pounded me to pieces. I really can't take such treatment at my age—it's awful.

1959
Mealtime

President Eisenhower was nearing the end of his second term. Bonny, Linda, and Larry flitted about the house playing dolls. Battle lines solidified between Barb and Herman. Looking back, the marriage seems analogous to World War I trench warfare, as each side licked their wounds from the previous encounter, fully aware that another attack was imminent. My siblings and I were cannon fodder forced into a no-man's land of alliances, confused by explosive rages and cloying poison of sweet-smelling deception. Mealtime often triggered confrontations.

Summer crept in with warmer days as the garden developed. Poplar and bass trees leafed out, and bees were thick in the blossoming orchard. Summer was officially in swing with the hanging of the first fly-ribbon over the table. Within three weeks the glue-covered strip was coated with dead flies. Crisp wings shed and fluttered down to whatever might be on the table.

With ten people living in the little house, the spring-loaded screen door was constantly opened and closed by kids running in and out. Rusted, holey window screens provided easy access for flies. The kitchen sink drained onto the ground below the front window. Dirty dishes in the sink, manure-crusted shoes, and garbage proved a fertile breeding ground. The outhouse, thirty feet from the front door, was busier than ever—one indoor toilet couldn't accommodate all of us. Flies swarmed. Money was grudgingly spent on new glue strips. When flies landed on our plate, Herman grunted, "Brush them away. They don't eat much."

By the time I was eleven Barb had relegated Herman's place to that of an animal. His feeding dish, a relic from his bachelor days, was a chipped white-blue enamel rectangular bowl with two-inch sides and a lip around the edge. Barb refused to contaminate the other dishes with Herman's bowl. After each meal it was placed in the oven until the next meal. She scraped the past meal's residue out before placing it at his wooden chair with the cracked seat, along with his special, quarantined fork, knife, and spoon. Family mealtime conversations spiraled down— not exactly conducive to appropriate social development for children.

"For cripe sake, we out of bread again?" Herman grumbled. "Windy, after breakfast you make a batch—your mother don't know how." And he'd toss the bag of leftover homemade bread-ends across the table toward me. The stale crusts thudded like the clay dinosaurs Chris baked in the oven. "Make a batch of pudding out of them."

"Out of those," Barb corrected. "We ate at white-tablecloth restaurants and had the maid prepare meals. Bakery was delivered with the dairy," she said. "Only peasants eat bread pudding."

"Useless bitch—don't do nothing."

"Doesn't do anything," Barb amended.

Herman ignored her. "Chris, pass the sugar."

"Say please," Barb insisted. "I want my children to use proper manners."

"Shut the hell up, you damn battle-axe. Chris, Tim, after breakfast you help me fork over windrows. Sun's dried the top of them by the time we get out there. Windy, you weed three rows when bread's done. Randy can help." I was thankful I was smaller than Chris and Tim. I'd much rather knead bread dough and weed garden rows.

Breakfast seasons blend: summer, a bowl of corn flakes or cheerios: winter, farina, oatmeal mush, or corn meal with one teaspoon—level, not heaped—of sugar.

"That's enough." Herman's hand would shoot forward like a striking rattler and whack the offender with the back edge of a butter knife — always it seemed, across knuckles. The reprimand wasn't really two words; they slurred together into a drawn-out monosyllabic statement, "thashnough." For several days the bruised knuckles were a livid reminder. As the bruises faded, so did the memory, and again the offender reached for an extra bit of sweetness.

"You expect my boys to do nigger work yet they can't even have sugar," Barb said.

Herman answered with silence, tapping his empty mug on the table, signaling for a refill. She slammed the re-warmed coffee down in front of him.

"Tastes like skunk piss," he said after a slurp.

"You would know."

Barb loved extra-strong Hills Bros. coffee. In the morning, the moment Herman was out the door doing chores, she'd dump yesterday's grounds and make herself fresh coffee. Even today, when I smell my morning coffee brewing, I remember back to Barb's brew. I can still smell that rich aroma wafting: summers, blended with blossoming lilacs and curing clover. Barb loved cut lilacs on the table. Winters, the coffee aroma blended with drying muskrat and weasel pelts stretched on hand-carved boards, hanging behind the woodstove. Across all seasons, coffee aroma blended with the odor of unwashed clothing, cow manure, and tension.

Dinner was at noon. In the summers, we had fried perch or bullheads that Chris, Tim, Laurel, Randy, and I caught down at the lake, or a fresh-killed leghorn chicken, mashed potatoes, and cucumber salad or garden lettuce drenched in milk and vinegar. Homemade bread was the gut-filler; sliced thick, with oleo margarine and rhubarb sauce. In the winter, when money was scarce, lard and molasses—blackstrap we called it—was glopped on. Kool-Aid or skim milk was the standard drink for us kids.

Potatoes were a part of every dinner and supper: boiled, fried, mashed, or riced. Herman didn't like potato skins. He demanded they be peeled before cooking. Barb boiled them peel-on. Herman loved mashed potatoes. I imagine they were easier to chew with his false teeth. After the unpeeled potatoes were boiled to mushiness, Barb would drain the pitted cast iron pot and have us squish them with the hand potato masher. Her final touch was to pour in a bit of skim milk and whip them with the electric mixer.

"What's these goddamn skins doing in the spuds?" Herman muttered, as he picked the bigger bits out with his fork and flicked them on the table.

"They are nutritious," Barb said. "We always ate them in New York. And do not swear in front of my children."

"You're not in New York. I want my damn spuds peeled."

"Then cook your own food," Barb said as she wiped Kool-Aid from Larry's chin with a dish towel.

"Useless bitch—what the hell I keep you around for?" He grudgingly ate the brown-flecked potatoes rather than see them go to waste.

"It's not my fault you were only fit for KP (kitchen police), peeling potatoes when you were in the army."

"That's enough, bitch."

Barb flipped a chicken leg, tail attached, into Herman's dish. After eating the thigh, he held the tail and asked, "Who wants the pope's nose?"

"The pope's nose," Herman said again. "Windy, you like the pope's nose?"

I shook my head, no.

Though Barb had been raised Episcopalian, she fancied herself a devout Catholic even though she had become a member of the Lutheran church. "Don't be sacrilegious—he is the head of my church."

"Ain't no damn Crow living in my house—pack your bag."

"Rot in hell, you bald bastard. My sons will have this farm when you are dead."

"Them goddamn chow-hounds ain't getting nothing." He tapped his coffee mug for a refill. Lunch coffee was the third time through for the grounds but Herman gulped the tepid brew and pulled a used toothpick from his sweat-stained denim shirt.

Barb's hands went to her hips. "Aren't getting anything. And I told you not to swear. Take that vulgar toothpick out of your mouth. If you must suck on it, do it outside where my children won't see you. And if I leave here, my children go with me."

"You take the four you came with. My sister'll come and take care of my children."

"Over my dead body, you shell-shocked bastard."

He ignored her, leaned back in his chair, and watched the little kids who were done eating, race around the table chasing each other.

Hot west wind whistled through the holey screen. A blowfly, like the ones that spread maggot larvae on the bloated cows, dropped from the crowded glue strip and crawled sluggishly across the table.

Linda, Barb's youngest daughter, a chubby little girl, raced after her dress-clad younger brother.

"Take that damn dress off him—he'll grow up thinking he's a girl," Herman said. He reached out, grabbed Linda by the wrist as she raced past, pulled her onto his lap and began chanting a ditty as he bounced her on his knee.

"How's my little girl?

My little Fatty-R-Buckle—

Apple of my eye

The puddin in my pie..."

"Get your filthy hands off her. Keep that filthy Kraut pecker away from my daughter," Barb screamed as she grabbed Linda by the wrist and yanked her away.

Herman leapt from his chair and backhanded Barb, knocking her to the floor, then kicked her in the side.

"You slut." He kicked her again as he unbuckled his belt.

Barb scampered under the table and jumped to her feet across from him.

"You may force that filthy Kraut pecker on me, but not my daughters."

The arguments were not rational—he often alluded to Chris and Tim, apparently thinking that would infuriate Barb. "Them goddamn Mexican bastards are useless as the tits on a boar pig. Nothing but goddamn chow hounds." The belt lashed back and forth across the table, the end snapping at Barb's bare arms.

Linda, hands covering her ears, screamed in terror. Bonny and Larry laughed in the front room, wrestling on the floor, dresses tangled. Laurel sat at the piano, slamming keys, playing "Chopsticks." Chris and Tim jumped up, away from the table, and moved toward the door. I grabbed Randy's hand, shoved past them, out to the porch where we turned and watched through the open window.

Rewarded with hisses of pain, Herman re-looped the belt in his dungarees and pulled his sweat-stained engineer cap on.

"Mind your damn tongue, bitch. Next time, you will get the buckle end." The screen door slammed behind him.

Rubbing her arms, sobbing, Barb scuttled around the table and scooped Linda up with a hug. "You poor darling—I've told you to stay away from that bald bastard. What were you doing so close that he reached you?" Her fingers moved up the underside of Linda's arm, above the elbow, and pinched until the sniffling little girl squealed in pain.

Barb's pinches were a furtive punishment—less painful than the sit-on-your-head-pummel-your-body-until-exhausted beatings. She'd squeeze the underarm tissue as hard as possible, and then twist until it left a dime-size welt that took weeks to heal. I learned early not to trust her overtures for affection.

Warm weather limited meals to fresh meat. Chicken, killed at 10 A.M. and fried for noon dinner, was the number one summer entrée. Herman grudgingly authorized four chickens a week. With all the cows freshened, it was necessary for him to haul cream into the creamery three times a week. Often, he went alone, and it was an opportunity to splurge.

"You boys catch two chickens and butcher them," Barb said. "Do it in the weeds behind the garden where He won't find them." She used 'He' like a proper noun, refusing to use Herman's name. "Windy, if you tell, we'll never do this again," she finished.

I craved the extra meat ration, too, so I promised not to tattle.

Chris and Tim had a *Pogo Possum* comic book they'd memorized and we'd often play roles of favorite characters. Chris was Pogo, Tim was Turtle (Turkle), and I was Porcupine.

It was great sport. Chris got the .22 rifle from the garage and loaded it. We became big game hunters, Chris in the lead carrying the gun, followed by Tim, then me, bent low creeping around the chickenhouse corner.

He raised the gun, fired, and ran forward. "Dish one is dah trophy," Chris chimed, mimicking Pogo, holding a headless, flapping Leghorn by the neck. "Dah res has fled to Okefanokee."

Chris handed me the dead chicken and held the gun out to Tim. "You is mah gun-bearer, I has dah bullet. Follow close, Turkle. Porky, stay behind."

"I want to shoot the other one," Tim complained.

Through the barn, out the back door, we crept. Again, Chris loaded then raised the gun and fired. We rushed forward only to discover that he'd wounded the chicken and it was running blindly, stumbling up the side of the manure pile, blood spraying from her beakless face. We rushed to catch her, afraid that Herman would spot the stains.

"I has caught dah emeny," Tim proclaimed, holding the flapping bird by the neck. He whipped it around and snapped the chicken's neck.

Retrieving the empty .22 shell casings, we carried the birds to the garden, plucked them, and buried the evidence. Over dinner, we joked about the chicken's head spurting like Old Faithful.

"You mean there is blood on the manure pile?" Barb asked.

"Yes," Chris said.

"Windy, go unhook the dog—he'll clean it up."

I returned in time for a dessert of purple plums dished from a gallon can that Barb purchased with our AFDC and kept stashed upstairs. The money was supposed to be used to buy food and clothing and help with other necessities for the four children Barb brought to the farm with her. By 1959, I rarely saw any evidence of the money.

Butcher Day

Butchering was done in early winter, after Herman was confident of freezing weather. A cull cow, one that probably would not live through the winter, was selected. After slaughter she was quartered and hung in the granary. As I mentioned earlier, he would take the axe or Swede-saw and cut a piece for that day's supper. One might have a prime rib, a bony pot roast, or a grisly flank. By mid-winter, when the cow was gone, a hog was slaughtered and hung in the granary. Oftentimes, as the meat thawed in the kitchen sink, rodent gnaw marks and bird droppings had to be trimmed from the edges.

If an animal became ill or crippled, we ate it. One spring a cow went down after having her calf. She lay in the barn for a week and we milked her by rolling her onto her side. Herman tried to get her to her feet. When he couldn't get her to stand up, he lost his temper and shot her. We butchered her and ate the bruised, manure-tainted meat.

"Put mustard on it," he said.

During the 1950s and early '60s, I witnessed Herman commit various acts of brutality—beyond assaulting Barb. When I was about thirteen, home for a visit from the foster home I was living in at the time, I watched him destroy a first calf heifer. It was the first time she'd been locked in a stanchion and had a milking machine strapped on. She kicked when Herman washed her udder.

He expected that and stood back, talked soothingly, and reached forward with the warm washcloth. The young cow stood rigid as he buckled the surcingle around her middle. When he hung the milking machine from it and connected the pulsating teat cups, the cow twitched and kicked her hind feet forward, attempting to escape from the noisy machine pulling at her udder.

Her foot caught beneath the surcingle, and the old strap broke, dropping the milking machine to the concrete between her legs. She began bawling as she kicked hysterically, causing the other cows to bellow. She knocked the milking machine into the gutter behind her where it broke open.

Furious, Herman grabbed a pitchfork—a hay fork with three slender, sharp tines—and began stabbing her in the back legs. I watched in horror as the cow attempted to break free. Herman stabbed repeatedly, the tines going in several inches, blood dribbling to the milk-and manure-covered concrete.

I stepped forward and wrapped my hands around the fork handle, interrupting the attack. "Stop—you're killing her. Stop."

He looked at me with a blank stare and froze, the fork poised behind the screaming cow. He let me take it, and he walked into the manger. I could hear him talking low to the young cow as he stroked her quivering jaw. He went to the little medicine cabinet, dug out a jar of udder balm and rubbed it on the cow's injured legs.

Her udder shriveled and she lost weight over the summer. She went into autumn unbred and thin. Because she wasn't going to make it through the winter, we butchered her. I remember the puss pockets that we cut out where the tine wounds had gotten infected and healed over. We ate the scarred gristly meat.

"Put mustard on it," Herman said.

We got a free goat at the livestock sales barn—a curve-horned, bony, mean, stinky billy. We loved playing with him, trying to hold on and ride—especially at the top of the ridge overlooking Maple Lake. Our game was this: Get on the goat, aim him downhill, and hold onto the horns for a wild ride. The goat often fell halfway down, and the rider, legs wrapped around the billy, rolled as one with the goat to the bottom.

The sneaky critter used to run up behind and butt us. He was free to roam the yard, and Barb hated him. The garden was fenced and off limits, but one day somebody left the small gate open, and the goat found his way in. Herman spotted him, got the .22 rifle from the garage, walked to the garden and dropped him. That night we ate goat, and the next night. Within two days the gut-pile in the garden became a living maggot mass. We poked sticks at the slimy intestines, exposing maggots and black beetles hiding beneath the lungs.

By the third day, goat meat smelled the kitchen up when the refrigerator door was opened. After breakfast Herman took the meat outside, scrubbed it, put it in the roasting pan and said we'd finish it for dinner. It lasted for dinner, supper, and the remains were heated for dinner the next noon. The rancid tallow stuck to the roof of our mouths—the decaying taste and smell seeped through the yellow mustard. Nobody missed the billy.

Surprisingly, that experience came in handy. Ten years later while serving on the riverboat in Vietnam, our crew stole a sixty pound case of frozen meat while making a supply run. We had no refrigeration on the boat, and in the tropical heat, after three days, the steaks were slimy. I taught the rest of the crew how to rinse the meat in the Mekong River before grilling the slippery steaks over small clumps of C-4. We didn't have mustard so I told them, "Put Tabasco on it."

Grandmother Elsie Visits

On July 4, 1959, the new 49-star flag honoring Alaska led the parade in town. We clustered on the sidewalk and dashed out for candy tossed from passing floats. We couldn't know it then, but that summer's events set in motion the path some of us children would arbitrarily take. Chris bought a 1946 Chevrolet Club Coupe that he was allowed to drive to Bemidji on Friday and Saturday nights. One night he and his friends were caught siphoning gas. By the autumn of 1959, both Chris and Tim were on probation for petty juvenile activities.

Elsie continued to reach out. After so many years, why was Barb still angry with her mother? The summer of 1959, Barb was pregnant with her ninth child. Perhaps that had something to do with her silence. Or was she ashamed of what she had done with her life? As I've mentioned earlier, I discovered no letters from Barb to Elsie during the 1950s. That changed beginning in 1960, but I'm getting ahead of myself.

In the chickenhouse I discovered a letter from our teacher, Mrs. Cheney, to our grandmother.

Blackduck, Minnesota, July 31, 1959. My Dear Mrs. Philips; I received your letter Wednesday. In reply to your query, I'd have to say that Bemidji is the nearest place for accommodations that you require. Blackduck has a motel but it would be farther to drive than from Bemidji. There are countless motels and cabins around Bemidji and it wouldn't be necessary for you to be secretive about who you are or what your mission is, as no one there will know your connection with Mrs. Affield. I have seen none of them since June first and have heard nothing about them. I hope you get to see and know the children. Tim and Chris are big as men now. I had Wendell and Laurel last year and will have them again. They are both nice children to work with but I have to say Laurel is by far the better worker. I hope you are not disappointed in your trip. I should be happy to meet you if you happen to drive our way. Sincerely, Katherine Cheney.

Why did our grandmother want to visit Bemidji incognito the summer of 1959? I remember the constant friction between Barb and Elsie. We didn't know it at the time, but Barb was obsessed with leaving Herman and the farm, and I'm sure she begged Elsie to take us with her.

(August 1959) Lake Bemidji waterfront.
(Standing, left to right) Tim, Elsie, Barb, and Chris.
(On bench) Laurel, Bonny, Larry, Linda, Randy, and Wendell.

Shortly after the visit, we received the following letter. To the uninitiated, this letter sounds reasonable—the suggestions for improvements make sense. What can't be seen are the cow manure, flies, smell, and never-ending conflict.

All My Dears, Barbara, Herman, Chris, Timmy, Wendy, Lori, Randy, Bonny, Linda and Larry, Here we are at home again after that long interesting trip to see you all. I thank God that we were able to make the trip and that we found you all in good health and spirits and that we were able to have quite a lot of fun together. And that we were able to return home again safely with no more mishap then the car rolling backward on a steep hill and injuring my foot but by a miracle not breaking any bones!!! I begrudge any time it made me miss with you but I can only thank God that I was not laid up with a broken leg which would have been impossible. I still rub it with Analgesic Ball but the pain is almost gone now.

The time with you went all too fast. I wish we could have stayed longer, but now that dear grandpa is gone and grandma is a widow we can't do what we used to do and there are always so many things that must be attended to here, just to keep us going. So we are most thankful for the wonderful visit that we did have; it caught us up on all of the happenings that had been going on for a long time—4 years since we had seen you, longer for dear Aunt Polly, and almost as long since we had heard from you. Let's not ever let that happen again. You all promised that you would write -- almost all of you can write and, in fact, I had hoped a little bit that I would have heard from some of you by now. Did you know that this is "Write to grandma month"!! I know how hard it is to get down to writing. It always seems as though everything else has to come first, but it shouldn't. We should keep track of each other, we are all one big family.

Because of a habit you have, and I don't say it isn't a good one, the habit of all talking at once, it helps self-expression, but it has some disadvantages. Number one, it's difficult to put over the idea, such as when Barbara wanted to tell you what the mechanic said about her car, hardly anyone got it because everyone else wanted to talk. Also I wanted to tell you that on Monday, when you couldn't see me, I called up Mrs. Cheney's home. She was away judging the Blackduck Fair but her Granddaughter answered and asked us over to "Tea." She made a delicious cake like the delicious one Wendy made and very delicious coffee and we had a good time. After a while Mrs. Cheney came home and I was so glad to meet her. What a wonderful woman she is. She said you were all marvelous young people to teach, that it was most evident that your mother is the most educated woman in the District—that you've all absorbed quite a bit of it. It made me feel good because I was glad that all of her fine education hadn't gone for naught. She said that Herman was a fine father and that all the children show their great interest in him and fondness for him. She said that if it was too hard to find the time to write at home to me, that time could be found in school to write. I do think that was good of her.

Do write and tell me how the project is going forward this fall of improving your home. That is really the most important thing of all. Your home is your Castle and there are so many of your willing hands to make it beautiful. Think of it—twenty willing hands! Mother won't be able to do very much because she won't feel very good at all for at least a year, [Barb was pregnant] *but she has given all of you the greatest gift of all— that of being alive—and you could all do it for her, as a special gift for her. In that way you could see if it didn't help her to get well faster. Now what were all of these things that we talked about?*

First, fix the furnace so it runs all right. I believe all of these could be done without so very much expense—no more than you would put into the farm to make it run all right. Put the ventilator or radiator in so that the heat would go upstairs. I think the idea of a stairway with a railing would be attractive and let the heat go up, too. Bringing the porch into the living room is almost a must because you are twice as many as you were and therefore you need twice as much space. The porch is wasted space, now. Perhaps there would be room for the freezer in the basement. I wish you could have two more bathrooms built on the side with showers, so that when you come in from the barn and fields you could freshen up, and I wish one room could be your office, Herman. You really need it.

Then two nice "G. I." cans by the kitchen door to take care of the trash. A sweet little kitchen garden could be built near the door. It would be fun with a path with whitewashed stones lining the path and flowers blooming in it. Also a winding fence being put up will make a lovely place for the lovely young children to play, free of dirt from the cows and a pretty entrance off the main road would add a lot to your pride of ownership.

Don't put any more money into expensive furniture. As you know it isn't worthwhile until the children are grown. Plenty good enough furniture can be purchased quite inexpensively. I believe the little children could be trained not to tear down the curtains. You never tore down curtains when you were little, Barbara. You played nicely with all of your animals and games and took good care of everything.

Oh yes, Herman, ask Mother to give a little concert every few evenings— it is very soothing to tired nerves. I still have here a great deal of your valuable music which I meant to bring. I had quite a bit more in the car, which every time there was a disturbance I was thrown off track and didn't deliver to you. I did bring a great deal though, and I had hoped by now to hear from you how much you appreciated it. I hope you took good care of everything, saw that all of the clothes were hung up and the books put in bookcases. The fishing tackle is here. It doesn't seem like so much, but I know Grandpa paid over $12 for it. That was a fun fishing trip we had. Had I known that there was a fishing instructor around, I would have had him go, too, and he might've shown us how to do it, especially this year when even uncle Nubs writes that the fish aren't biting very well. I'm glad we got one good picture. I wondered why I had wool clothes and then remembered that after church, we picked flowers on the way home and then you all changed but Aunt Polly and I didn't have a chance to. What a shame that the other picture was a double exposure when you have so little opportunity to have pictures of you. Timmy, Windy and

Randy got in twice, amazingly it is very good of both Lori and Timmy.

We looked at farmhouses all the way home and all seem to be busy making repairs and enlargements. We went through Cherry Valley, and it has been completely ruined by one great highway going through and ruining all of the properties and its great beauty. We stayed overnight in Cooperstown and it, too, has been taken over by tourists. There is much more to talk about but this is already long and I must get it in the mail. It has taken me several different days to write it. Love, Grandmother

The reason Elsie mentioned placing "two nice 'G. I.' cans by the kitchen door" was because trash and garbage overflowed the can that was by the stove and then spread across the kitchen. Usually Herman was the one to say, "Enough is enough," and make us all clean the house. Elsie's idea about upgrading the landscaping on the farm wasn't practical because the cows free-ranged right up to the doorstep.

Goose Hunt

As I grew older, I started shooting ducks in flight. After the firing pin broke on our old shotgun, I filed a rusted spike down so it fit in the hole. It worked fine except I couldn't shoot at flying ducks because, with the barrel elevated, the improvised firing pin slid out when the hammer was cocked.

One Saturday in early November, I crept through the willows to the water's edge at Nebish Lake and spotted two Canadian geese feeding about thirty yards from shore. I raised the gun and fired. Beyond the smoke haze and lily pads, one goose lay flopping while the other fled. Wings beating water, feet racing across the surface, the survivor struggled to get air-borne. For me, it was a coup—neither Chris nor Tim had ever shot a goose.

I knew Herman would be very proud of me. Thanksgiving was near and he wouldn't have to buy a turkey. I stood in awe, first staring at the huge gray bird, then casting a wistful glance skyward at the escaping goose. To my astonishment, she circled and returned. In disbelief, I crouched down and reloaded the gun. The goose settled and swam up to the dead one, nosing inquisitively. I fired, and then laughed in satisfaction as the second goose lay kicking. I was on the lee side of the lake, but the wind was picking up, pushing the geese away from shore. The willow-covered bog floated on muck-bottomed water. We called that kind of lake bottom "loon shit."

Wind ruffled loose feathers and I made—in retrospect—a very foolish decision. I stripped naked and stepped nearer the edge. I sank and was up to my knees in ice-crusted water. The spongy layer slipped from beneath my feet and I dropped below the surface, into water clouded by silty muck. I kicked up, body numbed by the sudden plunge, and dog-paddled toward the geese, pushing lily pads away from my face as I glanced back at my muddy wake. I was shivering and winded by the time I reached the dead birds.

I side-stroked back, slender necks clutched in one hand, the other cupped and pulling me toward shore as I kicked my feet. I tossed the geese onto the swamp grass. When I tried to climb out, the bog disintegrated in my hands. Small pieces broke as I grabbed, feet thrashing. Kicking in terror, I imagined sinking through thirty-foot-deep muck. No one would find me. Numb hands gnawed at the bog's edge, feet churning until I worked my way inland to a willow root. Teeth clenched to control my shivering, I gently tested the root with stiff fingers. It held fast and I was able to climb out. Holding a supple willow, I stood, shaking as I crawled back into my clothes.

I don't remember the cold walk home, carrying my trophies. I don't recall that anyone noticed my wet hair when I proudly walked into the house. Herman said they were tame geese—belonged to Tom, our neighbor on the far side of the lake. I told him how the one had flown, circled the lake, and returned. Tom's geese couldn't fly. We dry-plucked the geese and baked them for Thanksgiving dinner, the fluffy feather evidence buried at the back of the garden in case Tom came looking. Years later I learned why the second goose had returned: Geese mate for life.

In November, the Clutter family was murdered in Kansas. It created conversation because it happened on an isolated farm. We talked about it at school. I asked Herman about it and he said the killers wouldn't come to Minnesota because it was too cold. Six years later, *In Cold Blood* was published. Truman Capote had created a new genre of literature—the non-fiction novel, when he reconstructed the crime and its aftermath.

Herman and Barb's rancor increased. Because Chris and Tim were in high school, they sometimes didn't come home to help with chores, and that angered Herman. In his opinion, if they ate and slept at the farm, they should do their share of work. The confrontations with Barb usually evolved to, "You bald bastard, when you're dead my sons will have this farm."

Looking back, there was really nothing in particular that stands out in my mind that triggered Barb that December of 1959. During one of our interviews a few years before she died, I asked her why she ran away in the dead of winter. She said she didn't feel right with the pregnancy and didn't trust the hospital in Bemidji. But I wonder, after a decade of hardship—financial, psychological, and physical—had she reached the point of those pioneer women a century earlier who had prairie madness?

Hillsboro, Texas, Saga

I found many documents relating to this next escapade—documents that provide at least three points of view. I think they best reveal the Affield family situation and Barb's downward spiral. I must jump ahead a few months for a moment to the court report given in mid-July1960. Here is the legalistic point of view from the Beltrami County welfare worker. The court document began, "Vera Graves, first duly sworn...."

were at time dressed in dirty clothes, or not adequately clothed. She described
her flight last winter when she picked up all the children in the family, the oldest
two who were on probation of the court and violated the court's probation rules,
left her husband and home and left for the west coast, that she was hemorrhaging
at the time she left the home under these circumstances, and ended up in the

Excerpt from a 1960 Beltrami County Juvenile Court Record

She described her[Barbara's] flight last winter when she picked up all the children in the family, the oldest two were on probation of the court and violated the court's probation rules, left her husband and home and left for the west coast, that she was hemorrhaging at the time she left the home under these circumstances, and ended up in the hospital at Sioux Falls, South Dakota, where she was operated on by Caesarean Section giving birth to the younger of the children here involved. During her hospitalization the younger children were cared for by the Lutheran Welfare, the two older children were placed in the Y.M.C.A.. That upon her release from the hospital, she spent a few days in a motel with the children where it was reported they were very rough on the equipment. Arrangements were made for her transportation to western Minnesota and for her to be picked up and returned to her home. Sometime before arriving at that location, she changed her mind and ended up in Hillsboro, Texas, where she was in a couple of run-down motel rooms and almost without funds, and the children were reported to be

destroying the motel. The old car they had had broken down and the
same was sold. Money was sent down for their return home.

I remember the December afternoon in 1959. We were in the middle of the final rehearsal for the Nebish School Christmas play. Wind rattled the eight-foot windowpanes as an Arctic Clipper moved into northern Minnesota. The boiler moaned, struggling to keep up with the thermostat. Worn bearings in the blower fan made a *peew-peew-peew* sound. I sat on the stage, cloaked in my mildew smelling royal scarlet robe.

"King Herod, straighten your crown," Mrs. Cheney, the big room teacher, said. "Show more anger when the messenger tells you that a King is born."

Perched on my piano bench throne, I straightened my crown and watched my teacher walk to the back of the room where Barb stood; Larry perched on her stomach, Linda and Bonny at her side. A few moments later, Mrs. Cheney came to the stage and told me to get Laurel and Randy and join our mother. We were going Christmas shopping in Bemidji. I walked out to the maroon 1950 Ford, surprised at the two bed-sheet-filled bundles of clothes covering the floor and back seat.

"Sit on it," Barb said simply. I climbed to the top of the pile and pulled Bonny and Linda in with me. Randy and Laurel got in the front seat, and Barb handed Larry to Laurel. Barb was so pregnant that she had the seat wedged back, tight against the bundle of clothes. She had trouble reaching the accelerator. Bonny and Linda chanted a little ditty, "Mommy go-ee fasty, Mommy go-ee slowy," because her speed ranged from twenty to forty.

As I worked on this story, a thought occurred to me: How was Barb able to wrestle those cow paunches of clothing out to the car? She must have done it when Herman was gone to Bemidji—he certainly wouldn't have helped. The bags were unwieldy and weighed at least fifty pounds each. She was nine months pregnant and hemorrhaging. There's a clinical term, "excited delirium" that may be the key to Barb's spurt of strength and determination. Or had Chris and Tim carried them out a day or two before, when Herman wasn't around?

I try to think what may have been going through Barb's mind as she drove out to the airport and left us in the small terminal. Did she realize, as the court report states, that she was already hemorrhaging? What must the ticket agent have thought—a nine-month pregnant woman dropping off five children, including a two-year-old, and then driving away? About an hour later she returned to the airport with Chris and Tim, having pulled them out of high school. As I write this, I wonder why she didn't go directly to the high school and have us wait in the car. Was that action another in a series of irrational decisions?

We all piled into the car and went west into the December twilight. Chris drove, Barb sat in the middle nursing Larry, and Tim sat on the passenger side. Randy, Laurel, Bonny, Linda, and I were wedged between the back doors on top of what we came to call the "cow paunches" of clothing. It was before seatbelts and I cringe, thinking about what would have happened in an accident.

A few years ago Chris told me that Barb paid him one hundred dollars and Tim, fifty to go along with her scheme. Tim said that Barb ordered them to obey her because they were on probation. The court report states that in taking Chris and Tim out of state, Barb had "violated the court's probation rules." If Tim remembered correctly, Barb knew she was breaking the law, but I believe by that time, she didn't care.

She knew Randy and I wouldn't go along willingly, so she told us that she had found an afternoon job for us stacking firewood in Shevlin, a small village west of Bemidji. Half an hour later I yelled at Chris, "Hey, you passed Shevlin."

Tim cocked his head around and looked at me. "Don't be stupid."

Looking back almost sixty years, I think Barb must have shared her plans with them, and they whole-heartedly joined her scheme because of the open hostility between Herman and Chris and Tim.

In studying a 1959 Texaco Road Map, I realized that our trip was before the four-lane interstate system was completed. Was Barb delusional? I imagine she plotted a route from the maps I found tucked in our Encyclopedia Britannica. We probably drove west on US 2 to Highway 75, then south. I wonder what passed through her mind when she saw the highway sign directing traffic toward Fergus Falls. (Herman often threatened to have her committed to Fergus Falls State Hospital.) At Ortonville we probably crossed the Bois de Sioux River into South Dakota and jumped onto Highway 77. Or we may have taken US Highway 2 west into North Dakota, Barb reasoning that she needed to escape across the state line as quickly as possible.

In 1959, after dusk, especially in winter, there were very few vehicles on the highway. As I reflect on the trip, studying the Texaco map, I remember the dark miles between towns and wonder what would have happened if, during the night, we'd hit the ditch or the old car had just died. Fourteen years later, during the OPEC oil embargo of the 1970s, Chris and I, while driving through the night from Chicago to the farm, rescued a car load of young people at about 2:00 A.M. We were north of St. Cloud, Minnesota, when we spotted their stalled car. We stopped to investigate and discovered several young people huddled together, hypothermia beginning to set in. We piled them into Chris's little Maverick and brought them to their home town, about twenty miles up the highway. That December night in 1959, Barb and all of us kids were at just such a risk.

At some point we all dozed off in the back seat, huddled together for warmth. We reached Sioux Falls, South Dakota, as the sun rose over the snow-swept horizon. The sweet sticky smell of Barb's hemorrhaging blood was trapped by the frost-covered windows of the car. The only clearings on the windshield were the two holes above the dashboard where the defrost heater blew. At the hospital emergency entrance, Barb was placed in a wheel chair, admitted, and by 6:00 that evening, our youngest brother, ten-and-half-pound Daniel Paul, was born. Barb was in the hospital for a week.

Chris and Tim argued about who was in charge at the motel we stayed in. On the second morning, four-year-old Linda locked herself in the bathroom and Chris boosted me up to the outside bathroom window to unlock the door. Later that same morning I was rummaging in the car, searching for coins in the crack of the frozen, blood-stained front seat. In the glove compartment I discovered a sock with something in it. I slipped my hand in and pulled out another wadded sock. Inside of it I discovered twelve crisp hundred dollar bills and gave them to Chris. Barb had recently received an inheritance from a relative in Seattle. Years later, while discussing the cash stash, Chris recalled that one time he was upstairs rummaging through piles and found an old camera. When he opened it he found a wad of cash.

The motel management must have called the police or family social services. Chris and Tim went to the YMCA; the rest of us were sent to a foster home with an old lady. Each day the lady gave me sixty-five cents and I walked six blocks to a small grocery store for powdered milk. Each night the old lady put Larry to bed screaming because he wanted mommy and his milk. After the old lady went to bed, I'd sneak a bottle up to Larry.

After Barb's discharge, we were reunited at a motel where she recuperated. A few days before Christmas, church groups brought us food and presents. The motel was near new highway construction, and Randy and I broke down cardboard boxes and used them as sleds to fly down the steep ice-covered slopes. Christmas morning brought more gifts and food boxes.

As children, we were oblivious to the drama playing out. The following documents illuminate the situation. The first is a letter from Herman to Barb's mother, Elsie.

Dec 22, 1959, Puposky, Minn.

Dear Mother, Barbara left and took the kids out of school. Mrs. Cheney will probably never get over that. Besides it must have been very hard on Windy, Randy, and Laurel they were studying hard on the pieces

(Christmas play) also they had the exchange presents. Now for the hard part, believe me I'm almost going nuts here. She got as far as Sioux Falls, So. Dakota when she had to go to the hospital and the welfare took the kids. I was ready to go and bring them home but they will not give them up until they have done a lot of investigating. It seems Barb went in and told them I would shoot her if she ever came back. So far they have not found anyone that will agree with her lie. I have a deep affection for my family and fight for them I will, but absolutely no threats or killings, that's not in me. I may have to sell everything to pay all those bills. Understand its costing $30.00 a day to keep the kids, alone. I was in Bemidji checking up and they told me Barb had a very bad hemorage. I would've rather had her in Bemidji Hospital where I could keep an eye on things. I will keep you posted on futher developments if I don't crack up first, although I have a couple of neighbors that come every day for a while. Since the welfare stepped in, I think that's the end of the trip. Have not learned a thing about the baby yet. Affectionatlly, Herman

We must have stayed at the motel in Sioux Falls until about December 28. Pastor Daniels, the minister who had baptized and confirmed us, drove down and visited. Barb agreed to come home. Again, Herman shared his angst with Elsie:

Puposky, Minn., Jan, 4, 1960.

Dear Mother, The Rev. Daniels was just here and his report is bad - very bad. Matter of fact it's so bad that I'm afraid for the kids' sake what will happen to them and I'm at a loss as to what to do. First, Chris and Tim are out of hand. Barb cannot handle them The Minister seemed to think they would take off, steal a car and land in jail. Barb still insists she is going to Seattle, and if they forced her to come back she would put in for a divorce. The Rev told her she would not gain anything by that. The welfare would step in and take all the kids and put them in homes, one here and another there and she give him a big horse laugh. He said he could not handle her and wondered how I did, and I told him I have not always been too fortunate either-- that if she got a brainstorm in her head, all hell and damnation could not stop her. He said I see what you mean. He said she had another boy and a big one -- weighed 10 lb 10 oz and she did almost die. No wonder the hospital sent word to get me at her bedside, but the welfare did not tell me that. Oh Boy, Oh Boy, what a headache. No wonder men get gray, bald, and die ahead of time-- these women. If this one quits me there will never be another. One is enough for me, and if I lose my family I'll sell everything I got as there will be nothing to look forward to, nothing to work for. In plain English I'll just give up, quit. Your true son (we hope) Herman P.S. Will keep you posted.

I never heard Barb laugh out loud, yet she "gave the [minister] a big horse laugh." Did she become hysterical when he told her she must return to the farm? The day after the minister visited, we left the motel and drove east into Iowa, into a raging storm on drifted, ice-covered roads. We drove through the day and into the night. Chris said we slipped away from Sioux Falls without paying the motel bill.

What triggered Barb to leave the farm? In the past, she had arranged for a neighbor lady to stay with us while she was in the hospital giving birth. Was that lady no longer available, and Barb didn't want her daughters alone with Herman? Or was there a deeper, more sinister reason?

I mentioned before how Barb had attempted suicide in the past, and her mother lived in terror of that threat. I discovered this yellowed newspaper clipping in Elsie's "Mental Health Journal" about a suicide where a mother drowned her three children, then killed herself. The tragedy took place in June, 1958. The article was titled "The Bad Seed" after a 1956 movie about a mother who realizes that her daughter, a young girl, had committed murder.

Documents I discovered in the "Mental Health Journal" reveal that Elsie carried the fear for many years that Barb would kill us all and then herself. Was driving into a raging storm with nine children, including a two-week-old infant, in subzero temperatures on remote roads in the dark of night in an unsafe vehicle, Barb's solution to ridding the world of her bad seeds?

In reconstructing our travels, I wonder if Barb had a plan beyond escaping the farm. Upon leaving Sioux Falls, why had she turned east, into Iowa? Had she called her mother, in New York, from our hotel in Iowa? Had Elsie advised Barb not to come—that she didn't have room in her two bedroom apartment for nine children? What drew Barb south, toward Texas? Remember Claud B. Willard, Jr., the man who lived in Winnsboro, Texas? Did thoughts of him pull Barb south? After more than a decade and five additional children, did she attempt to connect with him?

The Ford's clutch went out in southern Iowa, and we stayed one night in an old hotel while the car was repaired. The following day just as the sun set, the auto repair shop finished, and we left town on the ice-covered highway. We drove through the night—drove beyond the ice. Chris recalls that by dawn he was in southern Kansas, cruising along at seventy miles per hour when smoke suddenly filled the car and began billowing from under the hood. Later we learned that it had thrown two pistons. In a small town in Kansas we traded for a 1950 Pontiac with fifty dollars to boot. I remember the Pontiac as a wonderful car with a loud radio and a big back seat.

The closer we got to the Texas border, the louder we sang Marty Robbins' "El Paso." The song had been released in October, 1959 and by early January had reached number one on the charts. The ballad pulled us south. It became our theme song and we belted it out. By the time we reached mid-Texas we drove with all the windows down, amazed that there was no snow and the temperature was above freezing. Eventually we reached Laredo and perpetual summer.

Did Barb plan to flee the United States but got skittish when she saw the border guards? We settled for lunch in a Mexican restaurant. I'd read about spicy Mexican food but had never tasted it. I ordered a bowl of chili and splashed a liberal dose of habanero sauce into it. Mild yellow mustard was the only condiment I was familiar with. The chili burned, but I was so hungry I forced it down. We turned north and spent a day in San Antonio.

First we visited the Alamo. On the farm we had all read about the famous fort and the gallant defenders. The cannonball-pocked doors confirmed what we had read, and to visit the shrine was awesome. Through the fog of almost sixty years, I recall that I was drawn to the cot that Jim Bowie had laid on in a cool dark corner of the fort and the display of relics supporting the Davy Crockett legend. Later, we visited a pioneer museum and an antique auto display.

We also toured a huge alligator garden—the first live alligators we had ever seen. Chris threw a Coke bottle at a huge monster sunning near the bridged walkway we were on. The bottle smacked the old bull in the snout and he bellowed at us. We were thrown out of the Alligator Park.

I don't remember the day we arrived in Hillsboro, Texas. We settled into a motel adjacent to a truck stop. There was no rational reason to stop there except that Barb was running out of money. She registered us in school. It was a very old school with plain wood floors and dim hallways. I don't recall if it was integrated—the concept was not part of my worldview.

I started out on the wrong track my first day. We had a history test, a blank U.S. map, and we were required to fill in state names and their capitols. We had just learned them in Nebish, and I got 100% on the test. The teacher, an older lady, harangued her class about this new-comer Yankee who was smarter than they were.

We must have lived near the city dump, because that was our playground. Some black kids taught us a new game. We stood about fifty feet apart and our opponent whipped a coffee can lid at us. We blocked the razor-edged metal frisbees with a four-foot board used as a bat. And like our game Stab, if you moved your feet, you lost a point.

On the farm we rarely had fresh fruit except what we salvaged from the dumpsters behind the grocery stores. Here we picked oranges and grapefruit off the ground, fresh from the trees, and gorged until we got the squirts. I knew we were running low on money. Chris, Tim, and I picked pecans and sold them to a local buyer. Barb had a hot plate set on a nightstand in the motel room. The maid who cleaned our room gave us a couple of stewing rabbits. Bonny and Linda were jumping on the bed, and Bonny fell, hit the pan handle on the simmering rabbit, and splashed it on her leg, causing third degree burns. I don't think she went to the doctor.

My shoes were falling apart—I had to lift one foot high each step because the sole was ripped loose from the front and it would double under. I tied string around it but the sidewalk chafed the string and it didn't last long. I tried to steal a new pair, but the salesman wouldn't let me out of his sight. I finally begged three dollars from Barb to buy a new pair. I purchased the cheapest tennis shoes I could find and spent the last dollar on hotdogs. The orange food coloring and fat ran down my arms and dripped off my elbows as I wolfed four down.

On January 7, 1960, Barb sent this telegram to her mother:

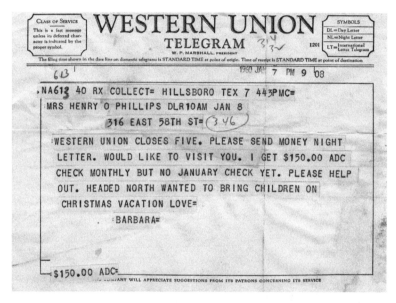

Hunger is the strongest memory I carry from Hillsboro. Randy and I begged food from the back door of the restaurant across the parking lot from our room. In return, we carried the cook's trash out each day. As on the farm, we created games to entertain ourselves. One day Randy and I were throwing rocks at each other in the parking lot. One of us dodged, and a rock hit the windshield of a new pickup truck just as the owner approached.

"You little bastards, I'm gonna whip the shit out of you," he shouted in his Texas twang. We took off running toward the nearest refuge: the back door of the restaurant. I yanked the screen door open, and we dashed in past the cook as she tended the hot griddle, the angry driver in pursuit.

The cook, a very large black lady, whirled on the man and waved a butcher knife. You can imagine her message. "You touch these boys, I'll cut your throat." I remember that the man cursed and huffed and stomped out and called the police. That was not the first time we appeared on the local law enforcement radar.

Chris and Tim had gone fishing and decided they needed a pitchfork, apparently to spear fish. Chris snuck into a barn to borrow one, discovered a horse, and clipped its tail off. By the end of two weeks we had worn out our welcome in Hillsboro, and we were broke. Barb sold the Pontiac for thirty dollars. Herman summed up our predicament in this letter to Elsie:

January 15, 1960. Puposky, Minn.

Dear Mother, I got a long distance call from the Hillsboro Police, and they told me to come and get my family or send money for bus fare and he would see that they got on. So I had to go to Bemidji and borrow that much money-- almost $200-- and wired it to the police not Barbara. I also told them to buy the fares and have the ticket agent stamp on them no refunds, no transfers, non-negotiable. I got the call Tuesday the 12th and the 14th went to Bemidji and done a little checking how long it would take them. Then went to the telephone office and put in another call to the Hillsboro Police, and he said she won't go. She sold her car for $30 junk price so she can live a couple more days. She told the police she was waiting for her welfare check -- it is not $150 as she told you, it is $134. I told the police there that her check would not come as they stopped that when she slipped through their fingers at Sioux Falls. They stopped that check, only she does not know it. How much longer she can hold out is anybody's guess. Now that she has sold her car, she cannot skip out too easy as bus fares cost money which I do not think she has too much of. She got the check from the Calvin Philips estate, there's a letter here that says so. She may have told you it was only a little bit, but I'll bet it was more than she says. If it was divided even, Polly should have been in on *it. But you know Barb spends money like water goes down a rat hole. That's about all I know. Have been busy moving the kitchen back to the other end of the house. I never liked it where Barb wanted it. You have to walk through the whole house and clean the whole house where as this way there will not be as much cleaning. Always me, Herman*

The Greyhound bus ticket agent decided that I should be charged the adult fare rather than child, so we lost the little food money available for the trip. Everyone—including Barb—blamed me. In Kansas City we had a layover, and Travelers' Aid bought us a meal. Afterward we were walking through the terminal, and I spotted a whole cigarette on the floor. I snatched it up and showed it to Chris. He demanded I give it to him, I refused, and he hit me on the side of the head, against my ear. I fell down, he took the cigarette, and my ear rang for two weeks.

We returned to Bemidji early in the morning and sat in the Markham Hotel/bus station waiting for Herman. Midmorning, Randy and I decided to hitchhike out to the farm. In retrospect, I am shocked that a parent would allow two children—twelve and nine—to go out into frigid January temperatures. I was so cold, walking north on Irvine Avenue in my two dollar tennis shoes. Fortunately, a neighbor stopped and gave us a ride to the farm. A few hours later Herman arrived home with the rest of the family and sent this letter to Elsie a few days later:

Puposky, Minn. Jan 26, 1960.

Dear Mother, They are all home but what a picnic I'm having. I'm catching Heck because I sent the money to the police instead of her, also the cop catches it because he sewed up the tickets and gives the bus drivers orders not to let her get her hands on them. It was not until the driver coming into Minneapolis turned soft and let her have the tickets. That was as far as she intended to go only she made a mistake of calling a

former minister from here, and the boys tipped him off, so he bought them
all dinner and said, since I bought your meal can I see your ticket, so she
handed them over and 10 minutes before the bus was due, he loaded them
in his car and put them in the Bemidji bus. She is a long way from being
herself, claims she will leave again Easter. At least the kids are all glad
to get home. Wendell and Randy hitch-hiked home. She told you that she
only got a little bit from the Calvin Philips estate, but the boys said the
check was $2200. But the boys said that Polly was to get half of that, also
the $1100 was to be divided between the kids but it's gone now. I estimate
she went through almost $1,000 and I bet I do not miss it far. This is the
second night I worked on this letter. Barb is doing her best to get it so I'll
either have to finish it in the barn or mail it as it is. Perhaps I can get the
boys to keep you informed. Randy likes to write letters. As Ever, Herman

Apparently Elsie replied to Herman's letters. He wrote this next
one on Randy's birthday about a second inheritance Barb was about to
receive. Herman made an interesting observation when he wrote about
the hot "Philips blood." Elsie must have told Herman about mental
instability that was passed forward from the Philips side of the family.

Jan 30, 1960. Dear Mother,

As far as I know there is not much we can do if they sent Barb that check.
But this I do know-- that I went into the Welfare Office and told them that
she received or was about to receive a sizable amount of money, so they
stopped her check again. The way they look at it, if she received money
from other sources, then she does not need the aid. It has been reported to
me that she consulted a couple of lawyers regarding divorce proceedings,
and they turned her down cold. She was told that she would lose all the
kids, but as you say that the Philips blood does the opposite. If she does
not wise up she may find herself working for a living as her Dad is not
going to come out of his grave to throw thousands of dollars at her. Windy

and Randy were really proud of the letters you sent them. Barb is having a fit because I am writing to you. Best Regards, Herman

Letter excerpt to my grandmother from Holt Law Office, Las Cruces, New Mexico, regarding Barb's 1947 divorce from John Curry:

January 20, 1947: [I received] Your letter from the 15th concerning your daughter's pending divorce suit. Under date of November 3, 1946, your daughter wrote us the following, to wit: "I have decided I don't want the divorce. Please hold it off. I think I refuse the divorce. I've written to my husband to tell him that since he has to send half his money to us anyway, he might as well come back here and live with his family."

Mrs. Philips, your last letter does not indicate that you have been or are in contact with your daughter. The failure of your daughter to answer our letter of the 9th, and the contents of your letter of the 15th, cause us to fear that your daughter's mental and/or physical condition may have become aggravated to such an extent as to preclude her answering our inquires....If her mental condition is such as to render her incompetent to give lucid testimony, we should know it at once in order that the situation is made known to the court. ...We have filed a motion for an Order requiring your daughter's husband to pay...such an amount in alimony, pending final hearing, and an additional amount toward support of the children.

1960
Barb and Elsie

I don't think it's possible to know the depth of Barb's despair. In late January 1960 she sent this note to Elsie.

Dear Mother and Polly, We hope you like all those nice letters from all my lovely children. And in return, how nice it would be if you found us a nice place to rent either out on Long Island or upstate New York. I'm sure you could do this for us, with just a little effort on your part. Perhaps we can come back East when school is out for the summer. Let's keep this confidential—shall we? Write to me personally—registered mail— thank you for the $30 you sent. I can repay it starting next month in $5 payments. Love, Barbara

Over the next several months, Barb sent Elsie six letters. I include them in their entirety because they give a glimpse into Barb's mind. In this first letter, Barb wrote, "Please let us not be jealous because of Grandfather." What was she alluding to? Documents from the 1920s and 1930s reveal Barb's affection for her father and resentment toward her mother. Or was Barb referring to Calvin Philips, her paternal grandfather who had never liked Elsie and left her out of his will?

Dear Mother,   *February 12, 1960*

I hope that by this time you have received my letter and that a registered letter from you is on the way. I must tell you first off—to make you feel better—that I never sold any of my dear Father's clothes—nor had any such an idea of such a thing. There aren't any second hand stores in Bemidji that buy clothing anyway. I've been to rummage sales where everything goes for a nickel an article so his lie (Herman had written to Elsie.) *is utterly fantastic. Now you see why we left. It is a good thing he made you sick with his lies because he goes about making me utterly sick 24 hrs per day. I have a tough row to hoe—I wish you would make it a little easier for me.*

He just sits in the house all day long, won't do anything—not even put up a clothesline so I can hang blankets and wash, outside in the sun. I know I had an impossible situation to face, so just before we left I gave up and sold the furnace. They came in a large truck and took out all the pipes, vents, etc. It was sad, but I wasn't going to leave it here to rust. He hasn't brought up one stick of wood since we got back; just sits and spits tobacco in the rusty old stove and seldom throws in a stick of wood. The rest of us freeze and he occupies the place, and the poor boys freeze upstairs with no heat at all and 20 degrees below zero weather. It's just horrible.

The minute you sent that letter saying you received word I had a considerable sum of money, he ran down to the agency and showed it to them. Now I don't know what we're going to do, cows don't give milk in the winter. Therefore we have no income whatsoever. I have always bought all the groceries in the wintertime. I don't know what you were thinking of writing that I had a considerable sum. Now that you know the truth—that sum should be put into a trust fund for the boys' college education—you better send that registered letter saying that it was a trust fund for the boys. Because if I do receive a sum of money, it seems the only thing to do would be to send it back immediately to be put in a trust fund for the boys' college education. Too bad your rich baron friends across the way don't know of a place where we could live. Please hurry that letter if you haven't already.

Well, I must sign off now—I'm very tired—tho the way you talk about me behind my back you'd think I was an automaton made of steel. Please don't write any more letters behind my back to Mrs. Graves or Herman, my husband. Please let us turn over a new leaf—you write to me and I'll write to you and no more outsiders involved. Please let us not be jealous because of Grandfather. Love, Barbara

P.S. I did receive a sum, you can rest assured and sleep at night—that I'll send it back without signing it and have it put in a trust fund in Seattle. If I kept it here it would be outrageous to use such an unusual gift for the children's college education. Something is going to have to be done as the situation is just unbearable here. Also I am thinking of the older boys, too. Chris is doing very poorly in school. We owe it to the dear boy to try to help him to graduate. His report card is terrible: 2 Failures, 2 Incompletes, worse than failure. It was my idea to leave here and put him back in the 10th grade. If he could just have a little encouragement to bring his homework home. (I forgot to tell you the sewer is completely frozen up—no bathroom—no furnace—can't use the bathroom at all.) It's pretty hard with so many children not to have use of the bathtub and other facilities. Everything that I paid money to improve here is gone out the window. While we were gone he moved the sink and stove into my living room so the picture window was for naught. He nailed up the service door to my former kitchen—which I paid a man a week's labor to put in that door. He's jealous because he never went beyond the 8th grade, so Chris and Tim get no encouragement about their school work. He'd be glad if Chris quit—even the principal told him [Chris] in his office that with his bad marks he might as well quit. That is one of the main reasons I wanted to leave—to seriously help Chris finish high school—he can if he gets some encouragement at home. But with a step-dad that wants him to quit, he hasn't got a chance.

Thanks for the music—the children don't have much time for music *lessons here. He never encourages anything but farm work. I repeat, the situation is unbearable or we wouldn't have left in the first place. I realize that with such a little baby and so many little ones, we must have a safe place to go—far away from highways—don't you have any friends that know of a place like this? A small farm would be the best because the boys are old enough to take care of a little livestock, etc.—which is very dear to their heart. I know it would have been best to stay with John Curry—but I've learned my lesson with these second marriages—he never has shown Chris and Tim any loving kindness, nor has this been a real home where they could do as they pleased—mostly they're ordered out . Poor things, freezing upstairs—to think we had to come back from warm Texas to this horrid freezing place. I wish we had gone to New York instead of Texas. I played a hunch we could get a good place. But we were too near Clifford Curry, John's father. I'm positive he helped to hurry us back—of course, too, my husband is liable to support us by law. I asked Mrs. Graves if she would send my money to your address—then you could give me the check wherever we lived. This sounds more legal to them because you are legally next of kin—that's why we should have gone to your place from Sioux Falls. I'm freezing cold but sincerely hope you find us a good safe place—Love, Barbara*

I could pay up to $50 per month rent I should think.

There are inconsistencies in the letter that question Barb's grasp on reality. Upon our arrival in Texas, did she contact the Curry family in Las Cruces, New Mexico? Otherwise how would they possibly have known we were there? Second, Mrs. Graves was the caseworker for Beltrami County Family Services; if Barb left the county, she would no longer be a resident—no longer eligible for the money.

About the furnace Barb sold: My youngest brother Danny recently told me that after Herman died in 1970, Barb got on a government fuel assistance program, installed an oil furnace, and from then on, she heated the upstairs.

Barb's rage toward Herman had no bounds. A few years ago Chris told me that not long after we returned to the farm, he and Herman had an argument in the house while Barb stood listening. Herman stomped out, slammed the door behind him, and Chris said, "I could kill that bastard."

"How would you do it?" Barb asked. Chris believes to this day that Barb was serious.

I remember returning to school, embarrassed, trying to explain why we had disappeared for a month. That late winter and spring of 1960 our family spun out of control as Barb withdrew even more from day to day activities and Chris and Herman were in open conflict.

I think we all coped differently when it came to schoolwork. With Barb and Herman constantly arguing and the distraction of four little kids racing around the table, it was difficult to concentrate on studying. I sat at the kitchen table, struggling with long division and trying to decipher the mysteries of prepositions, verbs, and subjects.

Chris recalls Laurel locking herself in her room to do her homework, but that must have been only in the autumn and spring, because in the dead of winter it was always below freezing upstairs. Laurel persevered. She is the only one of my siblings to earn her college degree. Chris and I both gave up on school at the same age—beginning of eleventh grade. But Chris struggled along and eventually graduated in a foster home after he got out of reform school. I dropped out and enlisted in the Navy.

Without a job, Chris and his friends resorted to petty theft and stealing gas to keep their old cars running. Several of them had already done time in reform school and were on probation. In May 1960, Chris was sentenced to Red Wing Reform School. He told me recently that it was during that time he discovered alcohol—Italian Swiss Colony Muscatel wine. "I drank a whole bottle and felt a new sense of empowerment," he told me. "Sixty years later I'm battling alcoholism." He rambled on about his mentor at AA. I wonder if that's why his grades plummeted the spring of 1960.

The next letter Barb wrote:

February 23, 1960. Dear Mother, I am very sorry you are sick with the flu, too bad you can hardly hold a fountain pen, but I understand. It is well that you had dear Polly to take care of you. Please wish her a Happy Birthday for the 28th. I'm just sick with worry over Chris and Tim—he [Herman] treats them so bad they don't want to come home. They chase around with hoodlums and are under the supervision of the juvenile court. You saw him hit Timmy for nothing once when you were here—he told Chris not to come home without his FFA jacket which poor Chris left in someone's car. I am not treated any better. His sister said, "Pa had to leave. Pa just couldn't get along with him at all." He's shell-shocked. When can you find us a place to live? I know it's not easy, but they would send my check if they knew we were well situated. When we went to Texas, they knew we were not well situated. I should have gone to my next of kin right away. That's what the District Attorney in Texas said, "You all hurry on to your mother's and get the children in school." Traveling is expensive, I have so much baggage. I really would like to get settled and not go traveling all over. I know why the Seattle relatives don't answer. They're afraid if I moved out there, they would be investigated.

Please send me a registered letter—otherwise I won't get it—saying that you have a nice safe place for us to come to. Write me two letters in one envelope—one nice chatty letter saying you have a place for us to come to and describing how much it is a month etc. This one I will show the social worker so she O.K.s our coming. The other one you can tell me anything you have to say. Perhaps I could invest my inheritance in something so I could have a steady little income—what do you know about this? This must all be confidential in a registered letter as I will keep denying I have ever gotten an inheritance. I figure this way—I never got any alimony from Chris, Tim, Windy, Laurey so why should I be cut off? Too bad Richard [Barb's uncle who lived in Seattle] can't get us a small farm in Washington or Oregon. I feel that out west things are less crowded. Can't you ask him to invest my inheritance in a small farm out there? Chris and Tim really enjoy cutting timber—that's what they do all weekend—every weekend—there's a reasonably good amount of money to be made this way, and we could be clearing land at the same time. Why can't Richard find us an investment—a nice farm? No cars for me this time. I want to travel to the place where we are going to settle down.

A good way to squander money is in cars—mine's going to be spent on a farm this time—just why won't Richard or John help us to this extent?

Chris and Tim and myself—we are treated just awfully badly here—no groceries at all except what I buy. I buy all the clothes for all the children and myself—it's not fair. I'd like to sue him for non-support, but instead I'm going to try to support the children if I had a farm—with Chris and Tim's help.

Hope you haven't been writing any letters behind my back as you haven't written any to me—don't forget the two letters—registered. You're the only close relative next-of-kin—I know you will feel a responsibility about this soon now—I hope. The boys are treated worse every day—no wood in that measly wood stove -- we have to get it ourselves. Hope you are well enough to find us a country place where 9 children can't disturb the neighbors. I suppose it is not easy. Then write Richard to find us a place out there. Love always, Barbara (answer by registered mail)

As I transcribed these letters, I tried to imagine how tormented Barb must have been. Why did she think moving to Seattle would trigger an investigation on her relatives? With Chris and Tim acting out, I wonder if Barb remembered her teenage years and how she rebelled against her parents. In the letters, she talked about suing Herman for non-support, but in the dead of winter there really was no income because most of the cows were dried up.

Barb's scheming to keep a second inheritance confidential was a glimpse of her lifelong financial deception. Barb's father wrote about her dishonesty in the 1940s. After Barb died in 2010, after I received a

$128,000 bill from Beltrami County Human Services, I discovered that she had defrauded Beltrami County and the VA for twenty years.

In this next letter, Barb's writing is small and tight—very unlike her usual large, flowing prose. Here is the beginning of the letter.

Full transcription follows.

March 15, 1960

Dear Mother, How are you and Polly? Fine I hope. I have been looking for a little loving kindness from you toward me and my new baby—but apparently you don't love your daughter any more at all—because all you do is write letters behind her back to her husband, social worker, etc. Now you have put me in the worst spot I have ever been in—you have actually turned your own daughter in to the Welfare so that her monthly check for food and clothing shall be cut off. There is only one thing you can do now, and that is to write me a registered (circled) letter so that only me and my social worker will see it, since my own mother is the one that turned me in. Haven't you any love for your daughter? The only thing that will save me now is for you to write me a registered (circled) letter saying that you heard (underlined) I was going to inherit a considerable sum of money but that now you understand it is being sent to you—that's all you have to say. I will show it to my social worker, and then I will continue to receive my check out of which I buy the family groceries $25 per month, (circled) *for school lunches alone—school supplies, etc. clothing, boots, rubbers, winter clothing, bedding, etc. I have promised everyone including you not to take off again unless I have some specific safe place to take the children—such as a farm for the summer near you—by Shipways or wherever you go in the summer.*

Please have enough love, religion and consideration for me and the new baby so that you won't knife me in the back ever again. If you could just write me a loving letter and say that you made a big mistake and there will be no money distributed to the grandchildren but it will go directly to you—or whatever you consider diplomatic. I need a little advice from my dear mother right now—other daughters seem to depend on their mothers for everything and anything. Couldn't I ask this one wee favor of you? Write me a friendly, loving, kind, congratulatory letter about what a wonderful mother I am, what a fine job I am doing raising nine children and maintaining a lovely, charming, hospitable home. Then, at the last you can say that you made a big mistake about my inheriting any money and that it went directly to the closest relatives. If you can and will send me a registered (circled) letter like this—I will be more than delighted to mail you the check which you imagine I will get. Otherwise I shall be forced to mail it back to Uncle Richard to keep in a trust fund for Chris and Tim's college education, or perhaps I might even ask Aunt Ruth and Uncle Nubs what to do—they always managed Grammie's affairs.

Anyway, thanks a million (dollars) for not saying how much was involved. I can't thank you enough for this—you at least went this far not to knife your daughter in the back—oh please (underlined) don't knife me in the back—oh please please (twice underlined) don't knife me in the back—"United we stand, divided we fall." I think a mother and daughter should stick together, don't you? Please send me a registered letter that I may show her—since that was the whole source of the damage. I promise not to leave again. We have no other income now. I buy all the groceries, etc. Love, hugs and kisses for this gift to my new baby, Barbara

In the midst of the family turmoil, one event does stand out in my mind from the spring of 1960—an event that, as I look back, had a major impact on my future. All eighth grade students spent an orientation day at Bemidji High School. One of our tasks was to fill out class electives for the ninth grade. I selected two— Debate and Drama. The school counselor glanced at my choices, crossed them out, and said, "You're a farm kid. You take Shop and FFA."

I've never been mechanically inclined—still am not. From the very beginning I hated those high school shop classes. I hope today that counselors are less biased toward students' backgrounds.

Barb's next letter to her mother:

April 10, 1960. Mother dear, Happy, happy Easter to you and dear Polly. How have you been this winter? It is too bad that our Easter letters will cross. Did you like the picture that I sent you of Randy? You didn't mention in Bobbie's card. [Barb had named the new baby Daniel, the same name as Polly's ex-husband. Elsie refused to call him that and referred to Danny as "Bobbie".] *Times are very, very difficult here. As usual there is no money; and he seems to want to starve the children on purpose. Today we went to town and he bought $12 worth of feed for the livestock and a sack of cornmeal for the family's Easter dinner, plus some yeast for me to make bread.*

It does not seem fair that nine such lovely children should suffer so. I know it is just too much to expect you to help out—but something should really be done, about the one who causes this suffering. And here the poor mother wants to buy eggs and Easter coloring for her children and she is penniless. It is truly a sad state of affairs.

Before I forget—I think it would be best if from now on you addressed all correspondence directly to me, as long as this is such a queer household. Even the dollar you sent the baby today was locked away and he didn't get to spend it. Then too,--Windy and Randy each have over $100 in the bank from the frequent sale of livestock; and they're *not allowed to contribute to the family living expenses. Nor did Randy buy any pants with the money you sent him. If you had sent it to me, his $5, I would have seen that he got a shirt and sweater to show for it. Also I could have bought Windy socks and handkerchiefs as a gift from you. This way there is nothing to show for your sending them money. Well—it is a sad state of affairs and I do hope you have some pity in your heart for your daughter.*

Do you think you could send me the addresses of all the Philips so that I could send them pictures of the children? Also please send Uncle Nick's address and the rest of your brothers and sisters if you think this is a nice idea. Much Easter Love, Barbara

P.S. Too bad I have no phone to talk to you. You will be pleased to know that Laurel sat down this evening to write you a letter. She fibbed and said I didn't send you her letter. Only one about Judge Reed and Mrs. Hanson (another social worker)

I smiled as I transcribed this letter because by 1959 Herman was protecting Randy's and my money. We each had a savings account at First National Bank in Bemidji. Herman had specifically written, "Do not let Barbara Affield withdraw." For years I had been purchasing my own clothes with my trapping money. I imagine Barb wanted all the relatives' addresses for a money phishing expedition.

May 1, 1960. Dear Mother, Thank you very kindly for all the Easter presents you sent my children. You know I wrote Uncle Dick about what happened to Chris. He wrote right back (a registered letter) and said he was very sorry to hear of my predicament but that Grandfather had sold all (he underlined all) of Greenbank. He said you and I should work something out together. Yes, I think perhaps he has the answer there. You and I love all of these dear children equally. Starting with dear Chris and fine bright Tim. Next dear Windy whom you tended when he was tiny, Laurel who is a wonderful little student, Randy (still a baby in many ways), Bonny so cute she could play "Silent Night" at age 3—Linda Darlene, such a good helper and babysitter at 4, curly topped Larry and last of all little Danny Paul. Please think this is a cute name—I like the name Paul from the bible so much and I could think only of "Daniel in the Lion's den" I have had so many "roaring lions" around me through the years.

I believe all in all Uncle Richard has the right idea after all. Perhaps you could show my letter to Ned Shipways and they might know of a farm we could rent or buy. Why don't you ask dear Polly if she would like to use her inheritance of $1,500 plus perhaps you have some money and I could send you about $1,000 immediately toward the purchase of a farm. If each of us, you, Polly, and me, contributed $1,000 that would make $3,000 toward the purchase of a nice farm. With dear Chris and Tim to keep it going—all of us to help out—we couldn't go wrong. We have had 11 years experience here. Just last night Tim said one cow consumes as much hay per year as eight sheep. Many around here have sold their cows to raise money from sheep. There is much to be said for sheep as far as less work. The lambs are very delicate but can be raised to sell for good money. Also the wool at shearing time brings a good price. Don't you think it would be nice if all three of us went into partnership on a farm? Banks loan money if there is livestock concerned.

I thought perhaps we could purchase or mortgage a farm for $3,000 if Mr. Shipway knows of one. Then I would borrow money from the bank for the purchase of 50-100 sheep. This would be a start. Believe me, Chris and Tim are old enough and would love to help. Please don't get me wrong, but this would be my idea of supporting myself and children. This man is no better, nor any worse than Frank Schoenwandt. Worse as far as money goes. My sweet dear little baby whom I just know you'd love, he's going on 5 months old May 16th. He's a real bright little baby boy. You can just tell that he needs vitamin drops, orange juice, baby cereal, and apple sauce, etc. But this man will not buy him a single thing, nor us either. Never any oranges in the house in 11 years, except when I buy them.

I tell you I'm so sick of Welfare -- they cut off my check because you told them I had a large sum of money. I feel it is time to strike out on my own, support my own kids and I have outlined what way I plan to do this. Many people around here have a trailer with some other members of their family living in it. You told me last summer that you and Polly might buy a trailer. The heating problem isn't so much then. You could live in a trailer on our property or do whatever you saw fit. Uncle Dick is right. It is up to us to work out a happy life—you in your old age and me at the end of my younger section of life. I know you love each child and take a lively interest in educating each one of them to the good things of life. This is good. I told the Welfare I was taking the children to my mother because she was a very cultured lady and it would be very educational for them to learn some of her culture. Too—I know dear Polly's future is at the back of your mind. What better plan can I offer than to take care of dear Polly in this partnership? I don't see how we can go wrong. With smart fine young Tim and dear Chris to help us. Let us pray together now that this solution can be worked out with the help of a good friend like Ned Shipway. I just know he will understand our predicament and help out. How wonderful this would be. Is Ann still on their farm? I trust they will know of a good farm (underlined) for sale! All we can do is pray together that this plan will be successful. Let bygones be bygones—much water has gone over the dam since our youth—let us lend all our culture to these dear young people of whom I am the mother and you are the grandmother.

Much Love, your daughter, Barbara

P.S. Have I done anything sly to you? Why do you write the minister behind my back and even give him a letter to give my husband behind my back. Isn't this cruelty? What reason have you? I must have a registered letter. This means the mailman gives it to me personally and I sign for it. Otherwise I wouldn't get your letter. I forgot to say that my husband is making good money now, but I can't squeeze a penny out of him such as food and medicine for my baby. If I go to court for non-support I would just get the "shitty end of the stick" in most unladylike language.

Comments on the letter: Barb was married to Frank Schoenwandt for a several months in 1948. He was an extremely violent man and the marriage was annulled. Out of curiosity I Googled "Farms for Sale" on Long Island, New York. According to my inflation calculator, in 1960 dollars, Barb would have needed approximately $380,000 to purchase a seventy-acre farm.

At some point that spring Tim, who was also on probation, was sent by the court to live in a foster home. This next letter is dated June 16, 1960. Barb writes a phrase I've seen a few times in earlier and later letters where she refers to herself as Elsie's "little daughter." There was no greeting at the beginning of this letter.

Elsie wrote on envelope, *Last letter from Laurel June 11—also from Barbara before Fergus Falls [State Hospital].*

June 16, 1960. Don't pay attention to any letters you receive from my husband. Remember—he chased Chris and Tim away from here. He says he wants to get some money from you when you die. Please turn the page—the authorities were just out to see me. They want me to go down to visit Chris because he is very lonely. They want us to take Tim and the little ones because it will be good for Chris to see us. I will let you know when we arrive there—so there is no use of your sending any more letters here because authorities have asked me to go down to visit Chris.

We'll see you in Red Wing. I'll send you a night letter where we are after we get there. Love, Barbara

P.S. I know you still love your little daughter—Barbara Ann

That early summer of 1960, we children weren't privy to the drama being played out. Social workers, our minister, and law enforcement were all trying to gauge Barb's next moves. Eventually the situation came to a head. Barb was preparing to flee the farm again. In the chickenhouse I discovered letters Pastor Trueman Daniels had written to Elsie.

Postmark July 1, 1960. Dear Friend,

Thank you for your letters. I'm sure these must be very trying times for you; having to move and then your concern for your loved ones back here. Yesterday Mrs. Affield was in town and purchased a car and was in the process of buying a house trailer when I found them and convinced them into going home. I guess she was heading for New York. Two of the children, Randy and Windy were enrolled in a bible camp however and that put a delaying crimp in her plans. Tim also refused to go along. Tim is working on a farm east of Nebish and so he is free from some of the strife that goes on in the home. Tim was in to see me last night and we had a very good talk together. I believe Tim is today a more wise individual than many ever become. I hope he has the opportunity to use it. The welfare dept began neglect proceedings against the Affield household and I believe they have in mind taking the children from out of the home and placing them until better and more wholesome arrangements are made in their home.

Mrs. Affield is ill I'm sure and therefore I feel so very sorry for not only the children but her also. Mr. Affield is ~~a good deal~~ also to be ~~pity~~ pitied but could do so much more if he only tried a little harder.

Chris is behaving himself at the school in Red Wing and will be released this fall in time for school. I believe it would be good if you stopped in to visit Chris on your way west. I also hope you have the opportunity to come soon. It seems as if Mrs. Affield is becoming trapped you might say for ways out and as usual you are the one she would naturally turn to.

If there are any late developments I'll write you if I know how to get in touch with you. Please forgive the messy and informal letter writing but I am on my way out to the Affield's and then to town to see what is developing today. Once again, bless you for your devotion and concern. Sincerely, A.T. Daniels

Barb was very secretive that summer. At one point she had Laurel and me carry a packed suitcase out into the woods and hide it in the shell of an abandoned car. (It might still be there.) Why didn't she pull Randy and me out of the Bible Camp the minister mentioned, the same way she had removed us from school six months earlier?

Family Court

We visited the courthouse several times that spring. I recall one of the last times, before we were placed in foster homes. Inside, the old building smelled like floor wax and Brasso. I spent the morning studying FBI Wanted posters on the bulletin board at the base of the wide circular staircase. They were boring—only two wanted for murder—most were wanted for mail fraud. I climbed the stairs and joined my six brothers and sisters sitting on the floor beside the heavy oak door labeled Family Court. Herman and Barb, a black-robed man, a lawyer, and a court social worker were in the room.

I tried to decipher the muffled voices behind the oak door. A policeman brought bologna sandwiches and milk cartons for lunch. A picture of President Eisenhower looked down on us, his stern eyes compelling us to finish our dry sandwiches and Land O' Lakes milk. In the early afternoon, Randy and I were upstairs in the rotunda looking through the balusters, down through the large oval opening to the floor below when the Family Court door opened and Barb and Herman stepped out. The side of Barb's face was bruised and swollen.

They'd had a vicious argument on the way into town earlier. Randy and I had been sitting in the front seat beside Herman. Barb sat in back holding baby Danny, Laurel on one side holding Larry, and Bonny and Linda on the other side of her.

Barb was flustered. She yelled to Herman, "You bald bastard, you drove my two oldest sons out. Now I suppose you'll get rid of my other two children." Herman clutched the steering wheel and stared ahead in silence, color rising in his cheeks.

"You stupid German immigrant, I never should have moved here. I should have stayed in New York," she continued. "You come in from the barn smelling like cow shit and want to rut. That's all I am, a baby-machine, another breeding animal to you. I'll have you know, I'm a sophisticated lady. I am a Daughter of the American Revolution. My descendants were crossing the Delaware while yours were living with cattle in Germany. My parents were building fortunes as timber barons when yours passed through Ellis Island."

"Why didn't you stay back east then, bitch?" Herman asked, rising to the bait.

"I should have. I'm a concert pianist. I was playing in Carnegie Hall while you were shoveling shit after the army sent you home, unfit for duty. Why is it that you were sent home after North Africa while the rest of the army continued on? You weren't wounded. I'll tell you why. You broke down. You're a coward. You didn't have the courage to fight for this country like my ancestors."

Herman glared into the rearview mirror. He gauged the angle, the distance, and like a rattlesnake, struck—one hand on the steering wheel, the other back-handing Barb across the face.

"Happy now, bitch?" he asked, the car swerving into the tall grass on the dirt shoulder. "Shut the hell up or I'll pull over and take my belt off." That seemed to have the desired effect. "It's your fault we have to go to court. You, taking AFDC checks for those four—then running off. You dragged us into this mess. Last time we were in court, Judge Reed said you were the one with the nervous breakdown. I'm going to see about committing you to the nuthouse for shock treatment," he finished, eyes locked on the road.

"You'd like that, wouldn't you, you eighth-grade idiot?" Barb screamed, spit flecking her lips. "Then you could rut with my daughters. I'll see you in hell first."

"That's it. Enough is enough." He hit the brakes, swerved to the shoulder, and opened his door as the pistachio green '54 Chevy four-door crunched to a halt. He yanked the back door open, grabbed Barb by the hair, and pulled her over the top of Bonny and Linda. She fell on the road, dress around her hips. "You asked for it, now you're gonna get it, bitch."

Laurel scampered out of the car and picked up baby Danny who was screaming on the ground where Barb had dropped him.

Barb scrambled around the back of the car as Herman unbuckled his belt. "You bastard—I found out why no local woman would marry you—because of your vile temper."

It was a wooded curve between farms—past the TB Sanitarium, before the ski hill. Late morning sun sparkled on dew clinging to the dusty clover blossoms in the shadowed side of the ditch. Sweet smelling bass trees hung out over the clover, bees among the leaves that shaded the car. Puffy white clouds sailed high in the distance above the road that curved out of sight.

They ran around the car, screaming incoherent accusations against each other. Several times, closing in for the kill, he swung the belt, and the brass buckle clanged against the side of the car.

"You're a sorry excuse for a man, you stupid immigrant," she screamed. "One day my boys will come home and run this farm."

"You slut whore, those Mexican chop-cocks will never have my farm," he shouted, panting, as he circled the car.

"You filthy peckered bastard, you're jealous because my sons are circumcised. They will get the farm when you're dead."

In the hot car we listened and watched.

Why did she antagonize him? I wondered. She knew how it would end. She'd bait him, insult him, increasing taunts until he snapped, with the inevitable result that she would limp around the house for weeks until her bruised legs turned pale egg-yoke yellow and finally healed.

They circled the car until they were both winded. Herman stopped by his door. "Get your ass in the car," he said, as he re-looped his belt.

Herman climbed in, put the car in gear and, even as Barb still had one foot on the road, drove away. The little girls pulled her in. Panting, she daubed an old towel on her face, soaking up sweaty dust. Rouge and lipstick smeared across her cheeks. The rest of the trip was silent. At the courthouse she went into the bathroom and cleaned up.

As I look back, I don't understand why Barb didn't go directly to the Sheriff's Office and press charges against Herman. The side of her face was bruised and swollen, proof that she had been assaulted. Or, why didn't the judge intervene that day?

JUVENILE COURT REGISTER "E"   565

FILE NO. 2170

State of Minnesota,
COUNTY OF BELTRAMI
IN JUVENILE COURT

In the matter of the Welfare of Wendell George Curry, Laurel Roselinda Curry, Randolph Leonard Affield Bonita Rose Affield, Linda Darlene Affield, and Lawrence Roswald Affield, Minor Children.
Daniel John Affield
(Re: Brothers: File No. 2103 and 2114)

June 30, 1960. Petitions of Vera Graves alleging neglect of the above named children, received and filed.
July 1, 1960. Affidavit of Vera Graves showing need for immediate custody of the above named children.

June 30, 1960. Petitions of Vera Graves alleging neglect of the above named children received and filed.

July 1, 1960. Affidavit of Vera Graves showing need for immediate custody of the above named children.

July 1, 1960. Summons to Barbara Ann Affield and Herman Arthur Affield, parents of above named children, and order for immediate custody also directed to the parents, issued, and delivered to the Sheriff for service. A Representative of the Beltrami Welfare Department accompanied Sheriff to the Affield home and took children into immediate custody.

July 7, 1960. Hearing held, present in the court were all of the seven Affield children concerned who were excused from remaining at the hearing because of their age; Mr. and Mrs. Affield, Douglas Cann, counsel for Mrs. Affield; Paul Kief, Assistant County Attorney: Vera

Graves, Beltrami County Welfare Department; Reverend Daniels, of Puposky, Minnesota; Pastor Thompson of the Community Church of Nebish; and later Russell Schrupp appeared. (Schrupp was Chris and Tim's probation officer.)

Reverend Daniels and Mr. Russell Schrupp presented testimony substantiating the filthy condition in which the home was maintained. Reverend Daniels also recited his part in getting her returned from her escapade in Texas and also how he urged her to desist from embarking on her new proposed escapade.

Upon questioning Mrs. Affield herself, the story of this escapade was for the most part substantiated and she also substantiated that she was making arrangements to go on a vacation, anticipated going to Red Wing where her oldest son is incarcerated, and that she was going out west to visit relatives and she intended to take all her children on this trip, as well. Mrs. Affield indicated in her testimony that her husband was not providing her and the children with adequate support.

The court determined that the children are neglected because they are without proper parental care because of the faults and habits of their parents and custodians and that they are without proper parental care because of the emotional and mental instability and state of immaturity of their parents and custodians, and that the legal custody of the children be and hereby transferred to the Beltrami County Welfare Board to and until October 7, 1960 at 1:30 P.M., and that the hearing be and the same continued to and until that time when further disposition of the children will again be considered.

On July 1, 1960, a Beltrami County deputy arrived at the farm along with another car driven by Vera Graves. The seven of us were placed in foster homes. Randy and I in one; Laurel, Bonny, and Linda in a second; Larry and Danny in a third. A week later Barb and Herman appeared in court.

The Snake

Gray light filtered through dirty basement windows as the afternoon sun silhouetted brown lily-of-the-valley leaves stuck to the panes. No escape there. Too high. I could hold Randy up but even if he did manage to open the window and squirm out, he didn't have anywhere to run. Water trickled from cracks in the concrete basement walls, saturating my ripped tennis shoes—always it seemed, I was growing out of my shoes. The smell of stale earth rose from the dampness. Cobwebs wove between dangling electrical wires and caught in my hair. In a corner, remnants of past seasons' canned produce rested on metal shelves. A hose hung from a rusty spike that was anchored to an oak post in the center of the basement.

In the thin beam of light, a spider—the size of a .22 caliber bullet head—rappelled a silk thread from the ceiling joist. A chameleon frog the size of a penny leapt and caught the spider while it hung defenseless two inches above damp concrete. A thick garter snake shot from beneath the cement block furnace base. Jaws wide, he locked on the frog. From the snake's mouth two legs convulsed frantically as webbed toes clawed concrete. I felt the silent scream of helplessness as the kicks weakened.

The woman stood between Randy and me and the worn wooden steps. Her thick red arms protruded from a faded tent dress. Her gray hair, wrapped in a tight bun anchored at the back of her head, stretched the skin of her wide round face and underscored the hairy mole on the side of her chin.

"Sit on that stool by the window," she said. "I need to cut your hair." I meekly sat down and she buzz-cut my head while Randy stood watching. "You're next," she pointed at him.

I silently slid off the stool and lifted Randy up. It only took her a few minutes. I lifted him down and we huddled below the window as she wrestled with the corroded faucet. As her work-calloused hands unwound the hose, water pressure straightened it, and small misty leaks sparkled tiny rainbows where the hose had kinked over the spike. Reaching quickly back to the valve, she turned it off with a mutter about not wasting water. Eyes never leaving us, she stepped over to the furnace, reached behind it, and lifted out a small kerosene can.

The garter snake, startled by the intruder, slithered from under the furnace, across the concrete, and into a wide crack at the base of the wall.

Sidling over to the potato bin, the woman picked up a dented baking pan and poured kerosene. She set the pan on the floor and moved back to the stairs where she felt for something on a step. Grasping it, she returned to the pan and set the object in the kerosene. It was an old animal scrub brush, the kind with a leather strap across the top. Towering over us, she ordered, "Take your clothes off and throw them in the stove."

Randy began crying and shuffled behind me. I couldn't believe what I was hearing. Get undressed in front of this woman—this stranger? No way, not in a million years. We moved away from her toward the darkest corner of the basement.

Hose nozzle in hand, she turned the valve and stepped toward us. "Get those louse-infested clothes off. Now." I looked past her toward the stairs. "Don't even think about it," she warned. "My husband is up there waiting for you."

"I'm not getting undressed in front of you. I don't even let my mother see me naked."

"You're twelve years old. I have custody of you and your brother. Now get undressed and no more back talk."

How could we escape? I couldn't leave Randy behind. I edged toward the furnace, shadowed by Randy. The woman shifted, staying between us and the stairs. "What's taking so long down there? I've got hay to put up and I need the big boy to help me," yelled a voice from the top.

"They don't want me to see them naked. You boys get undressed. Now."

"If you leave us alone we'll clean up and come upstairs when we're done," I bargained.

Cold water hit me in the face. "No more playing. I said to get undressed. Do it now. If he has to come down, you'll be sorry."

Randy's snuffles grew into a wail. "What are we going to do? Why does she have that pan of gas? Is she going to burn us in the stove with our clothes?"

"No one's going to burn anyone," the woman said. "You need to strip your filthy clothes and scrub in kerosene and soap to get rid of the lice."

Kerosene. I couldn't believe it. We didn't have lice. Besides, kerosene burned. But there was no escape. Slowly I pulled my shirt off. "Let's just do it, Randy. We'll be all right."

With Randy naked and my shirt and shoes off, the woman picked the dripping brush from the kerosene and told me to scrub Randy. "Keep your eyes tight shut and start with the hair. Soak it good, then scrub. Work your way down, between the legs, and down to the feet."

We didn't have any hair left. I held my hand on Randy's forehead, shielding fuel from his eyes. But he screamed, rubbing them as kerosene leaked in.

"Keep scrubbing. We'll rinse it out when we soap him down. Shut up, boy. You want my husband down here?" She grasped Randy by the neck and bent him over. "Spread your legs, scrub up between, get those critters out."

Satisfied with the fuel scrub, she produced a Lava soap bar and a tattered washcloth from her apron pocket. "Soap him down with this, then it's your turn," she ordered, and drenched Randy with the hose. I lathered Randy's hair, telling him to keep his eyes tight shut.

"They burn," Randy complained. I scrubbed until the woman grunted in satisfaction. She hosed the fuel-Lava paste from Randy while I held him by the wrist as he tried to dodge the cold water.

"At the top of the steps you'll find a towel and some fresh clothes. Leave the towel for your brother. It's your turn now," she added, eyes directed at me. "Take those pants off and start scrubbing. You know what to do."

There was no way out. I glanced about the cold basement, knowing I was trapped. At the top of the stairs, the man's voice soothed a sniffling Randy. Perhaps the old man would rescue me. The woman, as if reading my thoughts, warned me again not to even think about it. Tears welled as I begged her not to make me get undressed.

"Take those pants off. Now."

I undid my belt, eyes locked on the snake's haven. My back to the woman, I stepped out of the wet trousers ringing my ankles. She told me to start scrubbing. One hand covering my front, I picked up the brush and held it to my scalp. Kerosene poured down, across my eyelids and over my cheeks. Rivulets merged on my chin and trickled to my chest. The woman grabbed my arm and demanded the brush. I opened my eyes in panic, fuel flooding in. My shielding hand came up as I rubbed burning eyes.

"No more lice in them."

Clutching my wrist, she dipped the brush and scrubbed. I stood sobbing, hands covering my front. That night I lay awake in a moonbeam on a sweat-stained bed beside Randy, reflecting on our situation.

Randy and I joined four Red Lake Nation Native brothers in this foster home: Peter, the oldest, Lance and Lars—twins—and Ervin, a toddler, who could only speak Ojibwe. I was the oldest at twelve. The social worker told the foster parents to allow only English to be spoken, so many evenings over the next year, Ervin went to bed without supper as a punishment.

Later, after the old people had gone to sleep, I tiptoed down to the kitchen and made Ervin a sandwich and got him a cup of water. As I look back, I think the woman knew I brought Ervin food because in the morning she'd sometimes wink and smile at me with a comment about a mouse getting in the fridge. I remember them as decent people. I think that during the 1950s and '60s it was common for farm families to become foster parents when all of their own kids had grown up and left home. It was an additional source of income to fill those vacant bedrooms, and we were cheap labor. I spent that summer harvesting hay—just as I had done at home.

A few years ago I discovered Lars' obituary online and realized that he was one of the homeless men I often saw wandering around Bemidji. Lars was fifty-three years old when he died. It's a heart-wrenching story. "He was preceded in death by his parents, three sisters and four brothers, including his twin brother Lance," reads the obituary. I'd heard that Lance died in a fight. I wondered how the foster home experience impacted their lives, ripped from their Ojibwe culture and forced into the white man's world.

Peter and Randy became close friends. Several years later, after we all returned to our homes, Peter and Randy played baseball on opposing teams. By then I was in the Navy, but I imagine that they got together socially. Not long ago, my sister Laurel and I were visiting and discussing that era, and she commented that the Native girls she lived with were the sisters of the boys Randy and I lived with.

(July 1960) unnamed Native children and *(left to right)* Laurel, eleven years old, Bonny, six, and Linda, four, at foster home.

(July 1960) Laurel wrote on the back, *To our wonderful Mommy from Laurel, Bonny, Linda*

(August 1960) in our foster home. Randy, nine years old, standing; Wendell, twelve, sitting. Our hair is beginning to grow back.

July 15, 1960, File # 33966

State of Minnesota, County of Ottertail, Probate Court:

Report of Examination and Findings:

In the matter of the Mental Illness of Barbara Affield

Insidious onset of symptoms. Patient has fared poorly in selection of her three (perhaps four) husbands. (The possible fourth husband was the Polish soldier in 1939 that I'm quite certain Barb did marry.) *One was unable to hold a job for more than a day or two.* (John Curry). *Another actually carried a gun and was brutal in his treatment of his previous wife and of the patient.* (His name was Frank Schoenwandt. Barb had Frank arrested in 1948 after he stabbed his daughter from an earlier marriage with a pitchfork.) *He was 16 years older than the patient, as is the present husband. Patient met her two most recent husbands through "Lonely Hearts" clubs, either in person or through correspondence. Both recent marriages seem to have been of convenience to provide support of the children. Grossly abnormal behavior began in December 1959, when she loaded her eight children into a car and left town without notifying her husband. She got as far as Sioux Falls [SD] and had to have a Caesarian at term. More recently she planned to load her nine children in the car, meet her mother in another town, and just set out anywhere "to get away from home in order to get a rest" from her household duties. She is receiving ADC because of their low income. Her emotional response to life's problems is inappropriate to the seriousness of these problems. Her behavior represents a danger to the safety of the children. The seven youngest children are in the custody of the welfare board because of maternal neglect, and the oldest child is in*

Red Wing Training School. (Tim, the second oldest, on probation, had been placed in a foster home earlier.)

Frank C. Barnes, Probate Judge   *July 15, 1960*

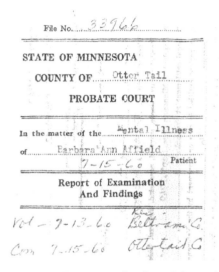

Barb's commitment order raises more questions than it answers. The order states that the "...patient has been confined in Fergus Falls State Hospital since July 13, 1960." In Beltrami County, Barb had voluntarily signed herself into the State Hospital.

On July 15, the Probate Court in Ottertail County issued this statement: "From examination of the patient [Barbara Ann Affield], and from the evidence submitted at the hearing, we find the above named patient to be a mentally ill person and the court finds that commitment to an institution for the mentally ill is necessary for the welfare and protection of the patient and society." The commitment order is signed by two medical doctors and Judge Frank Barnes.

I found a letter from July, 1960, in the chickenhouse, from our Beltrami County case worker to my grandmother. I apparently thought our grandmother might rescue us.

BELTRAMI COUNTY WELFARE DEPARTMENT

Mrs. Henry Phillips
316 East 58th St.
New York 22, New York

                                          Re: Affield Family

Dear Mrs. Phillips:

   We have been asked to write to you by your grandson, Wendy, who has given us
your address.

   You have been aware for some time of the problems that have existed in your
daughter's home. During the past two weeks, much has happened that hopefully will be
a first step in helping Mrs. Affield to again function well as a mother and homemaker.

   The seven youngest children have all been placed under the legal custody of the
Beltrami County Welfare Department for a period of three months and are presently
receiving care in three of our licensed boarding homes. Wendy and Randy are in one
farm home; Laurel, Bonnie and Linda in another about three miles from the boys; the
two little boys are together in a third home. The children are adjusting very well in
their boarding homes actually, their mother did a wonderful job in saying goodbye to
make it as easy as possible.

   Your daughter, at the recommendation of Dr. Reid, psychiatrist of the Bemidji
Mental Health Clinic, was voluntarily admitted to Fergus Falls State Hospital on
July 13th. I think one reason she was so willing for treatment was that she knew that
the children would be cared for while she was in the hospital.

   We understand that you were planning on coming here for a visit soon. We most
urgently want to see you when you are here and I know Pastor Daniels feels as we do.
Mrs. Vera Graves is your daughter's case worker in our agency and I am the worker
that will be in close contact with the children.

   If there is any further information that you might want, prior to your visit,
please write to us.

                                          Sincerely yours,

In later years when I asked Barb about her sojourn in Fergus Falls State Hospital, she said it was just a way to get a free hysterectomy. From the documents I recovered, I created a timeline. Is it possible that Herman contacted his relatives who lived in Ottertail County, where the State Hospital was located, and through those contacts he arranged a court hearing to get Barb committed so she could not sign herself out as Dr. Reid had promised?

(August 1960) Barb and her mother, Elsie, cornfield in the background, while Barb was a patient at Fergus Falls State Hospital. Elsie was traveling cross country, moving from New York to Seattle. Author discovered this picture tucked in Elsie's "Mental Health Journal."

FF-70   Discharge from Hospital
DISCHARGE & VISIT RECORD
Bond $_____
Provisional Discharge
No. ___33,966___   Straight parole
Voluntary
Visit
Name: ___Barbara Affield___   Ward ___3 WC___
Goes to ___Lake Region Hospital, and then Puposky, Minn.___
Accompanied by ___Self___
Date: ___12-15-60___ Time: ___4:30 P.M.___
Property ___$290.61___
Unimproved ___ Improved ___ Recovered X Unclassified
_____
Clinical director – Superintendent
Follow up:
Deportation _____
Transfer _____
Degree of Psychiatric Impairment _____

Six months later, Barb was discharged from Fergus Falls State Hospital, declared "Recovered." From the discharge record, it appears Herman did not go down to pick her up. I wonder if she returned to Bemidji on a bus or a train. Herman's actions must have elevated Barb's loathing to crystalline hatred.

Banded in a bundle of letters from the late 1960s that Barb wrote to her mother, I discovered an undated, mouse-chewed fragment: "Things will be better soon." Was it written shortly before Herman died?

Over the next three years, we children were in and out of the farm home and bounced between schools and foster homes. Not long ago Laurel and I were trying to figure out how many foster homes we passed through—I put mine at five.

(July 1960) Danny, seven months old, Larry, two years old. In a foster home.

It was a time of transition for Barb—her chicks were beginning to fledge. Chris and Tim were permanently gone from the farm. We came home for visits and vacations, but always we were sent back to the foster homes.

The late winter of 1961 Barb and Herman were alone on the farm, all of us kids in foster homes.

From this court excerpt dated the spring of 1961, it's obvious that Barb and Herman had learned nothing.

April 7, 1961. Continued hearing was convened as heretofore ordered by the court. Present at the hearing was Mrs. Barbara Affield of the children. Herman Affield, father of the Affield children and step-father of the Curry children (Laurel and Wendell); Mr. Douglas Cann of the firm of Cann & Schmidt, counsel for Mrs. Barbara Affield; and Mrs Hanson, child welfare worker of the Beltrami County Welfare Department. The court furnished Mr. Cann access to the report of Beltrami County Welfare Department, showing the adjustment of the children in and out of the home since the last hearing before this court, the present location of each of the children, and their adjustment in the home was discussed as was the relationship between Mr. and Mrs. Affield. It became apparent that Mr. and Mrs. Affield are not getting along well in their marriage, and many of the same things that brought about the conditions leading to the neglect proceeding herein had not been corrected. The older boy, Wendell, who is 14 years of age, was talked to separately without the presence of his mother or step-father, and he complained about his mother, claiming that she talked constantly; that lately she has been talking about a divorce from her husband and constantly claiming that her husband was no good. That she claimed that her husband shouldn't get to handle the kids and that she prevents Mr. Affield from spending time or paying attention to any of the children. That sometimes she screams and throws things around. In his opinion she doesn't know how to bring up kids, and lets the younger kids run around and do as they please and that when Dad tries to correct them there is a fight...

The fact that the Court, on two occasions, been stopped by Mrs. Affield since the last hearing while shopping for groceries and had been shown welts and bruises on her face and arms which had been inflicted by Mr. Affield was discussed....

May 23, 1962. Order Transferring and Continuing Custody issued and filed.

October 31, 1962. The court ordered that custody of said children be continued in the Beltrami County Welfare Department until April 30, 1963...

And so the years dragged by.

As I mentioned earlier, Elsie visited Barb the summer of 1960. I believe Herman also drove down during that visit. Was he standing next to his mother-in-law, cornfield in the background, when this picture was taken? I found another photo from the 1940s while Barb was living in New York where she "photochopped" a person from the picture. Was this a symbolic way of deleting people from her life?

In the chickenhouse I discovered *Rabbi Ben Ezra* by Robert Browning. Inside, Barb signed and listed all her children. The hard cover edition was published in 1902; one of the few surviving books Barb had brought to the farm. Tucked near the front of the little book was a picture of Barb and her two school friends standing in front of St. Mark's Basilica in Italy. Browning's poem is about growing old and the folly of youth. Had Barb, during her time in Fergus Falls, come to realize that Elsie was not her enemy? The photo and poetry were tangible links to Barb's past. Was she extending an olive branch?

1962
Surprise Visit

After a lifetime of avoiding her mother, Barb requested that we all remain in foster homes so that she could go to Seattle. What was her reasoning? She was forty-two years old. Her nine children had been taken away. She was forced to live with a man she detested. With her children gone, she had absolutely no income from AFDC. I remember Barb's subdued disposition after her stay in Fergus Falls. I don't think her spirit was broken. As future events played out, I think, like a caged prisoner, she was biding her time.

Elsie wrote in her diary,

Tuesday, July 17, 1962. Biggest surprise in years. Dear daugther Barbara walked in at 8 a.m. She had arrived at 5.

Barbara, visiting Elsie in Seattle, Washington. On the back of the photo Barb wrote, *Mommy and Grandma, July 21, 1962.*

Elsie's diary continued, *Sat. August 21. My Birthday. As usual a lovely birthday. Wonderful to have Bobby [Barb] here. The first time in twenty-five years. Shopped for me—Bobby and Polly did up presents. Then we went to Dee's for a dessert party and have Bobby see the Fairview.* (An apartment building.)

A few years later, when I visited Elsie, she told me that she opened her apartment door early one morning, and there was Barb, sitting on the floor. "Your mother didn't want to disturb me," Elsie said.

The summer that Barb visited Seattle, our minister wrote Elsie another letter.

Mrs. Henry Olmsted Philips

Dear Friend ,

       Thank you for your letter .I received it April 3rd in the evening and therefore was unable to comply with your request . I have not been in contact with any of the Affields except the children through our church's education program for many months so I am totally unqualified and uninformed as to what is transpiring in that home . This is the way they have wanted it and I haven't seen fit to disregard their desires.

       I wish there was something I might do to help the situation at this time , if there is a need. But until I have their confidence , I am helpless to do anything and it would only cause added turmoil if I were to intervene .

       I Have done all I know how and have prayed for them faithfully , but it just seems that what a person sows , sooner or later , they reap it , desirable or not.

       I do hope that what is best for all concerned is done , and if ever I am asked by the parties involved to help and if I can ,I will .

       Thank you again for your concern and confidence .I hope your faithfulness will be rewarded .

       Sincerely ,
       A.T. Daniels

       April 8 , 1962
       Puposky , Minnesota

I spent the summer of 1962 in a foster home in Waskish, on the shores of Upper Red Lake, about sixty miles north of Bemidji. The autumn of 2015, fifty-three years later, Patti and I visited Waskish along with my sister Laurel and her husband. We spent the afternoon on the Big Bog Boardwalk. Later we drove past the house I had lived in that long ago summer only to discover it was gone and a new one built in its place. We had dinner at the West Wind Restaurant in Waskish. As we were leaving, a man in a Veterans of Foreign Wars (VFW) uniform invited the public outside to participate in a flag replacement ceremony. Afterward I gave him two copies of my Vietnam War memoir, *Muddy Jungle Rivers*, for a drawing at their local Veterans Day dinner. As I visited with the VFW member, a man in his mid-seventies came up and asked if he could buy a copy of the book.

"Can you sign it?" he asked.

"What's your name?" I replied, as I opened the front of the book.

"John Olson."

I looked up at him, surprised. "I lived with a John and Anna Olson the summer of 1962 when I was a foster kid."

"They were my parents." He told me he was gone in the army during the summer I lived with them. The house burned down a year after I lived there. He recalled that they did have foster kids for a few years. He invited Patti and me to stop and visit sometime.

I found it disconcerting to reconnect with that distant past. The Olsons were very nice people. I helped John stucco the exterior of a small airplane hangar that summer. I remember his patience, as he taught me how to attach the chicken wire to the wooden end of the Quonset building and how to maintain the proper consistency of the stucco as we troweled it on. Fifty-three years later, the building stood solid, a fresh coat of paint on the stucco. I think that Quonset hut—the concrete image from the past—and reconnecting with the Olsons' son jarred me, yet validated a past that I sometimes wondered about—Did it happen? Why?

Over the next few years, Herman's children—the five youngest kids, returned home, with the condition of periodic inspections by the case worker. Laurel and I went through a series of foster homes.

On Palm Sunday Barb wrote this letter to her mother.

April 7, 1963. Dear Mother, How can I ever thank you for all of your kindness, thoughtfulness, and generosity? First, I will thank you for the $10 for Chris and Tim. These poor boys—I truly don't know what will become of the homeless waifs. If I find out they are penniless this will certainly pay their bus fare home. Next, no one could surpass your cleverness in sending each child, all the way down—Windy 15, Laurel 14, Randy 12, Bonny 8, Linda 7, Larry, 5, Bobby age 3, plus the $5 for my Easter. I truly apologize that you never had a fine son-in-law. But we must face the facts. Even the Welfare says that he (Herman) has this hate for lovely Chris and Tim, that he can't overcome it. The poor boys, they don't hate him. How well I remember you tried to stop me from divorcing Curry. Youth will never learn from the experience of old age. Especially Laurel thinks she knows it all and I do need help in steering her right. The main reason I have not called you is because why should the neighbors know our business? All I want to ask you is, what plans have you made for coming here? I am so sick of the Welfare having custody of the children. We have a good lawyer—if you were here to push, perhaps we could get legal custody of the children back. For this reason I hope that you can come. There is no reason why they should continue to have custody. The social worker is just awful. I have gotten so I want to be like you; and refuse to see her. That is how you could help push the legal custody of the children back to us.

The courts are so slow, they want to hold Laurel and Windy all summer, and Laurel and Windy even want to come home. Isn't that ridiculous? What would you do? Come here on the bus? We have bedrooms upstairs where you can stay. I think it would be very nice to have a good long visit for a *month or two with you and dear Polly. Could you sub-let your apartment? Could you see the Post Office about having your mail forwarded here? As I started to say, please address your letters exclusively to me. As long as H.A.A. (Herman—she refused to use his name) is so bitter about our dear boys it is useless to try to coddle him, on this subject or any other. Families should really stick together. It is the style now to call babies by two nicknames so if you want to call my youngest Bobby-Jim, it is alright with me. Please do not call him Junior. I don't see any of the other neighbors with juniors—so apparently it is out of style. Well none of this conversation is good for party-line telephone ears—so I saved you $2 or more! Can't you trust your intelligent daughter, Barbara, with your business? You don't believe I have turned over a new leaf to be sweet and kind and generous to you both and take care of dear Polly, do you? Come and see—start over! Please give me a definite date when you and dear Polly can come and stay at my home for two months. What is the earliest day you could make it? Love to you both, Barbara*

This was Barb's first attempt to manipulate her mother and Polly financially. Over the next two decades, it escalated to Barb attempting to get both of their bank accounts put in her name.

It was a time of change for all of us. Herman had less than seven years to live. I wonder if he was beginning to slow down, tired of fighting. Chris and Tim were gone, and I think he realized that I, too, would soon leave. In his opinion, Randy spent too much time with neighbor kids playing baseball and had not enough interest in the farm work. But he didn't discipline Randy as he had Chris, Tim, and me.

(Late summer 1962) Herman and Barb putting on a happy face. Laurel took this picture during a weekend visit from her foster home. By then the court was questioning us about conditions in the home during our visits.

Note the original barn, on the left side of the new barn.
A few years later it collapsed.

1963
Breakaway

Snowmelt made the farmyard a quagmire. The odor of the past season's thawing cow pies wafted across the yard. I was in the ninth grade, recently returned from a foster home in Blackduck, and anxious to take my first bike ride of the season. Barb came out of the house and asked where I was going.

"Over to the neighbor's," I told her. They had many children, including a girl my age.

"I want you to stop going over there," she said.

"Why?" We were in the same grade at school. I put my foot on the pedal, ready to kick off.

"Because." She grabbed the handlebar, my front wheel jackknifed, and I tipped over into the mud. "I forbid you to go by that girl. She's old enough to have a baby." I got up, angry, muddy water dripping off my elbows and running down my legs. I pushed Barb down. I was embarrassed that she had alluded to my sexuality. Plus, we all did our own laundry and I think that's what angered me most—I had been wearing clean clothes.

I again straddled the bike and pedaled beyond her reach. Almost sixty years later I recall Barb, sitting in the mud, shouting, "You stay away from her. She could get pregnant."

The younger kids don't recall Barb's violence. I wonder if her stay in Fergus Falls State Hospital did something to change that behavior, or perhaps, she simply was afraid to harm Herman's children under threat of retaliation.

On a November afternoon in 1964 I walked up to the house from the school bus. Barb met me on the step, which seemed odd. Her voice sounded scared as she asked, "What would you do if Chris got a girl pregnant?"

When Chris and Tim had moved to northern Illinois two years earlier, they initially found work on Northwoods Mink Ranch, near Harvard, Illinois, but later worked in area factories.

I imagine I told Barb, "It doesn't matter to me—it won't change my life." As it turned out, Chris's daughter was born a few months later, in early March, 1965, the same day I enlisted in the navy.

Barb was always flustered at the idea of her chicks being with a boy/girlfriend. I wonder if the roots of that apprehension date to the winter of 1936 when she was sixteen and deeply in love with a boy named Bruce Mims. It was the winter Barb's parents lived at the Waldorf Astoria in New York City and left Barb in Darien, Connecticut, to live with family friends.

From a 1963 farm kid's perspective, the social structure of Bemidji High School was reinforced by the faculty. At the top were the jocks and academic nerds. Lower on the food chain were the farm kids—rural, mostly poor, not privy to high society cosmopolitan Bemidji. We never went to the movies, ate at fine restaurants where one could order an extra-thick slice of fried bologna; we didn't purchase the latest fashions at Gill Brothers' clothing store. We shopped at Troppman's, a musty smelling store that carried utilitarian clothing and army surplus.

When a younger sibling entered high school, he or she invariably inherited the reputation of an older brother or sister—automatically categorized by the faculty, a clone of the one who went before you. If your older sibling was a good student, it was expected of you. If he was incorrigible, you started out with a deficit. Neither counselors nor teachers were about to waste valuable time.

Chris had become a symbol of rebellion during his short tenure at BHS, so my presence was synonymous with classroom rebellion, challenging authority, and showing disrespect.

(Spring 1963, *left to right*) Randy, Linda, Bonny, and Wendell, standing near the corner of the chickenhouse and corn crib.

By spring I had morphed into a rebel, my hair groomed into an acceptable DA. I had bling-studded black engineer boots that I kept my pants tucked into. I ironed my own shirts and used extra starch in the collar so they would stay turned up throughout the day and wouldn't wilt by afternoon classes. I still received decent grades in school—B average.

I began getting notes from girls. One in particular tagged along each day to the Mileage Cafe and sat by me. She was a townie and I felt like she was way out of my league. Her parents were divorced and she lived with her mother and little brother. As the weeks slipped by, she sat closer to me, until I was wedged into the booth corner, her leg pressed against mine, the front of her sweater pushing on my arm as she fed dimes into the juke box tune selector.

I was a closet rebel. Each afternoon before I got off the school bus, I'd adjust my clothes. I'd pull the pants out of the boots, let them hang down, tuck my shirt in, turn the collar down, button it all the way up, mess my hair so there was no DA.

Herman made it very clear that there would not be another Chris in the family. He and I had always gotten along because I did my chores and enjoyed reading history. He was an avid reader, so we also shared that.

Barb sent this letter to her mother.

October 4, 1963. Mother Dear, You are the kindest most wonderful mother in the whole world. Please accept my most humble apologies for not having written sooner. I know you will forgive me because my work here is so difficult. Thanks for the five lovely postcards. I want to make this letter pleasant but on the other hand you should know of the hard life I lead. Six children to get off to school in clean ironed clothes—every day. Up at 5:30 to start breakfasts; clean and wash; bake bread, make butter, butcher chickens, all this in order that the seven children can eat and not starve. Mr. Affield has stopped buying bread in the store until next summer. I haven't received any check

(AFDC for Laurel and Wendell) as yet and do not know if I will. That worker is all on his side, no matter what he does. I'm going to petition the court for another worker. I am not even given money for Laurel's necessities such as stockings, etc. Consequently your four dollars that you sent to Laurel and me—went for her basic necessities. However none seems to appreciate this. Please, I want to thank you ever so much for sending us this money. If you can spare $5 from time to time as a donation to the "humble servant," your generosity will most certainly be appreciated. Thank you for the nice pictures. I guess I will have to forget the phone because they want $25 at the least to reconnect it. We'll write you soon again. Love, Barbara

At the time, none of us kids realized how destitute and desperate Barb was for money. All our lives we had considered it greed when she took our money. This next letter was a blatant manipulation attempt.

October 22, '63. Dear Mother, This is certainly wonderful of you to send me $5 when you have done so much already. I hope your shoulder doesn't ache any more now. You know this Thursday, October 24th –the day you receive this letter is Linda's 8th birthday. Then next Wednesday, October 30th is Windy's 16th birthday. Well, I hope you send him a card and me his birthday money so that I can buy him a present. He sold his calf, so it is unfair that he has more money than I. Promise to write you a long letter tonight. Lots of love to you and Polly, Affectionately, Barbara

On a Friday afternoon, Herman and Randy drove into town and didn't return until Sunday evening—nobody had any idea where they went. I was left alone to do the chores Friday evening and again on Saturday morning. By Saturday afternoon I was bitter that I'd been left behind. Coincidentally, Chris and Tim came home from Illinois to visit that weekend and invited me to go into town with them on Saturday evening. I jumped at the offer.

Sunday morning I was hung over and sat in the house visiting until they left at noon. The chores were overdue by that time, so I set to work. The gutters were running over, the mangers were licked clean, and the cows' utters were bulging. I cleaned the barn and fed and milked the cows. I was impressed with how much milk I got from them. I had just finished the separating process when Randy and Herman returned. They'd gone to visit the Affield relatives over in Breckenridge, Minnesota. It was a time in my life when I hated the farm and everything it represented.

The fact that I wasn't invited reinforced the fact that I was not truly an Affield—as Ervin, Herman's brother, had told me during a visit the past summer, "You're one of Barb's kids." I guess in his mind, the younger ones were the only legitimate Affields. The following morning the cows gave about half the milk they usually did. Breaking the twice-a-day milking cycle must have triggered an internal response to dry up. Milk production dropped at an alarming rate over the next few days. We only separated once a day and Herman began rationing milk to us. The tiny cream check for several weeks, until calving started and milk began to flow again, made for an extra hungry late winter. I wonder if Herman ever wondered why the cows had all dried up so suddenly.

The past autumn I had done well trapping skunks and raccoons. Their pelts were prime and I received top price. After the lakes froze, I set my trap-line for muskrats, beavers, and weasels. Between trapping and working weekends for a neighbor, I accumulated a few hundred dollars.

Life on the farm assumed an uneasy truce. On the Friday preceding Hair Saturday, I had my hair trimmed in town at the barbershop. Herman saw this as an extravagant waste of money but conceded that it was acceptable. I caught him glancing at my haircut on the sly while we ate breakfast that morning. Later, when he clipped Randy's hair, it wasn't quite as short—a victory of sorts.

Letter written to my grandfather from his English cousin, Eloise, in 1949:

March 30, 1949,
My Dear Henry, Your letter of March 23 reached me on March 28. No matter how bravely and cheerfully you may write, I cannot get out of my head the idea that you and Elsie are beset with very great problems indeed. For once in my life, if never before, I read between the lines. Do you mean that Barbara and her four children have come home [to New York City] to stay for good? Please don't think I am asking for more information than you wish to give me, or that I am just displaying a vulgar curiosity. I do indeed hope you will not think that of me, but it really grieves me more than I can possibly say for both you and Elsie, if my surmise is correct. I cannot think of any more unselfish, patient and loving parents then you have both been, and it hurts me terribly if you have more trouble on your hands.

In writing thus plainly, you will of course let no one but Elsie read this, and will tear it up when read, and you may be sure I shall make not the slightest allusion to anyone in the family.

Last time I heard of Barbara she had two children—now you speak of four, but I never knew she had had two more. I don't know anyone at all so brave over problems as you and Elsie are.

With much love to you both, Ever your devoted cousin, Eloise

1964
"Times are so terribly hard"

As I read this next letter Barb wrote to her mother the winter of 1964, I tried again to imagine her sense of abandonment.

January 17, 1964. Dear Mother, Thank you very much for your lovely letter to Laurel. She is so wrapped up in her homework and Confirmation work, that I do not know when she will write to you. The weekends are taken up with much washing, ironing, and getting clothes ready for the next week of school, she accompanies her chorus classes and practices for those, plus speech and drama. As you say, there are many things in life to make one sad. The frames on my glasses were so old, that they finally broke to pieces. So I just have the lenses Scotch-taped to the frames. They look so awful that I am ashamed to even go to church. I thought that he would at least buy me some frames for Christmas, but I've been going around like this for over two months: and no telling when I'll be able to afford new glasses. I know I need them because the eye doctor said so. Also—I get terrible headaches and stomach upsets unnecessarily—due to my eyes. He (Herman) won't even buy me the pills I need to keep well and care for my family. This makes me very sad. Also, to think I have to ask you for a little donation, in order that Laurel and Windy will be secure for their lunch money, the last two weeks of this month. It costs $2.50 per week for Laurel and Windy's lunch. Bonny, Linda, and Larry need boots for the deep snow and what was I to do? I wonder if you could help me out a tiny bit? This also makes me very sad; that I should have to bring my burdens to you when you are already so burdened. Hope you *and Polly are keeping comfortable and warm this winter. Did you ever ask Uncle Nubs and Aunt Ruth to send us a box of clothes? Sorry I'm in such a tight spot. Lots of Love, Your daughter, Barbara. What woes!*

P.S. I never mentioned that Bonny and Linda have toothaches and must get to the dentist.

Late winter of 1964 weakened as the spring sun rose higher and stayed longer; snowbanks shrank, and water trickled across the driveway. Early morning, walking our quarter-mile driveway out to the bus, we crunched across crusted mud from the night's cold temperature. By afternoon, as we stepped off the bus we waded through a quarter mile of muddy clay gumbo. Each evening it took me half an hour to clean my leather boots. I pulled my trap-lines in for the season; I had begun to move farther out as I depopulated the fur bearing critters close to home. Besides, the ice was starting to crack, and I didn't want to fall through again.

In the chickenhouse I discovered this letter I wrote to my grandmother.

March 10, 1964. Dear Grandma and Polly, I'm sorry I never wrote sooner but I've been kind of busy with my school work and such. I hope you are fine. Everyone here is o.k. Chris and Tim haven't been up since the first of February. I'm expecting them home soon since Chris will be going into the Army. I need your help. In school I have to write a report of the family ancestry. This report is very important to my grade. I would really appreciate it if you would send me all the information you can. Mother was telling me Calvin Philips knows quite a bit on this subject. (Little did we know he had died five years earlier.) *Also I would appreciate it if you could tell me about some of Grandpa's achievements from when he was in the Army. I suppose I better quit before I have you writing a book. Mother doesn't know much about her ancestry but what she knows may be about people several generations apart. I don't know what I should do on my father's side. I don't know who he is, I think you do but don't want to tell me (no offense). I almost know for sure John Curry isn't my father, even you said that last summer. You don't know how much it would mean to me if you told me. If you don't tell me I may never find out. These aren't happy thoughts but that's just what I think.*

The army didn't want Chris because of his juvenile record. I don't remember the ancestry project. I've always been curious about who my father was. After studying the chickenhouse documents I'm confident that my grandmother didn't know. In the spring of 1964, Barb wrote this letter to her mother.

Monday, March 9, 1964. Mother Dear, It is certainly a shame that I haven't written you a lovely Easter letter sooner than this. I have been sick with a flu bug this past week. I think it is so kind of you, to write to Linda, Bonny, Randy, and Windy. I want to thank you right here and now for sending each of my two little daughters One dollar apiece and Windy and Randy two dollars apiece; you are truly a charming grandmother. It is honestly a shame that you do not live in Bemidji. How terrible it is that you live so far away. Could you ever possibly consider another move? The cold winters aren't so bad with a well heated house.

Well—here are a few newsy bits. I never knew you sent Randy that card with the Indian and the two dollars. I found your card all water-soaked and illegible in a snowbank. So you see I never even knew there was a letter from you last week. If you want your daughter to know that perhaps you better address all mail to me. I strongly doubt that I would have seen your letter to Windy today—except for the coincidence that we were right there at the mailbox. I don't like to ask you to send registered because it is extra trouble and expense for you. But it would really be nice to receive a letter from you that hadn't been all torn open in advance. Oh well, such is life. The children need everything imaginable in the way. The house needs refurnishing—I would like to buy curtains, furniture covering, rugs, etc. But where could such expensive things come from? And I haven't told you the worst yet.

It wasn't bad enough that we went all winter without heat. Now, no water. The pipe leading into the ground broke and we have to dig a hole in the Spring to reach this pipe. I bet a plumber could fix it though. But there is no money to hire plumbers. So, we'll just have to go without water. I've never been without water before.

Times are so terribly hard here—no heat—no water—no money to fix the house. At least you have heat and water and comfortable furnishings. I hope it would not be asking too much that you could spare me as much as you did at Christmas time. Then maybe I could get the water pump fixed and the house fixed up for spring.

Please have a heart and realize that when I tell you all these troubles I hope that you can sympathize with me a little bit. I hope that "charity still begins at home." Laurel has the stamp and envelope and will write you for sure this week. She really is swamped with work.

Love, Barbara

We always had heat on the main floor of the house—otherwise everyone would have frozen to death. I do not remember us being without water in the house. As for furnishings, furniture never lasted long with kids jumping and playing on it.

At school, Mac, a senior who had known Chris, befriended me and offered me an opportunity to escape the farm; he suggested that I go to work with him in the carnival. Last season he said he'd returned to Bemidji with almost two thousand dollars. I hesitantly broached the idea at home and received an adamant "No." I was needed on the farm to help put up hay. Visions of past summers raced through my mind. With those memories I made a fateful decision. I would go with the carnival.

I did finally convince Herman to let me go. The two thousand dollar carrot was irresistible to a man who worked twelve hours a day for an annual income less than three thousand. As I look back, I think he knew I would go, regardless. He had seen my two older brothers leave, not on good terms. I think he valued the years he and I had gotten along. At the time, I had a twinge of guilt, knowing he would have a heavier burden, but I rationalized to myself that it was time to let my younger brothers pick up the load.

My last night at home is a vivid memory. My Fairlane convertible was tucked away, a tarp tied over the roof to ward off summer rains. My little brothers and sisters were envious of my leaving. I had trouble sleeping that last night, imagining what the future held. I got up early and went for a walk. Bats swooped around the yard-light, mouths open like funnels as they scooped insects. It had rained during the night. Red worms lay on the surface, scudding in panic at my approach. Robins fluttered up ahead of me as I interrupted their early morning smorgasbord. Walking the curved, wooded road to Nebish Lake, I saw the new shoots of what would be late summer daisies and Indian paint brushes peeking up through the new season's grass.

Further into the woods I could see moccasin flowers beginning to bud. The lake was high from the spring melt. As I walked around the lake toward the pier, I skipped rocks across the mirror surface. On the pier, with a handful of specially selected flat stones, I skipped them one by one, attempting to set a new record. I guess it didn't matter, with no witness.

The early June sun climbed, and steam rose from the night's rain, leaving a sense of the world shrouded in ground fog. I walked back to the farm, reliving the memories of the lake and its influence on my life.

Barb wrote this next letter soon after I left.

June 12, '64. Dear Mother, That was very fine and kind of you, to send me such a pretty letter on such lovely note paper with the two dollars enclosed. That was truly thoughtful of you. I suppose you have kept well this summer. Again our letters will cross. The letter I wrote you last week, saying that I was in tatters, you will be answering in your next letter.

Do you hear from Chris and Tim often? Well, the card you sent to "the King-pin head of the house" came—it was very helpful of you to try, this way, and I hope it did some good though I doubt it very much. Love to you and Polly, Barbara

Herman is "King-pin." I found Barb's letter curious in that it didn't mention me—that I had left home. Maybe she felt it was another failure she didn't want to acknowledge.

The carnival I went to work for the summer of 1964 was a scam. The first week, I was assigned to help assemble and disassemble the merry-go-round. I was quickly promoted to run the High Striker. My pitch went something like this: "Come-on fella, show your girl how strong you are—three swings for a quarter—ring the bell, get a cigar." It's amazing how gullible young men are when trying to impress their girls.

At the time, I was walking out of my shoes and the owners wouldn't give me my own money for a new pair.

"We hold your pay until the end of the season," they said, and gave employees two dollars a day to live on.

Two weeks after joining the carnival, I waited in a small western Minnesota farm town for the evening crowds to thin out. I skipped out with the money I'd scammed from farm kids that evening—it had been a busy night, so I had about two weeks' pay. Rumor was, at the end of the season, the owners never paid up.

I rode the rails that summer; visited my grandmother in Seattle, spent time in hobo jungles, bucked bales for an old rancher near Whitefish, Montana, and returned to the farm in time for school—but that's another story.

Barb sent the following letter after I left my grandmother's apartment in Seattle. Elsie had offered to buy me a train ticket home, but I told her to just drop me off at the rail yard—which she did. Barb was a master at covering pages and not relating meaningful information. A few years later, when I was in Vietnam, I'd sometimes pitch her letters into the Mekong without opening them because I knew she would only be asking for money. When Barb was just filling pages, her writing was large and flourishing.

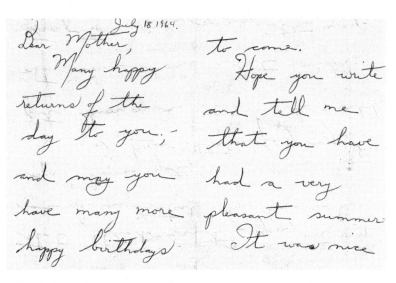

July 18, 1964. Dear Mother, Many happy returns of the day to you, and may you have many more happy birthdays to come. Hope you write and tell me you have had a very pleasant summer. It was nice that Windy visited you, but very sad for us, that he has not come home yet.

I knew that if you just put him on a train he would not come home but would stop to work along the way which he did. It did not do him any good to work out because he has no money to even buy a ticket home. How are you spending your summer? Please write soon and tell us all about yourself. Happy Birthday, Love, Barbara and family

Barb was right. I arrived home at the end of August, broke, and started school in the clothes I had worn the past spring. They hung loose on me because I'd lost weight. Begging for quarters so I could eat, living on hobo stew, or eating out of trash cans were great ways to shed a few pounds.

School never had a chance—through the autumn I stared out the windows, reliving the summer freedom I'd discovered. By early November I sat in history class watching snowflakes drift past, midterm test lying on my desk, blank. The teacher sat at his desk, radio low, listening to a football game. What's the difference between the Ming and Chin dynasties? Who cares? On the first anniversary of President Kennedy's assassination, our class listened again to his call to service. Vietnam beckoned. I'd turned seventeen in October—old enough to enlist.

The midterm tests came back with Fs, naturally. My report card was a dismal record of Fs and Incompletes. Barb wrote the following letter to her mother.

December 9, 1964. Mother dear and Polly dear, I just heard from Tim that he arrived in Phoenix alright. He gave me his address in Scottsdale, Arizona. He says he is sleeping in his car to save money. He did not even give me the name of these people. So if I were you, I would only send a letter, not money because he may not even be there anymore. Maybe he got a job 100 miles away or something. I will see that each one of these children here writes you a Christmas letter. And as you say—perhaps warm clothing would be the most important. Perhaps electric blankets, which cost $10-$15. Windy and Randy could share one and Bonny and Linda could share one. I will try to pick each one out a lovely present from Grandma and Aunt Polly. I think it is just perfectly sweet of you to offer to send fifty dollars, and I think you are the most wonderful Mother and most wonderful sister in the whole world. I should be helping both of you, too. And I hope I can help you in some way. Lovingly, Barbara and family.

I was tired of trapping. Tired of never-ending chores—tripled since Chris and Tim were no longer at home. Tired of Herman and Barb's constant bickering. A few weeks earlier, after Kennedy's speech, my history teacher had piqued my interest when he spoke of the mounting American presence in a little country called Vietnam. I remembered the Marine I'd traveled with the past summer, riding the rails. He'd just returned from Vietnam and told stories of fighting the communist insurgents—he'd called them Viet Cong.

"The Lord bless thee
and keep thee."
NUMBERS 6:24

Dear Grandma,
and
Aunt Polly,
With best wishes
for a joyous
Christmas
and a truly
Happy New Year
I am still
four years old
I hope you have
a very Merry Christmas and a
truly Happy New Year. Love B

On December 14, 1964, Barb sent this note to her mother.

Who was this little girl, reaching out to her mother and sister? Barb's childhood prose was usually signed "B." As an adult, she signed as "Barbara."

New Year's Eve, 1964

I remember it as a cold, still night. Weather station historical data shows it was -17.8°. Herman sat in his stuffed chair near the woodstove reading a dog-eared novel, Randy held the lid down and shook the old frying pan on the stovetop as popcorn popped, and the younger kids were in the front room watching *The Flintstones* on the fuzzy television. Barb turned the radio on searching until she found an opera.

"Turn that shit off," Herman said, glancing across the room.

"It's New Year's Eve. I want to listen to them celebrate in New York. They drop a giant ball at Times Square—music plays and everybody cheers. There is a world beyond this god-forsaken place."

"Turn that shit off."

"You might be content here, but I want to listen and remember life before I met you."

"You're the one that moved here. I didn't force you."

"You never told me I'd be a prisoner."

"You can leave anytime you like." Herman took his glasses off and looked up. "My kids stay."

"You bastard. You'd love to be alone with my daughters. Well, you can rot in hell first."

"You bitch, you have a filthy mind," Herman said, pushing himself up from his chair and unbuckling his belt.

"Well, isn't this a pleasant New Year's Eve," Barb said, racing around the table to escape. He swung but missed. "Let's sing, just like in New York," she taunted him.

"I'll give you something to sing about," Herman shouted, lashing out again, the belt tip snapping Barb's arm.

I came down the stairs into the kitchen and stood watching. "I'm tired of this shit," I said. "I'm leaving." I pulled on my school coat, hat, and mittens and walked the two miles to Nebish. I caught a ride into town with Red Lake Natives who had already begun celebrating. In town, I met some school friends. One of the Natives bought us wine and we drove around, listening to the radio. We drank the wine like beer and were soon puking in the snow.

It was about midnight when we went to the 24 hour truck stop west of Bemidji and had breakfast. I was tired and went out behind the diner—puked my breakfast out, then climbed into the empty sleeper of a semi truck, left idling, while the driver ate in the restaurant. Happy New Year's Eve.

Our teenage pictures on the wall in the old farmhouse living room:
Barb somehow didn't have one of Laurel.

1965
"Barbie's Ranch"

By 1965 we four children Barb had brought to the farm sixteen years earlier had flown the nest. (Laurel, in tenth grade, returned to the farm periodically from her foster home for visits.) With us gone, Barb no longer received a monthly AFDC check. She was completely dependent on Herman. I jump ahead a few months to a letter she wrote to her mother.

Dear Mother,   *September 24, 1965*

We received your nice postcards yesterday and we were all glad to know that you had a nice vacation. How long were you away? Did you have a nice time?

It is too bad that you couldn't have driven over here—but I suppose this is too great a distance, and would take too much time and money.

It is hard to believe that in less than two weeks Tim will be 21 years old— October 2nd. What do you think you will get him for his 21st birthday? Perhaps a grey button down sweater would be useful to him. Perhaps you would prefer to send me the money so I could buy Tim a sweater.

I want to thank you ever so much for the card and the two dollars that you sent dear little Larry for his birthday.

This is quite a birthday month. Linda will be ten on October 24th and Windy will be eighteen on October 30th. You may expect to receive another letter from me in a few days, but I hope you answer this letter soon.

I am quite bowed down with financial worries. You can imagine it costs a lot to dress the children for winter clothes, and I have no winter coat for myself. Anyway, I have been thinking that I would ask several little favors of you and I hope you don't mind.

The first is, that from now on—I trust you will refer to my home—in your daily conversations as "Barbara's Ranch," similar to the L.B.J. Ranch. I would certainly appreciate this because this is the official name of my ranch. It sounds quite insulting the way you refer to my home in your letters.

The second favor is this: I have absolutely no clothing at all. I am even ashamed to go to church in the one old coat I have. Now I know that Aunt Ruth has never been too friendly—seeing that she is not a blood relation. But in the past you have told me that she has offered a coat. Just think of all the clothes she must have that I could fix over. I think the main thing is, that she is far too busy to box up her old clothes and send them. Perhaps you could take the clothes over to your place in your car and I know this is a lot to ask, perhaps it is too much to ask—but you know it is embarrassing never to be decently dressed. There is a type of man who likes to embarrass the woman in this way.

I know you have received a lovely letter from Laurel by now. She is a sweet girl but she is suffering under the regime of this Hitler-like man. We are all suffering and there is a solution.

You know, if I only had the money I would buy his cows. Please do not look down on me for this; because you did live on the Shipway's ranch.

The cows are our pets, like the millionaires' race horses and they do give $50.00 average cream check per week. Furthermore, they like me better than they do him. There are 16 cows, and he says he wants $250.00 a piece for them—which is just as impossible as everything else on "Barbie's Ranch."

Last week I went and saw Judge Reed about sending him to Fergus Falls Hospital as you know he refuses to heat the upstairs in the winter and insists that the downstairs door be closed. Judge Reed says, "Now there's *a great deal of difference between a person being very ornery and being actually insane." He doubts if I have a case against him.*

Well in that case, the only solution is for me to buy this farm from him and support the children myself by milking the cows and selling the other various livestock. I would like to do this as I do not mind milking with my two expensive milking machines which I have been washing daily for 17 years. Do you know of anyone on either side of the family who would be willing to help me buy this farm?

Next April, at government expense, Herman can start drawing social security and also a soldier's pension. I think $100.00 a piece is plenty to pay for the cows—too bad I didn't pay for them with my inheritance money but it probably might not have worked out anyway.

Well, at least you would have a summer home to come to, and I could build you a pretty apartment if I were the owner here.

Do you know that years ago the Supreme Court of New York sent me volumes of legal papers, too? Perhaps the judge ruled that a sister is a closer relative than a mother. I sometimes wonder if you ever consider that I am just as close a relative to Polly as you are. Now that you chose to make your brother your business manager I wonder if you would feel free to discuss my letter with him.

As I understood from you, your brother, Norbert has knowledge of Polly's inheritance sum, plus all your various investments. (Incidentally, both your sisters chose to ignored my birthday, though Aunt Katherine sent a dress one year. It is too bad that relatives aren't more friendly.) Anyway, with winter coming on I felt I should tell you about my trip to Judge Reed.

Tim is all alone in a lonely boardinghouse. If Tim were home to help me, we could pay someone back in monthly installments if there were only someone interested enough to help me buy this farm.

Since your brother knows about your holding Polly's inheritance and other holdings—do you suppose that he would be willing to loan you the *money to loan me if I could pay back the loan at $20.00 per month.*

Please keep in mind that the reason Herman is alone when we came here so many years ago was because his father deeded this to him for about $500.00. Herman was so disagreeable that his father couldn't live here. Would you be so kind as to enclose a nice letter in answer to this letter? As long as we can't talk on the telephone, nor can we visit in person, let us keep our letters kind and good and free of criticism. To say mean and unkind things only hurts the other person and does not get you the confidence of the person you are writing to.

In conclusion, something (twice underlined) should be done about him. Someone should get him to retire voluntarily. Hope you find it in your heart to answer me in a sympathetic way.

Love, Barbara

So that was the corner Barb had painted herself into—back to New Years Eve.

Farewell to the Farm, January 1

I slept through the driver crawling back into his semi truck and leaving the truck stop in Bemidji. I awakened—gagging on diesel fumes and having to pee—to the swaying motion of a moving vehicle and a radio blaring Petula Clark, singing "Downtown." Gray light filtered through the curtains to the bunk I was lying in behind the driver's seat, and I remembered what I'd done the night before. I pushed the curtain open, leaned forward and shouted to the driver. "Hey, where are we?" He slammed on the brakes, throwing me forward against the back of the seat. The truck screeched to a halt.

"What the hell you doing back there? Get out of my bed—get the hell out of my truck." He reached beneath his seat and came up with a steel pipe. "Get the hell out before I bend this around your punk head." The pipe jabbed me in the ribs as I slid down to the passenger side of the cab. The enraged driver continued to poke at me as I tumbled out. I landed on the pitted asphalt, skinning my bare hands. "You little bastard, I've a mind to work you over."

Stunned, lying on the cold highway, I heard the driver's door open and looked under the truck. His feet hit the pavement on the far side.

I watched the feet coming around the front of the truck. I scrambled up the snowbank, across the ditch, and out onto the prairie, sinking into the crusted snow all the way up to my knees. The driver stood at the edge of the bank and shouted. "You little bastard, I hope you freeze out here—the buzzards and coyotes can work you over." He hurled a chunk of broken ice at me, climbed back into his truck, flicked me the finger, and drove away.

I followed my tracks through the broken crust back out to the highway. My hat and mittens were still in the truck. My palms burned where they had struck the pavement. Blood seeped through my jeans at the knees where they'd hit the ground. The wind whistled across the highway. Glancing behind me into the hard morning sun, I spotted a sign. U.S. 2 East—north wind, I thought.

It was New Year's Day. The highway stretched in both directions as far as I could see without a vehicle in sight. Icy banks formed ridges on both sides. I zipped my coat, lifted my collar up around the sides of my head and tucked my hands deep into my pockets. With my back to the sign, I began walking west.

My engineer boots weren't designed to walk on frozen pavement with a forty below wind chill. The cold began with my toes and ears—a tingling, aching, numbing sensation. The blood on my jeans crusted into ice and dug in with each step when raw skin rubbed the stiff surface. My ribs and shoulder ached where the driver had jabbed me. I kicked at wheat kernels lying on the asphalt—trickled from countless grain trucks hauling toward the harbor in Duluth. That's what I'd been riding; an empty grain semi, returning for another load.

Pheasants pecked at kernels where trucks had bumped over the frost-boiled hump of a small bridge. They flew away as I approached, swooping low into the arroyo, seeking shelter in the sage brushed gully. Two deer carcasses protruded from the wind-swept snowbank. It must be a prime feeding spot, I thought, kicking the wheat built up in the cracks of the shoulder as I walked over the bridge. My toes were numb and my fingers were stiff as I hugged the coat tightly around my waist. The wind was blowing harder, whipping in around my up-turned collar, freezing my ears. I walked to the south side of the bridge and looked over the rail. It looked sheltered from the wind. I could rest—perhaps take a short nap under the bridge. I walked to the end of the rail, climbed onto the snowbank and looked back.

I hadn't heard the car approaching. It pulled to the shoulder, and the driver rolled the window down and shouted. "What are you doing? How did you get out here in the middle of nowhere?"

I climbed down, back to the asphalt. "I was riding in a semi truck. The guy kicked me off about two miles back." I bent down and looked into the car. There was a woman in the front and two kids in the back seat. The man wore an Air Force uniform.

"You won't last long out here—get in." The woman squeezed to the middle and I climbed in beside her.

"Where are you going?" the driver asked.

I hadn't given it any thought—I was traveling in the direction I'd taken last summer, toward Seattle. I recalled the letters Tim had sent home about no snow and warm weather, and I remembered our time in Texas.

"Phoenix. I'm going to Phoenix to stay with my brother," I said through chattering teeth.

"That's a long haul—we'll take you as far as Rapid City, where we're stationed."

Early that evening they dropped me at a truck stop in southwest South Dakota. I snuck into the trucker's bathroom and took a shower. Warm and clean, I sat at the restaurant counter, nursing a glass of ice water. I knew what was in my wallet—three dollars. The buffet was four. When the trucker sitting next to me finished eating and left, I slid into his spot and sipped from his empty coffee cup. The waitress returned, filled it and winked.

"You want to get another plate of food?" she asked. I ate three helpings and filled my pockets with packaged bread sticks. I remembered the hungry days on the rails during the past summer.

Three days later I was north of Las Vegas—again at a truck stop. It was past midnight, and I was lying on a bench when two men sat down near me.

"I'm too tired to drive any farther—you drive. I've been doing it for the last eight hours," said the first, who had a hook nose.

"I can't stay awake either," said the other.

I sat up rubbing my eyes. "Where you guys headed?"

"El Paso," said the fat one.

"I'll drive you as far as Phoenix—my brother lives there," I offered.

"What the hell—you don't look old enough to drive," said Hook Nose.

I pulled out my wallet and showed them my driver's license.

"Well, hell, we got us a chauffeur," said Hook Nose.

"You got any gas money?" Fatty asked.

"No, but my brother will give you one hundred dollars when I get to him."

Hook Nose and Fatty looked at each other. "What are we waiting for? Let's hit the road."

I followed them out to their car. Hook Nose opened the trunk, rummaged in a bag, removed something I couldn't see, and tucked it in his coat pocket.

"We'll ride in back and sleep. Just get out on the highway and follow the signs to Phoenix. We just filled the gas tank," said Fatty.

I was nervous, having only driven between the farm and Bemidji. I pulled out onto the highway and followed the sign directing me south.

"Give me four of those," said Fatty. I heard a pill bottle rattle.

"Here, now stop whining and roll me one." A flaring match illuminated Hook Nose's face for a moment in the rearview mirror.

A strange tobacco smell came from the back seat. Ten minutes later I felt light headed and rolled a window down.

"Roll that damn window up," said Fatty.

"Yeah, keep this shit in here," mumbled Hook Nose.

I realized it must be marijuana—I'd never smelled it before but had heard of it. The Marine I'd ridden the rails with the past summer had bragged about smoking it every day. "I traded C-rations for rolled joints," he'd said. "I floated through the days."

Fatty and Hook Nose snored as I drove south, happy with my good fortune. I knew Tim didn't have a hundred dollars. I'd have to ditch these guys when I got there. As I drove through mountains in the early morning darkness, I wondered what the future held.

I knew I'd never return to the farm. Perhaps Tim could get me into school in Phoenix—Barb had, in Hillsboro, a few years earlier when Danny was born. Except, I was seventeen now and I could join the military. I recalled the history teacher talking about the growing battle against communism. Driving through the night I thought about Audie Murphy, John Wayne, and the Marine, and how crazy he had been—fearing no one.

Maybe I should join the Marines—if things didn't work out with Tim, that's what I'd do, join the Marines. I'd heard that you could enlist without a parent's consent at seventeen.

To the east, the horizon began to lighten. I looked at the fuel gauge as I passed a sign that read, Needles, 40 miles. The sun peeked over the horizon; it was going to be a clear day. I was happy to see no snow covering the brown hills.

"Where are we?" asked Fatty, through a yawn from the back seat.

"I just passed a sign that said Needles in forty miles."

"Needles. What the hell you doing in California?" shouted Hook Nose.

"I followed the sign that said Phoenix—I must have missed a turn. We need gas. We're below a quarter tank," I said.

"Just get the hell out of this state," said Fatty.

I pulled up to a pump at a packed-dirt gas station. "Fill'er up?" the lone attendant asked.

I turned to the men in the back seat. "Do you have enough to fill it?"

Fatty and Hook Nose pulled their wallets. "We're broke," Hook Nose said. "How much do you have?"

I pulled my wallet and held it open. "I'm broke, too—like I said, my brother will pay you when we get to Phoenix."

"What about that wristwatch you're wearing." said Hook Nose. "What's it worth?"

I looked at the watch my grandmother had given me—she said it had belonged to my grandfather. "It's Swiss—my granny said it was very expensive."

"See if he'll trade you a tank of gas for it," said Hook Nose.

The attendant agreed. He was a young kid, about my age. "Give me the watch and I'll fill the tank," he said. I remember wondering if he'd slip the watch in his pocket and not tell his boss.

"Do it," Hook Nose grunted.

"Stay off the main highway," Fatty said. Six hours later we were bumping over dirt roads on an Indian reservation in Arizona, Hook Nose directing me where to turn. We were hopelessly lost and the gas gauge was below a quarter. Ahead, finally, was a paved highway.

"Take a right—that must be south," said Hook Nose. I turned onto the road and soon spotted a sign—Phoenix 59 miles.

"We'll never make it," I said as we pulled into a small town. It was early evening and the one-street town looked deserted.

Three blocks past the police station, Hook Nose pointed to a laundromat that had no vehicles in the lot. "Pull in there," he said.

I turned in and parked near the door. Fatty and Hook Nose crawled out of the car and opened the trunk. Through the rearview mirror, I saw

Hook Nose tuck the tire iron under his shirt.

Fatty glanced up and down the highway. "This'll be a piece of cake," he said.

"You stay by the car," Hook Nose told me. "If anybody turns in, stick your head in the door and tell us."

The men walked into the laundromat. I climbed out of the car so I could get a better view up and down the road. A few minutes later they came out laughing, carrying three bulging socks, and climbed into the car.

"Payday," Fatty said with a grin, locking eyes with me in the rearview mirror as I pulled back onto the highway. "Here's a candy bar."

"We'll get gas in the next town," Hook Nose said. "Then on to Phoenix and another payday. Your brother better be good for that hundred."

I looked ahead, wondering what I'd gotten myself into.

"Give me some pills," Fatty said.

Hook Nose looked at him and rattled the bottle. "There's only three left and they're mine—I got them. Eat a candy bar." He unscrewed the lid and popped the pills into his mouth, followed by a long swallow of Coke.

"Drive faster," Fatty said, looking in the mirror at me. "I got to get something."

"Relax," said Hook Nose. "Eat another candy bar."

"Screw you. I'll puke if I eat another one. I wish there was something to put that candy in back there. They must have just filled the machine— it popped open like that Mexican's skull."

"Shut up," said Hook Nose.

It was dark when we pulled into Phoenix. "Find a drug store," said Fatty.

Driving slowly, I passed a police station; a block later, a drug store. "There's one. Want to stop?"

"It's too close to the cop station. Keep going," said Hook Nose.

"No. Stop there. I've had enough of your orders. I want to stop here," said Fatty.

"Okay, stop. You wait in the car," Hook Nose said, as he locked eyes with me in the rearview mirror.

I pulled into the parking place and the men got out. As soon as they entered the store I took the car keys, threw them into some shrubs, and ran toward the police station.

At the station I showed the desk sergeant Tim's address. "That's north of here—I'll give you directions," he said.

I didn't tell the sergeant that I was walking or about the two men I'd been with. I was worried that there might be a notice out for them about the robbery—especially if Fatty had broken open somebody's skull.

For the next four hours I walked along road shoulders—hiding in the ditch or behind bushes each time headlights approached, just in case Hook Nose and Fatty had a second set of keys. I finally found the address, a ranch style house in a new subdivision. It was after midnight but I knew Tim wouldn't mind if I woke him up, so I pounded on the door. Suddenly a porch light came on and the door jerked open.

I was staring up the barrel of a .45 caliber pistol with a crew cut skinny stranger behind it. "Who the hell are you, beating on our door at two in the morning?"

"I'm Tim's brother. Who are you?"

"What the hell—you almost got your ass blown off. We've been having break-ins around here. The whole neighborhood is nervous. You're Tim's brother? I saw him two days ago—he said something about his brother disappearing in northern Minnesota and nobody knowing where he was."

"You saw him two days ago? Doesn't he live here?"

"No, I'm Charlie's uncle. They use my address for mail. They're in an apartment across town—I'll drive you over there." Charlie was Tim's Illinois friend who had moved to Phoenix with him.

Tim and Charlie had a party going at his apartment—actually, I remember it as living quarters above a garage. Three girls and two guys raced down the stairs and around the building as we pulled up. I thought I heard somebody shout "cops" as they ran into the darkness. Tim came down the stairs with a small Italian man behind him.

"What the hell are you doing down here? Everybody is wondering what happened to you." Tim seemed kind of mad.

"I got tired of the bullshit at home and decided to leave like you and Chris."

We went up to the apartment. Charlie and his uncle were drinking a beer, the uncle telling about almost shooting me. Charlie thought it hilarious and went into a giggling fit.

"I'm going home to bed," the uncle said, "You knuckleheads can party the rest of the night away." For the next two hours I told and retold the details about my trip.

On Monday morning Tim brought me into where he worked and introduced me to his boss, a stocky man in his mid-thirties. "If he doesn't stutter, he's hired," he said.

It was a magazine sales business set up in a motel. Beds and furniture were stacked along a wall. Unpainted plywood boards divided the room into cubicles. Each workstation consisted of a chair, work bench, telephone, and cut-out pages of the Phoenix telephone directory. There was also a scripted message we read to prospects who answered their phone. It went something like this: "Hello, Mrs. O'Brian. This is Andy Williams calling from Des Moines, Iowa, and you are the lucky winner of *Good Housekeeping* magazine." More often than not the party silently hung up, but three to four times a day, leads developed and a closer went out to collect shipping and handling fees and funds for additional magazines the sucker may have purchased. It was a very monotonous job but we had light moments. Tim discovered a hot-headed old lady who cursed him out and slammed the phone down.

It was before the days of caller ID. About every third day, Tim called to antagonize her. "Hello, Mrs. Red Dick, this is Andy Williams…."

We crowded the cubicle, ears to the phone. "My name is Riddick, R-I-D-D-I-C-K. Mrs. Riddick. If I ever get my hands on you I'll strangle you." Slam, the phone echoed across the cubicle.

We stayed in Phoenix until early February. The telephone book was almost used up and Tim had several unpaid traffic tickets—squealing tires, speeding, drinking and driving—he knew he would eventually get arrested. He decided I must return to school—an honorable but misguided idea in my opinion. We needed a new battery for the 1955 Impala convertible but didn't want to waste money.

The night before we left, Tim, Charlie, and I snuck into a car dealer lot and stole a battery. When Tim installed it in the Impala, he over-tightened a cable clamp and broke the battery post—we went back for a second one. Late that night we drove through the Superstition Mountains, windows down in the warm night. We arrived back at the farm on a Friday afternoon. I don't recall any "return of the prodigal son" reunion.

An hour after we arrived, Herman said, "Windy, get your coat and boots on. It's chore time."

"I don't live here anymore. I'm just visiting with Tim and Charlie. I'm going down to Illinois with them tomorrow."

"No, you're not," said Tim. "That's why we drove up here—to bring you home."

"Get your damn boots and coat on. It's chore time," Herman reiterated.

"Thanks a lot," I said to Tim as I buttoned my barn coat. I trudged out, slid the door open and was greeted by a cloud of manure-scented steam. Inside, the body heat from the cows kept the barn warm and humid. Randy was in the manger distributing hay he'd pitched down from the loft.

"I'm glad you came home. I've been doing your chores and mine since you left."

"Well, get used to it," I said, "I'm not sticking around here for long."

"Dad says you're going to get on the bus and go to school Monday morning."

"We'll see about that," I said, pitching hay angrily into the cows' faces.

Herman came into the barn and began the evening milking. "Look at your heifer. She's going to calve pretty soon," Herman said to me. I walked over to the pen, looked at her, shrugged my shoulders and walked away.

Early Sunday morning Tim and Charlie left. It was a day of cutting firewood and carrying it into the house, cleaning the barn and throwing fresh bedding to the cows. That evening Randy and I sat at the table playing crazy eights.

"You better get ready for school—you're getting on the bus in the morning," said Herman.

"I don't want to go back. I've missed too much to catch up before the end of the year."

"I don't know what happened. You used to be on the honor roll. I saw your last report card—F's and Incompletes—why?" Herman looked at me, hard.

"I'm totally bored. Who cares about Chinese dynasties and if YxM=Z? I don't need to know those things. I want to see the world," I protested.

"Get ready for school. You're getting on the bus in the morning."

The next morning I climbed onto the bus and sat in my old seat.

My friend Steve sat behind me. "Where the hell have you been?" he asked. "We thought they'd find you when the snow melted."

When the bus pulled into the school parking lot I climbed off, looked at the entrance door to the high school and turned my back to it. I walked downtown to the Federal Building, went inside, and studied the directory. I rode the elevator to the third floor and followed directions to the office door labeled MARINE CORPS RECRUITER and knocked. Nobody answered. After several minutes, I went to the door labeled NAVY RECRUITER and walked in. A man in dress blues looked up at me from his desk. "Do you know where the Marine recruiter is?" I asked.

"No. Why, you thinking of joining up?" He eyed me up and down.

"Yes, I want to be a Marine."

"I'm going to tell you something—just between you and me." Cigarette in one hand, coffee mug in the other, he said, "The Marine Corps sucks. You ever think of joining the Navy?"

Two weeks later I was on my first airplane ride, flying to the Naval Training Center in San Diego, California.

Emancipated

In the chickenhouse I found this letter I wrote to my grandmother while I was in basic training. Elsie insisted on us giving Barb respect, thus I called her "Mom" in my letters.

May 12, 1965. Dear Grandma and Polly, I received your letter the other day. I am not too surprised that you didn't get a letter from the farm lately. Mom has probably told you that the check was put in her name. I guess there is going to be more trouble about it. I wrote Mom and Dad the other day and told them that if they didn't quit arguing about that check, the Welfare would step in and take the kids. I know they will do it if they find the least reason to. I am sort of worried about Mom, she is getting a bit old for all this fighting. As you know, her nerves are not too good as it is. I wish I could do something about her problem, but now that I don't live there I don't really see where it is my business. I am going overseas. I am almost certain of this because I have to get some extra shots.

Love, Windy

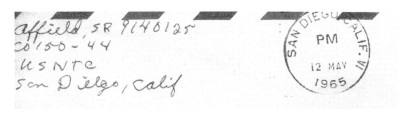

I don't remember what check I was talking about. Reading that letter fifty years later, I realized that I did worry about Barb even though I was angry at her. There are many more letters that show her misery and discontent. I discovered this little nugget in the court records.

May 10, 1966. Order Terminating Jurisdiction on Wendell George Curry for the reason that the youth has been out of the home in the service for over a year and can be considered to be emancipated and no longer in need of supervision.

May 10, 1966. Order Terminating Jurisdiction on Wendell George Curry for the reason that the youth has been out of the home and in the service for over a year and can be considered to be emancipated and no longer in need of supervision.

I was actually in the middle of my first Vietnam deployment when that order was issued.

(Autumn 1967, *left to right*) Chris, Tim, Wendell, Laurel, Randy, Bonny, Linda, Larry, and Danny. Last picture of the nine of us together.

I was home on leave just before redeploying to Vietnam. Chris and Tim came up to visit from Illinois. Laurel came up from Minneapolis. A few years later, Randy enlisted in the Navy and died in a plane crash in 1978.

1968
Convalescent Leave

I served two tours in Vietnam. Forty-five years later I wrote a memoir, *Muddy Jungle Rivers*, (2012) about my second tour. An excerpt from *Muddy Jungle Rivers* that took place late autumn, 1968, described my return home after being wounded:

North wind rustled dry ditch grass as I walked backward, thumb out, squinting into the cold white sun, wind biting at my back. Nobody knew I was coming in on the Greyhound—no phone at the farm.

"Didn't hear you were home," said Tom, a neighboring farmer who picked me up. "Heard you got wounded. Heard you were in the hospital."

"I got a thirty day convalescent leave—just got it yesterday."

Tom was quiet for the next eight miles of dirt road. Near the farm I spotted Herman at the edge of a field bent over pawing through dirt, picking potatoes, alone. The kids were in school.

"I'll get out at the end of the driveway," I told Tom. "Thanks for the ride."

Tom nodded.

Everything seemed the same. The loud slamming screen door. Barb, silent after a subdued greeting. Flypaper ribbons hung over the table, black with the summer's catch. Withered plants rested on window ledges—long-dead from neglect. Fluorescent tubes flickered, never changed until they went dark. The old-lived-in-house-smell flooded back as I walked through the house to the front room. The piano was still piled high with Bach and Beethoven and Mozart and Lutheran hymnals. I looked out the picture window toward Maple Lake, past the treehouse— now a relic—Randy and I had played in.

I jumped when the screen door slammed and turned to see Herman standing in the kitchen. His shoulders sagged beneath the weight of the mounded potato basket hanging from each fist, his baggy jeans bunched beneath the tarnished, brass buckled belt. A frayed, sweat-stained engineer cap shaded his eyes as he set the baskets down. Silently he crossed the floor and put his arms around me. Tears came unbidden.

He stepped back quickly, turned, and blew into a wrinkled gray handkerchief. "I gotta get these spuds to the basement."

Barb watched silently.

Not much had changed with the kids—they treated me the same. That night we all played cards and joked, like the old days. I think they'd been warned not to ask about the war. After the house went dark I tucked an old horse-hide robe beneath my arm and walked to the bluff overlooking Maple Lake. Wrapped in the bristly stallion hide, beneath the harvest moon I listened to skeins of geese wing south. Twice flocks passed between me and the moon. Frost settled and I remembered and cried and didn't understand why—why I was alive when so many others weren't. I drifted off—that was the first night I welcomed those faceless ones in my dreams. I felt safe with them. I woke shivering. As the stars faded in the east I listened to mallards feeding in the lake below and remembered the hundreds I had shot as a child. I crept back to the house and filled the stove. Herman heard me, got up, and shuffled into the living room in his ancient leather moccasins and droopy-bottomed longjohns and put the coffeepot on to boil.

"I saw you picking spuds yesterday. I'll help today," I said, as I watched him sprinkle coffee into the bubbling water. He stood for a while, *back to me, looking down at the pot as grounds rolled in the boiling water.*

"That's good. I got nobody to ride the digger and raise it at the end of rows. I was forking 'em yesterday," he said, handing me a mug of coffee, grounds still swirling. "How long are you home for?"

"Thirty days. You planted quite a bit of corn this year—cob corn or silage?"

"Silage. It froze early, kernels didn't dent."

"I'll help get it chopped—it'll go fast with both of us—maybe Randy can help get firewood up before I go back," I said.

Herman had aged. The halo of stubble surrounding his scarred skull had gone from gray to white. His shoulders drooped, as though he was still holding the potato baskets. He nodded silently, shifting the handleless mug between trembling palms.

Each day I walked the forests around the farm where Randy and I used to take turns shinnying up young maple trees. When the climber was about fifteen feet in the air, the person on the ground chopped the tree and it was an exhilarating ride down. Now I kicked at rotting stumps.

Many nights I crept out of the house and sat above the lake beneath the mildewy robe. The first flakes of winter brushed my cheeks and I recalled a strange thought I'd had during the memorial service for a boat crew killed when their boat hit a mine; how that past winter they'd flown west, died, and come home before the frost was out of the ground. This would be their first full winter beneath the soil. Why them and not me? My boat was supposed to lead that morning.

One day I rode into town with Herman. We delivered two cans of cream to the Creamery, then did errands; Co-op store, Red Owl, Surge Milking Machine dealer. It was the same at each stop, "This is my boy— he just got back from Vietnam." Herman didn't notice the silent nods and fixed-grin welcomes from the old men, all World War II veterans. He was proud.

We got out of the car at the little gas station downtown. "Put in a dollar's worth," he told Dale, the owner. We walked over to a truck where bushel baskets of apples were pyramided from ground to tailgate. It was an unspoken rule—if you bought gas you got a free apple. Dale came over, Herman handed him a dollar and said, "This is my boy, he just got back from Vietnam."

I had begged apples from Dale since I was a little kid. Dale looked at me, frowned, and said, "Take two." Dale had served during the Korean Conflict.

The kids found it humorous that I jumped at sudden noises. I learned to sit, back against the wall so they couldn't surprise me with the slamming screen door. One evening after supper Randy came around the table behind me. I caught a hint of burned cordite then a string of cracks like an AK-47 exploded beneath my chair. I hit the deck.

Herman jumped, too. "Take those damn firecrackers outside."

He'd served in North Africa.

Barb sat unmoving.

The kids thought the whole thing hilarious.

One morning, near the end of my thirty-day leave, I was filling the stove when Herman got up.

"Do the ducks still feed below the hill at night?" he asked.

I looked at him silently and nodded yes.

He put coffee water on to boil, then kneeled at the bottom step of the stairs and opened a hinged step, pulling out the .50 caliber ammo box that stored his treasures and removed an antique silver cigar cutter attached to a handmade silver chain.

"When I returned from the war, my father gave me this and the homestead—now I want you to have it." He held it out and lowered it gently into my open palm, chain links flashing beneath the flickering

fluorescent, then turned back to the stove and filled our mugs.

From fifty years out, I try to remember the family dynamics of that autumn, 1968 visit. There weren't any shouting matches between Herman and Barb, just a cold indifference. My youngest brother, Danny, was eight in 1968. His total memory of my Vietnam experience is that I ate his live goldfish because he dared me to. I know now that Herman was already sick—I didn't know he'd be dead within eighteen months.

The spring of 2017 I visited Indiana University, South Bend, and spoke to history students who used my book in their class. During that visit I reconnected with two men I did my 1966 Vietnam deployment with. Our last evening together, Chris, Ron, and I sat around a bonfire late into the night. I closed my eyes and once again, I was on the fantail of the USS *Rogers* DD 876, off the coast of Vietnam, joking with other teenage sailors in the dark night.

(Summer 2009) Wendell Affield hiking Lakeshore Trail toward the house
he lived in as a child in 1952. Lake Chelan in the background.

2009
Lake Chelan Revisited

In the summer of 2009, my wife Patti and I spent several days at Stehekin, Washington, located at the upper end of Lake Chelan. It's a remote area—still no roads in. From the ferry deck on *Lady of the Lake*, I spotted our old house tucked atop a bluff in the lee of a sheltered cove.

The mountain slopes were our playground in 1952. Three little boys free-ranged through pine forests. My four-year-old mind cached images of an unstable mother and an elegant old mansion with no plumbing or electricity. That's the remembrance I carried for almost six decades.

Stehekin, the nearest town to the house, is as close as one will get to Shangri-La in today's world. One day while Patti and I explored the valley, we expressed concern about leaving our bicycles unattended at Rainbow Falls trailhead. A young man, a crewman on *Lady of the Lake*, told us, "Don't worry, this is the last honest place on earth."

There's an almost numinous harmony of diversity and tolerance woven through the small community. The matriarch of one of the first families in the valley praised the knowledge of a barefoot, ponytailed, organic gardener who lived down the road from her home. "People come all the way from Seattle to ask him questions." Another local who lived in an old van with his cats was the "keeper of the local history." He humbled me when he asked if I would write and share my memories of Henry, our neighbor, when we lived on the mountain the summer of 1952.

Stehekin Pastry Company's cinnamon roll aroma wafted through the valley, drawing visitors as the Pied Piper's flute attracted the children of Hamelin. Patti and I took an afternoon break in the shaded restaurant almost every day. We noticed very little dust or noise pollution—I counted five vehicles; the historian's van, a forestry jeep, two tour vans, and the matriarch's car—she's about eighty, so I suppose she's earned it.

Even seasonal employees exuded a sense of belonging. Monetary position seemed not to influence one's social position. The pine-shrouded mountain slopes, waterfalls, flowers, and melting mountain snowcaps reigned supreme. In 1952, we were not a part of this harmony.

Symbolic of the valley's serenity was the lakeshore kneeler at Groseclose Meditation Site. Patti and I were hot and thirsty as we walked back to our lodge one afternoon from Buckner Orchard. I told her to keep going—I'd catch up after snapping a few pictures.

The Site is an amphitheater with forested mountain walls and a blue sky ceiling. I walked up the sandy aisle between the split-log benches to the shaded pulpit that had a hand-hewn cross silhouetted against the aqua lake. A scripture passage, burned into Ponderosa pine, jumped out at me. I traced my fingers over the charred Psalm: *Be still and know that I am God.* As I write this, I wonder if that message helped me make sense of that turbulent summer so many years ago.

Early on our second morning in Stehekin, I set out on the seven-mile hike to our old homestead. I detail this journey to emphasize the risks we children were exposed to as we roamed the mountain around our cabin the summer of 1952.

At the trailhead near our lodge, I discovered a seven-foot-long Ponderosa pine walking stick left by an earlier hiker. Staff in hand, I set off on Lakeshore Trail. Across the lake, the rising sun sparkled on snow, the mountain scene reflected in the crystalline water of the lake. Robins fluttered about on their incessant hunt. Hummingbirds and bees flitted through blossoms. Ponderosa pines towered above, many scarred by fires, new growth rising beneath them. Vanilla-scented sap, warmed by the sun, wept from charred bark. I took a break on a promontory and watched cloud banks build as wind kicked up dust on the powdery trail.

Distant thunder prompted me to move on, down into a cold gully where snow-melt flowed. This shaded spot was a different eco-system. Wide-leaf maples and other broad leaf trees flourished here in this mountain cleft, carved deep by eons of erosion. I waded the creek and began my ascent, following the zigzag trail up. Farther from the lodge, the trail was less traveled. Bordering the trail, Oregon grapes, like dime-sized blueberries, dotted knee-high bushes.

I approached a rock fence that paralleled the path, bleached cedar posts protruding from the stones. Exploring closer I saw it was an abandoned homestead. Somebody had spent thousands of hours building four stone walls to shelter an orchard about half the size of a soccer field. The relic reminded me of a crumbling French fort and cemetery I'd seen many years before, deep in the U Minh Forest in Vietnam. There, tropical growth had reclaimed the moss-covered headstones; the moist climate had crumbled mud-packed French fort walls. Here, on this semi-arid mountainside, naked stone dully reflected sun—tree roots snaked into rocky soil. One apple tree remained—a stunted apple high in the branches. How had that blossom pollinated? What happened to the people who tried to carve a homestead in such an inhospitable place? Storm clouds rolled over the ridge, and I hurried along the trail.

The twitching tail grabbed my attention and I jumped back. I slipped my camera from the pouch and followed the rattlesnake as he slithered off the trail. I followed him through dense undergrowth—for a moment I lost him—toward a charred blow-down Douglas fir. I stepped back and moved to the other side of the log where I spotted him, coiled, tail high, tongue flicking. I snapped a few pictures and moved on. Rain kicked tiny dust puffs on the trail.

Lightning struck close, wind picked up, and a torrential downpour drenched me. Hail stung the back of my neck and bounced on the bare gray rock face. I crouched in the shelter of an ancient Ponderosa. At the lodge there was a stump face, the rings dating back to Ponce de Leon in the 1400s. The tree that sheltered me probably dwarfed that trunk. The storm passed as suddenly as it had blown in and I continued along. Pushing aside fireweed that the wind and rain had knocked down over the trail, I jumped aside, spooked, but it was only a twisted, snake-shaped root.

My senses were heightened. Perhaps it was the adrenaline rush from the snake encounter or the reawakened memories from the French fort. Maybe it was the monsoon-like rain with only hail ricocheting. As I walked the now damp path, I was sharply aware of the wet fireweed drooped over the trail. I pushed my staff along ahead of me. Yellow arrowleaf balsamroot seemed brighter than before—I had read that the Okanagan Natives smoked the dried leaves before trappers carried tobacco west. Small blue flowers—lupines—seemed to grow out of rocks.

I passed through a recent burn area. Fireweed—one of the first plants to sprout after a forest fire—blanketed the mountain from lapping waves to summit, bees thick among the delicate purple flowers. Climbing over fallen tree trunks blocking the path, I poked my stick beneath them before I stepped up, then leapt clear on the far side. The sun was out, the trail steaming.

On another high point I looked down on a cove and spotted our old house. In the lee of the cove, rested the stone quay that Henry, our neighbor, had moored his barge to—the same quay from which he had tossed me into the icy water. It was a favorite play area for us that summer. I passed the trail to Henry's homestead, up the mountain where it sat in the pristine meadow valley.

I climbed the steep slope near the dock to a level area and found a section of rusted pipe and recalled how melt water was piped down the mountain to our house. I spotted the brown house around a curve and remembered it—the stone foundation, the screened-in upstairs sleeping area. It was changed, updated. The massive front yard pines were gone. I called out; no answer. I knocked on the door; no answer. I wrote a note and tucked it in the door jam. I walked around the front of the house. The steps I had slid down face-first in 1952 were gone. A new foundation covered the old. I walked to the edge of the yard, sat on the split rail fence and looked down at the lake. There was the long drop with the small stone dock at the bottom. My brothers had fished there with their Gabby Hayes fishing rigs.

It was a melancholy afternoon revisiting the past, enveloped in pine and mountain earth smell as I shuffled through needle beds. I remembered the little boy playing in the forest with his brothers and sister, hiding from his mother, skipping rocks out into the lake, bathing in the chilly water, waves splashing over his head. Late in the afternoon, *Lady of the Lake* steamed my way. I had planned to wave her down and catch a ride but decided to stay in this moment.

Later, as I hiked back to the lodge, I had a close encounter with a black bear—not really too close. I came around a bend and almost stepped in steaming bear scat, striped Oregon grape bushes strewn about the path where the bear had been feeding. As I hiked, I reflected on the summer of 1952 when we children roamed the mountain slopes around our house, and how our mother was the greatest danger to our well-being.

The next evening the owners of our old home stopped by the lodge and introduced themselves. As we visited, the lady was surprised at how vividly I recalled the interior of the home—how could I tell her that escape routes from my mother's wrath were seared into my memory?

The summer of 1939 when Barb was nineteen, she visited Poland and stayed with her school friend, Eva Barbacka, at Eva's family dacha in the Carpathian Mountains overlooking Lake Roznow. As I mentioned earlier, during that stay Barb met, became engaged to, and, I think, married a young Polish soldier whom she lost contact with after Hitler invaded Poland on September 1, 1939.

Lake Chelan has an eerie resemblance to Lake Roznow—both are narrow reservoirs tucked between mountain ranges. The summer of 1952, did Barb subconsciously revert to that summer twelve years earlier? We were in the Lake Chelan house late in the summer, the anniversary of her experience in Poland—trauma anniversary dates are powerful triggers to the past. I was only four but I remember her detached attitude, except when aroused to anger. I think now, it was that summer when I learned to read her moods.

I wish I knew more about our neighbor, Henry. In the chickenhouse I found evidence that he and Barb may have known each other in the 1920s—but that's another story. Henry must have been lonely, living alone with his mother up on the mountain after returning home from WWII. Was he sweet on Barb? He certainly made life more bearable for us—supplying milk and eggs and garden produce for so many young children. A few years before Barb died, I asked her about Henry. "He was a nice man," she told me. "But he didn't have much education."

I discovered that when Henry was five years old, he and his family moved to a ranch on Fish Creek. Contrary to what Barb thought, he was highly intelligent. According to his obituary, he designed and installed the hydro plant at Holden Village—near the place where my brothers attended school at Lucerne the autumn of 1952.

After the 2009 visit to Stehekin, I brought my laptop out to the farm and shared a slideshow with Barb. She traveled with me up Lake Chelan on *Lady of the Lake* and spotted our old house perched above the bluff. She hiked with me up and down the zigzag Lakeshore Trail. She saw the storm and the lightning and the flowers and the rattlesnake. She studied the many pictures of the old house and the area where we had lived in 1952. I was surprised at her response. "I worried about rattlesnakes that summer," she told me. And that was it.

By 2005 wild mint had spread across the lawn at the farm—the same mint Barb picked our first spring for icy lemonade. In later years I sometimes mowed the grass when I came out to visit her. Fresh-cut mint smell wafted across the old homestead yard and carried me back to that spring of 1950. After Barb died, I dug some lilac bleeders laced with mint and planted them in my yard. They're beginning to spread. Now, each spring, I rub mint leaves in my palms, bury my face in lilac blossoms, and remember a little boy's brain freeze when he guzzled ice cold lemonade.

(Spring 2008) Barbara, standing on her new deck, built over the crumbling steps we had peed on as children. Less than two years after this picture was taken she had a stroke and died.

2018
So Barbie, A Letter to my Mother

So, Barbie,

I told this story as true as I remember. After you died, I discovered the treasure locked in the chickenhouse. I've spent these last eight years studying it. You left so many stories, I hope to live long enough to tell them. As I pored over thousands of pages, I often wondered why you changed your will and left things to me. I know some of your children talked more than once about burning the chickenhouse treasures. I've come to realize that you wanted your story told. Did you, in your stroke-ravaged mind, conclude that I was your best shot? In telling *our* story, I've come to realize that, as a mother, you did the best you were capable of.

After your funeral I had to sell those old paintings, your Steinway grand, and all your other assets to pay for your funeral and settle debt you left with the county. One positive thing that came of my experience is that I've been in communication with the lady who owns your grandmother Fratt's home in Everett, Washington. She sounds lovely and has invited Patti and me to come visit her and her husband.

In the chickenhouse I found your "'38-'39 Memoirs" that you composed while enroute home from Europe. Near the end, you wrote, *We all have burdens and scars and roads that we might have taken—but one must never regret. I have many and bitter reasons for feeling that way. They say that in this world some are born weak and some are born strong and that each should accept his place.* Barbie, you were only nineteen that autumn of 1939, yet you wrote with an angst and knowledge beyond your years.

9293-B

Folded and tucked between pages in your mother's "Mental Health Journal" I found this picture of you taken two years earlier on September 24, 1937, aboard your ship, *American Farmer*. Now, eighty years later, I see a beautiful young woman wearing a pert dimpled smile that teases, "Look out Europe, here I come." Was that an early mask? What happened after you steamed east, past Lady Liberty?

From chickenhouse information, I learned that in 1939, on the eve of the German invasion of Poland when you were trying to escape, you had almost no money and were blocked at the Germany/Poland border. Your mother wrote in her diary about how you talked your way across. Later, the Wehrmacht kicked you off the train in Berlin. Somehow you regained passage but were stopped a third time at the Germany/Belgium border. Barbie, I've seen cruel things men do to women in war. Did you use your body to negotiate your way homeward, toward Brussels?

Chris remembers a homeless shelter in New York he called the "Green House." When you and Chris and Tim were homeless in the late 1940s did you use your body again to barter for food and shelter? Is that why Laurel and I don't have a father listed on our birth certificate? I know they are two different men because I had DNA tests done. As a child when I asked you, you told me that Chris, Tim, Laurel, and I, all had the same father. Was that one of your false memories or, perhaps, an alternate personality?

We all inherit genetic ghosts—good and bad. Laurel has two wonderful children and several grandchildren. She's made a good life for herself. She's strong and smart—genetic gifts from you I believe. She and I visit often—she too, struggles to make sense of our past. As a result of the DNA tests we did, Laurel discovered who her father was. The summer of 2017 she and I drove to Ohio and met her new sister—this past Thanksgiving she also met her ninety-year-old brother.

Barbie, in the chickenhouse treasures, I learned about the terrible sense of abandonment you felt as a child, when your mother left you at times and favored your sister Polly. Why did you separate me from my siblings and leave me with my grandparents when I was an infant? Speaking of childhood, why did you accuse Herman of molesting his daughters? You knew it was untrue. When he reached out to his little girls, did you flash back to something terrible that had happened to you when you were a child?

Not long ago, a lady who read this manuscript asked me, "How did you turn out the way you did?" I've certainly made my share of mistakes, but along life's path I learned empathy. I surely didn't inherit that trait from you or learn it from Herman. I like to think it was a quality gifted me from the father I never met. Like you, I drift away listening to classical piano music—perhaps a gift from you.

A love of the Arts has passed to your great grandchildren. Remember your last Christmas, in the nursing home, when Kadance and her dance group came and gave a holiday performance? I have a picture of you in your wheelchair holding Livia while Kadance pushed you toward the Day Room. You looked genuinely happy—as if all your masks had slipped away.

You were so proud of your great granddaughters. Eight years later Kadance has grown; she is a graceful presence on the stage. Livia has your gift of music. At your estate auction I purchased that old boxed xylophone and brought it home. Not long ago, I showed it to Livia. She took it out of the box, lined the keys up one above the other, and began tapping out tunes with the mallets. The last time I was at her house, the xylophone rested on one side of her piano, her guitar on the other.

Barbie, that day you crossed the river eight years ago, you asked my forgiveness and I granted it. Since then, I've come to understand that in August 1939, as Hitler's armies massed at the borders, you were forced to flee Poland and leave your new husband, Zdzisław "Kristaw." It must have been heart wrenching. A few weeks later, when you wrote, "Some are born weak and some are born strong," I'm sure you were alluding to yourself as weak.

After I learned details of your psychological struggle—the heartache and privation—I know that you must have been strong to survive. You passed that gift on to most of your children. I never told you, but for many years, when I called you Barbie, it was a term of endearment. I think you knew that.

Barbie, not long ago I asked the new owner if I could walk through the old farm buildings one last time. Bats have invaded the abandoned house. Holes in the granary roof have grown. Shredded binder canvasses still hang from the trusses. Herman must have hung them after the last season he harvested oats in the late 1960s. The log walls of the blacksmith shop are rotted at the corners after more than one hundred years. It will probably collapse within the next decade.

I visited the chickenhouse last. I stood, hand on the door latch, and looked east toward Maple Lake and remembered the first winter on the farm—when I was two— and how terrified I was of the Leghorn rooster that lay in wait to attack me each time I passed the little chicken door.

I recalled the first time I lifted the latch after you died and stood, looking at the piles of weathered documents and dry-rotted furniture. I remembered the musty rodent smell—Laurel and I wore masks when we cleaned things out. At first glance, I too considered burning everything, but then I discovered the 1822 letter and a newspaper scrap lying on the concrete, dated March 19, 1939. The headline screamed "Powers United To Curb Hitler" with a picture of the tyrant. It was in one of the early packets of letters your mother wrote that I learned about your first suicide attempt in 1937. I realized that here in this decomposing heap rested the truth of your struggle.

Seven years after you died, I lifted the chickenhouse door latch for the last time and slowly swung the door open. The concrete floor was swept clean—no ammonia manure smell left. The nesting boxes were gone. The little feed bin your father's urn was tucked into was still mounted on the wall. The two center posts still held the roof up. I searched for some hint of our having been there, but everything was gone—not even a scrap of your mother's brittle war-time newspaper clippings. The little chickenhouse door near the floor—the chicken exit that Randy and I had squeezed in and out of playing tag—caught the wind and swung open on a loose hinge. For a moment I saw two little boys playing again. I think about that door sometimes, rattling and clacking in the wind. I wonder if a small piece of us is still there.

Barbie, I've come to realize that we all left something on the farm—you left the most. I came home from my visit that day and began reading through the old letters again and realized that the chickenhouse was just a building—just as the memory of Randy and me playing in the chickenhouse lingered, your spirit remained with the treasure you gifted me. Your parents' urns are nestled in the steamer trunk you took when we left Chelan in 1952. One day Laurel and I hope to cast their ashes into the depths of the lake they loved.

I read again the letter your mother wrote to your grandmother in 1921 when you were ten months old: "Barbara Ann thrives over here on Whidbey Island—she's fatter than ever and quite brown."

Nineteen years later, your Polish soldier directed you to write to him in French and he would reply in Latin. Barbie, you were so intelligent—I can't begin to imagine how suffocated you felt on the farm. When I tell your story, I hope to do you justice.

Your Son,

Wendell

Afterword

Over the decades, when we older siblings got together, we rehashed our childhood from countless angles. When I first started this book I planned to fact-check stories with them. I did with Chris, my oldest brother, until he went off his bipolar meds. As I write this, he's homeless with no contact information. His wife of more than forty years recently obtained a divorce.

My sister Laurel was helpful, but younger than me, so her early memories were sketchy. Much of this story took place before the younger siblings were born or when they were so young they don't remember how it was on the farm in the 1950s.

I'm not a mental health professional. I've taken several university level psychology and philosophy classes, and I've spent hundreds of hours studying psychology because it interests me, but I have something few mental health professionals have—life experience living with very troubled parents. Many years ago, I was diagnosed with post traumatic stress disorder (PTSD) from service in Vietnam. So I believe I have authority to speculate on what troubled Herman and Barbara.

It's impossible to do a clinical assessment on a dead person. There's no chance to interview the subject, gather details, or question evidence. But I believe that all sentient, living things leave their mark in some fashion, no matter how infinitesimal. Dinosaurs left footprints in tar pits. We treasure insect inclusions in amber fossils. Barb and Herman left their *psychological footprint* in the chickenhouse and upstairs in the attic of our old farmhouse. Their documented footprints revealed two deeply disturbed people. The best we can do is study the clues they left behind and try to make sense of their lives and learn from them as we move forward.

Based on the postage date of the earliest lonely hearts catalogue I discovered in the attic of the old farmhouse (*The Exchange*, December 11, 1945), Herman had been searching for a woman for four years before he and my mother Barbara connected. Why did other women reject him? What spooked them? This excerpt from Herman's 1948 Veterans Administration (VA) medical report may offer some insight to understanding him.

February 4, 1948—41 years old, White, Male, 167 lbs., 5' 4" tall. In Africa (during WWII) *he was pulled back from the front for a rest and re-examination before being returned to the front. Blood pressure was found higher than normal, and he was taken out of combat. This was 1943. He lay around in a replacement depot and then went to work in a post office. He sat down at this job all the time. During the past year has had frontal headaches. His eyes smart on reading. He sleeps well after midnight and gets up at 6:30 with the help of an alarm clock. If he hurries in his work, his heart beats hard and fast. Is on a farm by himself and milks 3 cows now but has 7.*

For many years, I've believed that today Herman would be diagnosed with PTSD. The VA report supports my theory. Several of the findings mirror PTSD symptoms. In retrospect, his rage, isolation, and hypervigilance (traits that didn't appear on the medical exam) now make sense.

Unknown to us, our grandmother was haunted by Barb's mental instability. In the chickenhouse, in Elsie's "Mental Health Journal," I discovered this newspaper clipping, dated March 1, 1957. Was this how Barb attempted suicide, the summer of 1937?

Car Fumes Kill Textiler's Daughter
By EUGENE SPAGNOLI
Auburn-haired, attractive Carole Shernoff, 17, honor student and one of two daughters of wealthy textile converter Murray Shernoff, was found dead in her pajamas yesterday in the garage adjoining the family's $75,000 home in Harrison, Westchester.

Elsie's 1930s diaries document Barb's physical assaults on her. After we returned to the farm from foster homes, when we were big enough to defend ourselves, some of us nicknamed Barb "Schizo." Even today some of my siblings think she may have been schizophrenic. It's a natural assumption. Her younger sister Polly was diagnosed with schizophrenia and institutionalized in 1945.

When I first broached the idea of telling this story, I began reading mental health literature about schizophrenia. I often came across the term Borderline Personality Disorder (BPD). While killing time between flights in a concourse kiosk, I discovered *Borderline Personality Disorder Demystified* by Robert O. Friedel. By the time my plane landed several hours later, pages of Friedel's book were dog-eared and underlined. Notes filled margins with phrases such as, "This is Barb," or "her rage," or "hatred toward Herman" or "estranged from family." During that first read of Friedel's book, I realized that today Barb would probably be diagnosed with BPD. *Diagnostic and Statistical Manual of Mental Disorders*, Fifth Edition (DSM-5) states, "BPD is a pattern of instability in interpersonal relationships, self-image and affects, and marked impulsivity."

Adolph Stern first used the term "borderline personality" in 1938 to describe patients who did not fit the standard classification system. At that time they were often diagnosed as schizophrenic. Thus my grandmother's conclusion that Barb was schizophrenic makes sense, and I can begin to understand her frustration and lack of empathy with her daughter's behavior.

In *The Everything Guide to Borderline Personality Disorder*, Constance M. Dolecki, MS PhDc, writes, "Parentification is a process in which parents turn to their children to parent them.…They also look to the child to take care of them—plan meals, clean, cook, keep them on schedule, etc." As the reader has seen, Dolecki's description summarizes my childhood.

Over the past seven years, as I've worked on this manuscript, I continue to study BPD. Marsha M. Linehan's *Cognitive-Behavioral Treatment of Borderline Personality Disorder* section on "Characteristics of Invalidating Environments" is very illuminating as I juxtapose Linehan's findings to primary source documents from my mother's early life and the relationship she had with her parents—especially a child's sense of abandonment, which is well documented and I plan to explore in the next book in the *Chickenhouse Chronicles* series.

Several psychiatric disorders may co-occur with BPD including many of the mood disorders and personality disorders. Barb presented with symptoms of several disorders over the course of her life, including eating disorders. I single out symptoms of two possible comorbid disorders that my primary source documents chronicle.

First, PTSD commonly co-occurs with Borderline Personality Disorder because both disorders are most often the result of trauma. Early in Barb's life, she was exposed to traumatic events.

Second, and I think of greater impact, dissociation is a common characteristic of BPD. But at what point does dissociation become so extreme that it progresses from a characteristic of one disorder to a comorbid—additional—disorder?

Dissociative identity disorder (DID), formerly known as multiple personality disorder, is controversial. A primary cause of DID is attributed to a coping mechanism to deal with severe trauma. Some in the mental health profession do not believe it exists. Over the course of six decades, I witnessed Barb display bizarre behavior—at times violent.

Early letters document Barb accusing schoolmates of stealing things only for her to find them later. People suffering dissociative identity disorder harbor alternate personalities (alters) that perform specific tasks—revealing themselves as alter fragments. In later life Barb often wrote grocery lists in French. A person with dissociative identity disorder can speak a foreign language when an alter is in control.

Recall the Polish soldier? His name was Zdzisław "Kristaw" Konopka. On August 26, 1939, Elsie wrote in her diary: *A frightful shock this a.m. in the air mail, mailed by Bar [Barbara] from Poland enclosing a letter from a young Polish Engineer asking us for permission to marry Bar—apparently immediately.*

In researching Konopka, I discovered that his brother was a priest and two of his sisters were nuns in the Catholic Church. They died during the Nazi occupation of Poland. Konopka was forty-six years old and a Major in the Polish Army (Barb was nineteen in 1939. She had a preference for older men—later, two of her husbands were fifteen years older than she was.)

Barb was fluent in Latin. I can imagine her convincing a Church official that she was of the Catholic faith. Did Barb, in the hysteria of approaching war—less than two weeks out—become a member of the Catholic Church and marry the Polish Major? I found evidence that he was captured by the Russian army and murdered in the Katyn Forest Massacre.

When Barb told Herman, "Don't be sacrilegious—he is the head of my church," was that a Catholic alter speaking? Did Barb, in her acute stress of escaping Poland and abandoning her school friend and new husband six days before the Wehrmacht invaded, unconsciously create a new alternate personality to deal with the trauma she was living? An alter that despised German men? Is that why she often referred to Herman as an ignorant German immigrant and a Nazi stormtrooper?

Barb changed her name to Linda in 1948.

Was it the alter Linda who married Schoenwandt in 1948 and Herman in 1950? Was it the alter Linda who kept Tim home for sixty-four school days in 1951? Recall that Barb signed all four quarters of his report card, Mrs. L. Affield.

The afternoon Barb proposed to the neighbor while Herman and we children listened—was that Linda or another alter?

Was it an alter who danced naked on the table while her children watched? An alter who beat me when I was a child; who terrified me to the point that I jumped out a second story window to escape from her? Was it an alter who refused to unlock her door in the dead of night during a violent storm to give her children shelter? Was it an alter speaking, when Barb wrote to her mother in the 1960s: "I'm still your little girl"? We'll never know the answer to those questions, but as I reflect on Barb's journey, I'm amazed at her resilience.

In *The Dissociative Identity Disorder Sourcebook*, Deborah Bray Haddock, writing about bodywork therapy and memory, says, "An individual never completely forgets what has happened to her in the past. Sometimes, though, those memories have been dissociated and stored very far away, like stacks of boxes packed away in the corner of a basement." (p. 166).

Had a community of alter fragments relegated those "boxes" of memories to the chickenhouse? Had Barb, as a final act a few days before she died, regained control and put me in charge so her story would be told?

Acknowledgements

My grandmother, Elsie Fratt Philips (1893-1984), made *Chickenhouse Chronicles* possible. Elsie was a prolific writer who recorded our family history in diaries and saved primary source documents—thousands of pages from those she corresponded with. My mother, Barbara Philips Affield (1920-2010), inherited the treasure, preserved it to the best of her ability, and gifted it to me.

My sister, Laurel Affield Hofmann, has been a font of inspiration and was instrumental in salvaging the chickenhouse treasures before others had a chance to burn our family history. Laurel and I have spent countless hours rehashing our childhood; she has also contributed research. My oldest brother Chris and I had many phone conversations as I worked on this story. His memories often validated mine, and he resurrected new memory paths for me to follow. Youngest brother Danny filled in gaps about life on the farm after I left.

My writers group—Sue Bruns, Polly Scotland, Doug Lewandowski, Marilyn Heltzer, and Mary Lou Brandvik—thank you for the many hours you've spent over the past years reading my stories. Sue, thank you for proof editing my stories.

For many years I have been a member of IBPA (Independent Book Publishers Association). Their monthly magazine and on-line articles and workshops are priceless. Self published authors are held to a higher bar than traditionally published writers. In preparing this manuscript for print, I shared sections of it with many students and at last count—four editors.

Spring semester, 2016, I audited a Creative Nonfiction class with Professor Mark Christensen at Bemidji State University. As with my Vietnam War memoir, *Muddy Jungle Rivers* (2012), Mark and his students provided valuable insights.

While attending that class, I met an amazing young lady who did the first edit of this manuscript. Amanda Jo Klejeski's developmental edit revealed her innate gift for memory and organizational skills. She'll go far in the publishing industry if she chooses to travel that path.

Angela Foster, a fantastic editor I met and worked with on my first book, also edited *The Farm 1950s* and again did an amazing job.

Thank you Peggy Nohner for the great line edit job.

Thank you Dr. Marsha Driscoll for critiquing the "Afterword" for psychological accuracy.

Eleanor Joan Daniels generously gave me full permission to use letters of her late husband's, Pastor Trueman Daniels. They were instrumental in illuminating a dark time in my family's life.

Ron McGaughey, Manager, Chelan Museum, Lake Chelan Historical Society, supplied background information for my childhood memories.

And thank you, my wife, Patti; she traveled this memory story with me. We spent a week in Stehekin, Washington, while I chased sixty-year-old ghosts. She saw firsthand the beautiful mountains we lived in that formed one backdrop to my chaotic childhood.

I feel blessed to have so many people help me in developing this story. Any shortcomings are mine.

Book Club Discussion:

1. Some of Affield's experiences in Vietnam as described in *Muddy Jungle Rivers* are interwoven into this biographical account, just as some of his childhood memories from the farm appear in the Vietnam memoir. How does this criss-crossing or overlapping of experiences at different stages of his life enrich both stories? (Examples: pp. 29-30, Natives and peasant in VN; p. 56, contrast—afraid of water in Lake Chelan, but pilot rescue swimmer in VN; p. 90, outhouse experience at home compared to boat "relief" in the Mekong; p. 114, comparing scavenging for food behind grocery stores as a kid to the Chinese women in Hong Kong; p. 142, playing war vs. real war; pp. 167-168, Shep's death and returning after Vietnam to mourn so many deaths; p. 176, swatting mosquitoes after cleaning up in Nebish Lake, and mosquitoes in U Minh Forest, VN; pp. 197-198, Bible camp, eternal damnation, and the funeral service for fellow soldiers in VN; p. 229, after the story of the billy goat feeding the family for several days, the story about the steaks in VN, rinsing the meat in the river (Put mustard on it/Put tobasco on it).

2. As the narrator of this very personal story, Affield takes the reader back to revisit his life through the eyes of a child, an adolescent, and as an adult. How does the story evolve as the teller matures and gains life experience, including his time in Vietnam and at Barb's death bed?

3. Writers use the five senses to pull the reader into the story. Throughout the book, sensory details help the reader to visualize the scenes. What specific sights, sounds, smells, tastes, or sensations stand out in your mind?

4. Throughout the book, Affield reflects on individual differences as he becomes more familiar with people of different cultures and beliefs—the Native Americans in the movie theater, the Baptists from the Bible camp, local Croatian farm families, and later, the peasants in VN. In what ways does his home environment serve as a microcosm for differences and reflect the way people from different backgrounds fear, misunderstand, and sometimes show a complete lack of respect for others who are different? (Wendell talks about how his childhood prepared him for individual differences.)

5. Throughout the book there are examples of the hardships and often cruelty suffered by the farm animals, cats, and dogs. As a reader, which stories or details stand out in your mind? In what ways do these details and stories about the animals parallel the hardships and abuse suffered by Wendell and his siblings?

6. When Wendell is taken to the doctor and diagnosed with mumps, the nurse and doctor are both incensed about his condition and his lack of cleanliness. What details about this scene were beyond the control of his parents and which aspects show neglect?

7. As Wendell gets older, his bond with Herman becomes more complicated. He states at one point that this could be partly due to the fact that Chris and Tim were on Barb's side (pp. 162-163). Why might the two older boys have seemed to favor Barb?

8. Barb pushes Wendell down for eating off the same spoon as Herman (p. 25). She also segregates Herman's bowl and eating utensils from other dishes and silverware (p. 220). Why?

9. Barb uses *Aesop's Fables* as a teaching tool—a moral compass—for her children. Yet in her anger when Wendell lets the mouse escape, she does not forgive him—quite the opposite (pp. 56-57). What might be going on in her head as she jabs him with the broom handle? Is she flashing back to her childhood? Perhaps a child alter?

10. What in Barb's past may have motivated her to demand that her children address her as Mommy Darling (pp. 54-55, 187, 188)?

11. Wendell gives Herman the feeder pig check and Barb goes after him. He jumps out the window (pp. 188). Try to see the situation through child-eyes—what would you have done?

12. Barb is a study in inconsistencies and paradoxes. What details about her and her behavior as a mother contrast dramatically with her often-repeated claims of being a Daughter of the American Revolution, a sophisticated woman from New York, an accomplished pianist and lover of opera?

13. Do you think there is merit to Affield's theory that his mother suffered borderline personality disorder?

14. At times, the narration includes unanswered questions, speculation, attempts to answer questions that cannot be answered. How do these affect you as a reader? What additional questions do you have after reading the book?

A Conversation With Wendell Affield

This book is the result of several years of poring through the Chickenhouse documents, interviewing people, and processing your own memories. Can you describe the evolution of your feelings about Herman and Barb that you experienced as you were writing the book?

I came to realize that they were like all of us—flawed people chasing a dream—Barb wanted a safe place to raise her children. Herman wanted a wife and family. He had been sending out letters to women for four years before Barb answered him in 1949. I've spent seven years researching the old documents, and each time I look at them I have new revelations. For example, I just realized, in tracking Barb's timeline in 1949, that she, with four young children, had moved back in with her parents, Elsie and Henry Philips, into their two bedroom apartment in NYC. Polly, Barb's schizophrenic younger sister, was also living in the apartment. I gleaned that information from a letter Eloise, Henry's English cousin, wrote. I'm sure that is when the priceless picture in Central Park was taken — the one with Barb on a bench holding infant Laurel with us three boys clustered around.

Your experiences in Vietnam could stand alone as a story, but even in *Muddy Jungle Rivers*, you interweave your childhood experiences into things that happened in Vietnam. Obviously the treasure trove of documents you found in the chickenhouse helped you to piece together details in the lives of your parents and grandparents that

could probably not have been learned without these letters, diaries, etc. If the Chickenhouse documents didn't exist, would you still have felt compelled to write about your childhood? If so, how would you have gone about it?

I felt compelled to write *Muddy Jungle Rivers* because I knew I had lived a unique experience and that would die with me if I didn't commit it to paper. In retrospect, I realize that in writing my memories for ten years while I learned the writing craft, I was psychologically coming to terms with my war experience. But back to your question; yes, I did plan to tell my mother's story. A few years before she died I began interviewing her each week. I scribbled countless pages of notes as she spoke. It was only after she died and I discovered the Chickenhouse treasures and studied them that I realized Barb had her own version of the past—she was a very unreliable narrator. For example, she told me that Herman had advertised himself when in fact it was her advertisement in *Cupid's Columns* that Herman responded to. But if I've learned anything in my quest into the past, it's the fact that memory is unreliable. Each day I feel blessed that I do have the Chickenhouse documents. They reawakened memories that I imagine I suppressed. They add layers and intrigue that even the most creative novelist could not imagine. I think that in the end, my interviews with Barb made her realize that I was her best hope for her story to be told—that's why she changed her will eight days before she died. She knew some of her children planned to burn the contents in the chickenhouse.

If you could sit down today and converse with Herman or Elsie, what kinds of questions would you have for them that you wouldn't have thought to ask before examining the chickenhouse treasure trove? What additional questions would you ask Barb now that you have seen all of the items in the chickenhouse?

Tough question: I think with Herman I would focus on his war trauma—if he realized that it affected his life. While attending BSU I took a few psychology classes and they opened a new world to me—I came to understand that behavior is the result of nature and nurture. Herman's father was a strict man who believed in corporal punishment. I believe now that Herman's violent behavior was a result of his childhood and his war trauma. Herman was in fact a very mild-mannered gentle man unless someone or something—like an uncooperative animal—triggered his rage.

I hope to tell Elsie's story because with two mentally ill daughters she constantly struggled emotionally and financially. Her husband was a very meek, kind-hearted man who struggled to provide Elsie with the standard of living she was accustomed to—he failed. A question I would ask Elsie: Did you force Barb to have an abortion when she was fifteen?"

Three questions I would ask Barb: 1) While you were in Poland with your friend, Eva Barbacka, did you marry Kristaw Konopka in August 1939? 2) Why did you despise your mother and refuse to let her see her grandchildren in the 1940s? 3) Who was my father?

Barbara is the next book in the *Chickenhouse Chronicles* series. I already have a 500 page rough draft exploring my mother's life. Usually, the biographer is challenged to research his/her subject; I am challenged not to go down rabbit trails with the thousands of pages covering my mother's life, but to include what is most relevant to her journey—what formed her into the woman I remember.

Your war experiences and your childhood memories are often interwoven. How did your experiences in Vietnam affect your perceptions of your childhood, of Herman, and of Barb? If you hadn't ever been to Vietnam, how different would this story be?

Over the months I was in Vietnam, watching the peasants struggle for survival, I came to realize that, as a child, I had it pretty good. I don't really think that my Vietnam Experience impacted my perception of Herman or Barb. I do sometimes reflect on what life would have been if I hadn't gone into the military. Midway through my first deployment the

Education Officer on the ship I was on suggested I take correspondence courses to qualify for my GED test. I wasn't interested—after all, I had dropped out of school to go to war not school. The Education Officer and I stood midnight watches together, and over the months he must have seen a glimmer of intelligence in me because he offered to let me take just the test without doing the correspondence courses. I aced the test. The reason I tell that story is that if I hadn't enlisted and instead finished high school and attended college—who knows what path I might have taken.

You were diagnosed with PTSD after your experiences in Vietnam, which is not uncommon for men who have been to war. As I read your book, however, I wondered if you might not have already had PTSD from the childhood experiences you had.

I think all nine of us children were psychologically damaged. Danny, the youngest, escaped the least scarred. Over the decades, Barb, as dysfunctional as she was, kept a thread of familial bond alive. The moment she died the thread snapped. I haven't spoken to several of my siblings for many years. But that is their choice. When my son, Jeff, died in 2015, one of them was in town from Illinois and didn't attend Jeff's funeral— I'm still waiting for a condolence card. I tried to reach out to him one time, I sent him a rough draft of the chapter about when he cut his hand in the buzz saw and spent time in Gillette Children's Hospital in the early 1950s. He sent the essay back with hateful comments and said that my writing skills were atrocious. He suggested I follow Hemingway's lead. Ironically, this past summer, my wife Patti and I attended a luncheon at the Minnesota Humanities Center in St Paul where I was recognized for my work with the underserved in our community. A little plaque in the entryway of the Humanities Center caught my eye, "Gillette Children's Hospital." I had been in the building sixty-four years earlier visiting that brother after the buzz saw incident. Today, those sibs who wrote me off— truly are inconsequential in my life. Patti and I have our circle of friends and family.

I saw on Facebook that recently (summer, 2017) your sister Laurel met a sister she didn't know she had. Will the ongoing discoveries of your siblings and you become an epilogue for the Chickenhouse Chronicles?

I think not. Laurel has asked me not to write about her discoveries. I feel honored to be a part of her journey and respect her right to privacy. If she and her new sister, Grace, grant me permission to share their story I will. As far as the other siblings—let them write their own stories.

As I read your story, it seemed to me that at times Barb treated you differently than she treated Chris, Tim, and Randy—like sleeping in the big bed with the other children and having you sleep alone in Chelan, or when she denied you the Schwinn bike. Part of this, of course, is that the book is your recollections. The reader is getting your story, but did you ever feel as though Barb blamed you for something? Possibly something to do with your biological father? Or was it just your bond with Herman?

I'm sure, as a toddler on the farm, my bonding with Herman exacerbated Barb's displeasure with me. In the late 1940s, before Barb met Herman, while still in New York, she wanted very much to reconcile with Chris and Tim's father, John Curry. In the chickenhouse I discovered a divorce deposition dated late January 1947—she refused to divorce John. That deposition was done the exact week I was conceived. Barb's mental health is questioned in that document. I believe she was struggling with many issues including depression. As I discuss in the book, I think if Barb had been clinically diagnosed, she would have been found suffering with borderline personality disorder (BPD). One of the criteria is fear of abandonment and a classic result is unwise and impulsive relationships. The final divorce decree was granted in mid November 1947, two weeks after I was born. Did John Curry discover that Barb was pregnant and used that information against her? A few weeks after I was born Barb dropped me at her parents' apartment in New York and traveled to Las

Cruces, New Mexico, in one final attempt to save her marriage—stay tuned for details in the next book, *Barbara*.

Before Barb died, she told you she was sorry. Did you take this as a personal apology or as a statement of regrets for you and your siblings and the life you all had led?

I took it as a personal apology. In the book I don't really get graphic about her beatings but she would sit on my head and pound me with her fists until I was almost unconscious because I couldn't breathe. She didn't do that often—maybe half a dozen times until I got big enough to defend myself—but the memory is etched into my life narrative.

Your experience is unique to you, just as others' childhoods are unique to them; yet we all grow up with our own experiences as being our "normal." At what point in your life did you start to feel that your experiences were different from what others would consider "normal"?

Psychology teaches us that we are each the center of our own universe: I recognized as a young child that Barb treated me different than her other children. As you mention, that was my "normal." Thank goodness I had Herman as a protector and Randy to play with. Randy and I both learned to keep our distance from Barb and not to expect anything positive from her. But in Barb's defense, I realize now that she did the best she was capable of.

How did your experiences growing up and working on the farm affect your experience in Vietnam?

On the farm we lived a very spartan existence, so when our crew had to live on the riverboat the amenities weren't really that much different—at least it was mostly warm except for monsoon season and the cold rains. Growing up, I certainly wasn't taught empathy and yet one of my strongest memories of my time in Vietnam is how I felt bad for the poverty the farmers and fishermen lived in— thatched hooches with dirt floor—as if time was frozen in the 17th century. I carried those memories home with me and today are part of who I am.

You have never met, nor do you know the name of your biological father. As someone who has searched and researched everything you could to learn more about and make sense of your own growing up, I assume you would want to meet him if he's still alive. The reader gets many glimpses of the "nurture" or "environment" part of your life. In what ways do you think "nature" or "biology" may have affected who you are today?

I like to think my sense of empathy, my good looks (that's a stab at humor), and a full head of brown hair at seventy were gifts from my father. As a child, Herman, Chris, and Tim mocked me because I didn't know who my father was—again, that was my "normal" and I don't recall being troubled about it. Now, in the autumn of my years, I'd be lying if I said I didn't care—I think we all want to know our roots.

The chapter about you and Randy at play is a beautiful compilation of time spent with your next younger brother. The reader learns that Randy was killed in a plane crash in 1978, while doing what he said on several occasions he wanted to do some day—fly. It makes the afterword of that segment bittersweet. What do you think Randy would say about this book? What questions do you wish you could have asked him?

I remember Randy as having a kind, loving, full-of-fun personality. As I wrote the book I wished many times he was there to visit with—in spirit he was. I think Randy would be pleased with the book. His children never had a chance to hear our stories. His daughter was about five and his son an infant when Randy died. What would I ask him? I suppose I'd pick his mind about how life was on the farm after returning from the foster homes, after I left for the military.

Although Barb's sister Polly is not a major character in the book, her mental illness parallels Barb's in many ways. Elsie's diary entries sometimes briefly describe what is going on with one or the other of her daughters and their illnesses, and then comment on something completely unrelated and different in tone.

In the chickenhouse I discovered a thick packet labeled "Mental Health Journal." Beyond the diaries, Elsie delves into her daughters' mental issues and documents treatments and doctor visits. I think Elsie's bouncing around with subjects in her diaries may have been her way of sprinkling memory crumbs for herself.

From 1949-1960 Barb gave birth to six children. Over the course of eleven years she was nursing nonstop. Her last four children were cesarean. She must have been in a constant state of healing from the last birth or pregnant with the next child. How did that affect her psychologically?

For a woman lactating and pregnant, nutritional requirements are high. I think Barb, with the constant demands on her body, suffered nutritional deprivation and that affected her psychologically. The only form of birth control available was for her to sleep upstairs, away from Herman, but he would stand in the stairway in the dark of night and loudly demand that she come to his bed. She would go down, telling him to "Hush because the children will wake up." If I heard, I imagine most of the other kids did, too. I wonder if lashing out at Herman, triggering his rages, was a coping mechanism for her.

With the wealth of information you have, what is your plan moving forward?

As I mentioned, I already have a 500 page rough draft about my mother's life. Chronologically, her story begins in 1920, Seattle, Washington, but the back-story about her parents and grandparents is compelling so I probably will include an overview because long-range I plan to write about the earlier generations.

About the Author

Wendell Affield, the third of nine children born to Barbara Affield, grew up on a small farm in northern Minnesota. He was born in NYC in 1947 and moved to Minnesota as a toddler when his mother met his stepfather, Herman Affield, through *Cupid's Columns*, a singles publication. In 1960 Affield and seven of his siblings were placed in foster homes after his mother was committed to Fergus Falls State Hospital— her ninth child was sentenced to Red Wing State Training School.

At seventeen Affield enlisted in the navy. In January 1968 he returned to Vietnam on a second deployment as the cox'n of a river patrol boat with the Mobile Riverine Force. On August 18, 1968 Affield was wounded in an ambush and medevaced home.

After leaving the navy in 1969, he found work as a meat cutter apprentice in the Chicago area. A few years later he became a manager, a position he held with various companies for almost thirty years. In 1980 he and his family returned to northern Minnesota. After retiring in 2001 Affield enrolled in Bemidji State University, where, over the years, his Vietnam essays evolved into *Muddy Jungle Rivers* (2012).

In 2010 Affield's mother died. Locked in the chickenhouse on the farm where he was raised, Affield discovered thousands of letters, dozens of diaries, scrapbooks, and photo albums documenting his maternal past. He spent seven years unraveling his mother's history. In the process, he came to understand her struggle. Today, Affield works on his *Chickenhouse Chronicles* series, speaks to veteran groups about

PTSD, and leads a Veteran's Writer Group at his local VA Clinic. He is a 2017 recipient of Minnesota Humanities Center "Veteran's Voices Award" for his work with the underserved in his community.

He and his wife, Patti, live in northern Minnesota. They have two children and several grandchildren. Sadly, their third child, Jeffrey, died in 2015.

You can reach Wendell at info@wendellaffield.com

BOOKS BY WENDELL AFFIELD

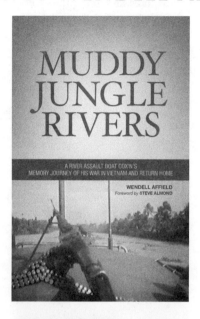

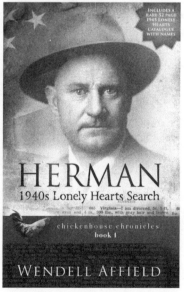

wendellaffield.com/books